The Prophet of The Nearness of God
-- *Isaiah*

The Prophet
of The
Nearness of God
--*Isaiah*

by the REV. H. RENKENS, S.J.

Translated by James M. Boumans

ST. NORBERT ABBEY PRESS
De Pere, Wisconsin
U.S.A.
1969

Excerpts from *The Jerusalem Bible,* copyright © 1966 by Darton, Longman & Todd, Ltd. and Doubleday and Company, Inc. Used by permission of the publishers.

Edited by Lisa McGaw

Translated by James M. Boumans

Originally published as *De Profeet van de Nabijheid Gods* by Uitgeverij Lannoo, Tielt, Belgium.

© 1969 St. Norbert Abbey Press

Standard Book Number 8316-1039-5
Library of Congress Catalog Card Number 77-87814

Printed in the United States of America
ST. NORBERT ABBEY PRESS
De Pere, Wisconsin 54115

CONTENTS

	Preface	1
	Reading Guide	5
	The Text (1-12)	7
1.	The Accusation (1:1-4)	32
2.	The Beaten Man (1:5-9)	41
3.	Worship in Spirit and in Truth (1:10-17A)	52
4.	The Redeeming Judgment of God (1:17B-28)	62
5.	The City of the Mountain (2:2-4)	74
6.	That Will Be God's Day (2:6-22)	87
7.	Between God and Chaos (3:1-15)	101
8.	Zion and Zions' Daughters (3:16-4:6)	112
9.	The Song of the Vineyard (5:1-24)	126
10.	The Experience of Holiness (6:1-13)	140
11.	The Decree Against Hardness of Heart (6:9-10; 29:9-12; 28:9-13)	154
12.	The Sign of Immanuel (7:1-17)	168
13.	The Waters of Shiloah (7:18-8:8)	184
14.	The Master and His Disciples (8:11-9:6)	199
15.	Yahweh's Outstretched Hand (9:7-10:4)	218
16.	The Rod in God's Hand (10:5-27)	220
17.	The Root of Jesse (11:1-16)	234
	Epilogue: Immanuel and His Mother (7:14)	247

PREFACE

This book owes its origin to the invitation of the Katholieke Radio Omroep to present a radio program about the Bible every other Sunday afternoon during its 1959-1960 broadcasting season. It became, in fact, a series of sixteen presentations which were afterward published individually in the weekly **De Bazuin**, usually in a somewhat abbreviated form.

In this book we offer not only the complete texts as originally presented, but also their thorough revision with many expansions for clarification. It is possible to convey more to readers than to listeners, since we are not hindered by the time limit of a broadcast.

The original method of approaching the Bible was conscientiously maintained. The title of the book shows this by retaining the title given to the radio broadcast. The subtitle indicates not only the material treated, but also the method of treating it.

It was decided from the start that I would not speak about Scripture, since my task was to let Scripture speak for itself: the listener had to be personally confronted with the text. In doing so we were primarily concerned neither with the literary beauty of the texts nor with the search for peculiarities in them, but with their import for the reader of Scripture, both as man and as believer. In other words, the reading of Scripture is at issue. This book offers a sample of Scripture reading in a way which corresponds to the goal for which the Bible has been written and handed down to us.

The texts treated here have come to us as Jewish literature, being originally the reflection of prophetic preaching in Jerusalem, the royal city. They are applied as generically human and more specifically as Christian literature. This book will prove this to be true, practically as well as theoretically, namely, by introducing the reader himself into the dialogue between Yahweh and Israel and by presenting reasons why he is indeed engaged in this dialogue.

This book, therefore, is no more than a specimen. As such it seeks to probe further than the texts which are presented here. It searches for an attitude by which, in principle, the whole Bible becomes readable. If this principle can be shown anywhere in the Old Testament, then it can be demonstrated in Isaiah. Hence my choice almost immediately fell on the nicely rounded entity which is formed by the first twelve chapters of that book. Although the New Testament can be made more easily accessible, I thought that as a student of the Old Testament I should restrict myself to my field. Isaiah stands at the turning point of the Old Testament. By referring to his oracles, I will be able to pinpoint what is at issue in the whole of the Old Testament. I chose him especially because he, as man and believer, is of such a caliber that his words can speak directly to anyone who is really man and consequently, in some sense, a believer.

That I was not mistaken in this has become evident from the manifold reactions. Among the listeners who were already familiar with the Scripture text, I have found a very grateful audience: in one way or another the radio program seemed to have given them answers to questions which the text had evoked in them long ago. Or they heard expressed in words what they had always sensed in the text without being able to formulate it. The presentations have also been fruitful for the listeners who knew the Scripture text only superficially or did not know it at all, insofar as they began to recognize their ignorance concerning these texts as a deficiency. Since they did not have any question with regard to Isaiah, the answer was for them too new and too strange to accept it and to digest it on first hearing, although they really felt that values were at issue, values by which the Church lives and by which they, as believers, should live more directly.

The reader is advised to study thoroughly the Scripture texts which are presented here. They are mainly poetry. How does one read a poem? Surely not superficially or just once. A poem has to be assimilated and digested. Discretion and silence are needed for this.

This is not a book to be covered in one reading. It should be used as spiritual reading. Every presentation should have a chance to penetrate, then one gradually gets into the spirit of it. The introductory parts are short; the text could therefore be treated at great length at first and the actual value of it could be illustrated more explicitly. Further on, the texts are longer and often more difficult. After a foundation has been laid, it will suffice to indicate the direction in which the reader can extend the theme to his personal life and his own time.

The only part that was not presented, although we referred to it casually (9:7-10:4), is now inserted in the translation: the completeness of the textual data seems to be an advantage in a book which has to remain incomplete in so many respects.

The epilogue concerning the Immanuel texts attempts to save the puzzled reader from any unnecessary questions.

Although some questions will inevitably remain, they do not necessarily make a puzzle of the entire work; they become unimportant once we have discovered that Isaiah and we as believers live by the same mystery.

If this book aids some readers on their way to this discovery, the publisher and author will feel amply rewarded.

H. Renckens, S.J.

Maastricht, Netherlands
All Saints Day, 1960

READING GUIDE

I. Collection of Damnation Oracles (1-5)

    A. Prologue (1)
        1:1 Title of the Collected Prophecies
        1:2-20 Concerning the People
        1:21-28 Concerning the City
        1:29-31 Concerning the "Heights"

    B. Insertion (2:1-5)
        2:1 Heading of the "Collection"
        2:2-4 Concerning the New Jerusalem
        2:5 Connecting Verse

    C. The Day of Yahweh (2:6-3:24)
        As a Day of Wrath for:
        2:6-22 The Pride of Man
        3:1-15 The Pride of the Leading Classes
        3:16-24 The Pride of Women

    D. Insertion (3:25-4:6)
        3:25-4:1 Connecting Oracle
        4:2-6 The New Zion

    E. Epilogue (5)
        5:1-7 The Infertile Vineyard
        5:8-25 Accusations ("Woe") and
                           Threats ("For . . .")
        5:26-30 The Great Threat: Assyria

II. The Vision of His Call (6)
    Apotheosis of the Preceding and Overture to the
    Following Collection:
        6:1-7 The Experiencing of God
        6:8-13 Mission and Instructions

III. The Immanuel Book (7-12)

A. The "Syro-Ephraimitic" War (7:1-8:10)
    7:1-9   The House of David in Danger
    7:10-16   The Immanuel Sign
    7:17-25   The Assyrian Plague
    8:1-4   The Maher-shalal Sign
    8:5-10   The Assyrian Deluge

B. Certainty of the Believer (8:11-9:6)
    8:11-22   The Discourse with the Disciples
    8:23   Connecting Oracle
    9:1-6   The Child with Mysterious Names

C. Insertion (9:7-10:4)
    "Yahweh's Outstretched Hand"

D. Reckoning with Assyria (10:5-34)
    10:5-19   The King's "Arrogant Insolence"
    10:20-23   The Shear-jashub Sign
    10:24-27   "A Little Longer"
    10:28-34   The Darkest Hour
                          Is before the Dawn

E. The New David and His Kingdom (11)
    11:1-5, 10   The Root of Jesse
    11:6-9   Paradise Regained
    11:11-12, 15-16   The Second Redemption
    11:13-14   Reunion of North and South

F. Psalm of Thanksgiving (12)

1:1   The vision of Isaiah son of Amoz concerning Judah and Jerusalem, which he saw in the reigns of Uzziah, Jotham, Ahaz and Hezekiah, kings of Judah.

2   Listen, you heavens; earth, attend
for Yahweh is speaking,
"I reared sons, I brought them up,
but they have rebelled against me.

3   The ox knows its owner
and the ass its master's crib,
Israel knows nothing,
my people understands nothing."

4   A sinful nation, a people weighed down with guilt,
a breed of wrong-doers, perverted sons.
They have abandoned Yahweh, despised the Holy
    One of Israel,
they have turned away from him.

5   Where shall I strike you next,
since you heap one betrayal on another?
The whole head is sick, the whole heart grown
    faint;

6   from the sole of the foot to the head there is not
    a sound spot:
wounds, bruises, open sores
not dressed, not bandaged,
not soothed with oil.

7   Your land is desolate, your towns burnt down,
your fields—strangers lay them waste before your
    eyes;
all is desolation, as after the fall of Sodom.

1:8 The daughter of Zion is left
   like a shanty in a vineyard,
   like a shed in a melon patch,
   like a besieged city.

9 Had Yahweh not left us a few survivors,
   we should be like Sodom,
   we should now be like Gomorrah.

10 Hear the word of Yahweh,
   you rulers of Sodom;
   listen to the command of our God,
   you people of Gomorrah.

11 "What are your endless sacrifices to me:
   says Yahweh.
   I am sick of holocausts of rams
   and the fat of calves.
   The blood of bulls and of goats revolts me.

12 When you come to present yourselves before me,
   who asked you to trample over my courts?

13 Bring me your worthless offerings no more,
   the smoke of them fills me with disgust.
   New Moons, sabbaths, assemblies—
   I cannot endure festival and solemnity.

14 Your New Moons and your pilgrimages
   I hate with all my soul.
   They lie heavy on me,
   I am tired of bearing them.

15 When you stretch out your hands
   I turn my eyes away.
   You may multiply your prayers,
   I shall not listen.
   Your hands are covered with blood,

16 wash, make yourselves clean.

   "Take your wrong-doing out of my sight.
   Cease to do evil.

17 Learn to do good,
   search for justice,
   help the oppressed,
   be just to the orphan,
   plead for the widow.

1:18   "Come now, let us talk this over,
        says Yahweh.
        Though your sins are like scarlet,
        they shall be as white as snow;
        though they are red as crimson,
        they shall be like wool.

19   "If you are willing to obey,
        you shall eat the good things of the earth.
20   But if you persist in rebellion,
        the sword shall eat you instead."
        The mouth of Yahweh has spoken.

21   What a harlot she has become,
        the faithful city,
        Zion, that was all justice!
        Once integrity lived there,
        but now assassins.

22   Your silver has turned into dross,
        your wine is watered.
23   Your princes are rebels,
        accomplices of thieves.

        All are greedy for profit
        and chase after bribes.
        They show no justice to the orphan,
        the cause of the widow is never heard.

24   Therefore—it is the Lord Yahweh Sabaoth who
          speaks,
        the Mighty One of Israel,
        "Ah, I will outdo my enemies,
        avenge myself on my foes.

25   "I will turn my hand against you,
        I will smelt away your dross in the furnace,
        I will remove all your base metal from you.

26   "I will restore your judges as of old,
        your counsellors as in bygone days.
        Then you will be called City of Integrity,
        Faithful City."

1:27   Zion will be redeemed by justice,
        and her penitents by integrity.
28   Rebels and sinners together will be shattered,
        and those who abandon Yahweh will perish.

29   Yes, you will be ashamed of the terebinths
        which give you such pleasure;
        you will blush for the gardens
        that charm you.
30   Since you will be like a terebinth
        with faded leaves,
        like a garden
        without water.
31   The man of high estate will be tinder,
        his handiwork a spark.
        Both will burn together
        and no one put them out.

2:1   The vision of Isaiah son of Amoz, concerning
       Judah and Jerusalem.
2   In the days to come
        the mountain of the Temple of Yahweh
        shall tower above the mountains
        and be lifted higher than the hills.
        All the nations will stream to it,
3   peoples without number will come to it; and they
          will say:
        "Come, let us go up to the mountain of Yahweh,
        to the Temple of the God of Jacob
        that he may teach us his ways
        so that we may walk in his paths;
        since the Law will go out from Zion,
        and the oracle of Yahweh from Jerusalem."

4   He will wield authority over the nations
        and adjudicate between many peoples;
        these will hammer their swords into ploughshares,
        their spears into sickles.
        Nation will not lift sword against nation,
        there will be no more training for war.

5   O House of Jacob, come,
        let us walk in the light of Yahweh.

2:6   Yes, you have cast off your people,
        the House of Jacob;
        the land is full of soothsayers,
        full of sorcerers like the Philistines;
        they clap foreigners by the hand.
7   His land is full of silver and gold
        and treasures beyond counting;
        his land is full of horses
        and chariots without number;
8   his land is full of idols . . .
        They bow down before the work of their hands,
        before the thing their fingers have made.

9   The mortal will be humbled, man brought low;
        do not forgive them.
10   Get among the rocks,
        hide in the dust,
        at the sight of the terror of Yahweh,
        at the brilliance of his majesty,
        when he arises
        to make the earth quake.

11   Human pride will lower its eyes,
        the arrogance of men will be humbled.
        Yahweh alone shall be exalted,
        on that day.
12   Yes, that will be the day of Yahweh Sabaoth
        against all pride and arrogance,
        against all that is great, to bring it down,
13   against all the cedars of Lebanon
        and all the oaks of Bashan,
14   against all the high mountains
        and all the soaring hills,
15   against all the lofty towers
        and all the sheer walls,
16   against all the ships of Tarshish
        and all things of price . . .

17   Human pride will be humbled,
        the arrogance of men will be brought low.
        Yahweh alone will be exalted,
        on that day,

2:18   and all idols thrown down.

19   Go into the hollows of the rocks,
into the caverns of the earth,
at the sight of the terror of Yahweh,
at the brilliance of his majesty,
when he arises
to make the earth quake.

20   That day man will fling to moles and bats the idols of silver and the idols of gold that he made for worship,

21   and go into the crevices of the rocks
and the rifts of the crag,
at the sight of the terror of Yahweh,
at the brilliance of his majesty,
when he arises
to make the earth quake.

22   Trust no more in man,
he has but a breath in his nostrils.
How much is he worth?

3:1   Yes, see how the Lord Yahweh Sabaoth
is taking from Jerusalem and Judah
support of every kind
(support of bread and support of water):

2   hero, man-at-arms, judge, prophet,

3   diviner, elder, ● captain, noble,
counsellor, sorcerer, soothsayer.

4   "I give them boys for princes,
raw lads to rule over them."

5   The people bully each other,
neighbour and neighbour;
a youth can insult his elder,
a lout abuse a noble,

6   so that everyone tries to catch his brother
in their father's house, to say,
"You have a cloak, so you be leader,
and rule this heap of ruins."

7   When that day comes the other will protest,

"I am no doctor,
in my house is neither bread nor cloak;
do not make me leader of the people."

3:8   Yes, Jerusalem is falling into ruins
and Judah is in collapse,
since their words and their deeds affront the Lord,
insulting his glory.

9   Their insolent airs bear witness against them,
they parade their sin like Sodom.
To their own undoing, they do not hide it,
they are preparing their own downfall.

10   Tell them, "Happy is the virtuous man,
for he will feed on the fruit of his deeds;
11   woe to the wicked, evil is on him,
he will be treated as his actions deserve."

12   O my people, oppressed by a lad,
ruled by women.
O my people, your rulers mislead you
and destroy the road you walk on.

13   Yahweh rises from his judgement seat,
he stands up to arraign his people.

14   Yahweh calls to judgement
the elders and the princes of his people:
"You are the ones who destroy the vineyard
and conceal what you have stolen from the poor.
15   By what right do you crush my people
and grind the faces of the poor?"
It is the Lord Yahweh Sabaoth who speaks.

16   Yahweh said: Because of the haughtiness
of the daughters of Zion,
the way they walk with their heads held high
and enticing eyes,
the way they mince along,
tinkling the bangles on their feet,
17   the Lord will give the daughters of Zion itching
heads
and uncover their nakedness.

3:18-23   That day the Lord will take away the ankle ornaments, tiaras, pendants ● and bracelets, the veils, ● headbands, foot chains and belts, the scent bottles and amulets, signet rings and nose rings, ● the expensive dresses, mantles, cloaks and purses, ● the mirrors, linen garments, turbans and mantillas.

24   Instead of scent, a stink;
instead of belt, a rope;
instead of hair elaborately done, a shaven scalp,
and instead of gorgeous dress, a sack;
and brand marks instead of beauty.

25   Your men will fall by the sword,
your heroes in the fight.

26   The gates will moan and mourn;
you will sit on the ground desolate.

4:1   And seven women will fight
over a single man that day:
"We will eat our own food,
and wear our own clothing," they will say
"let us bear your name;
take our disgrace away."

2   That day, the branch of Yahweh
shall be beauty and glory,
and the fruit of the earth
shall be the pride and adornment
of Israel's survivors.

3   Those who are left of Zion
and remain of Jerusalem
shall be called holy
and those left in Jerusalem, noted down for survival.

4   When the Lord has washed away
the filth of the daughter of Zion
and cleansed Jerusalem of the blood shed in her
with the blast of judgement and the blast of destruction,

5   Yahweh will come and rest
on the whole stretch of Mount Zion

and on those who are gathered there,
a cloud by day, and smoke,
and by night the brightness of a flaring fire.
For, over all, the glory of Yahweh
4:6   will be a canopy • and a tent
to give shade by day from the heat,
refuge and shelter from the storm and the rain.

5:1   Let me sing to my friend
the song of his love for his vineyard.
My friend had a vineyard
on a fertile hillside.
2   He dug the soil, cleared it of stones,
and planted choice vines in it.
In the middle he built a tower,
he dug a press there too.
He expected it to yield grapes,
but sour grapes were all that it gave.

3   And now, inhabitants of Jerusalem
and men of Judah,
I ask you to judge
between my vineyard and me.
4   What could I have done for my vineyard
that I have not done?
I expected it to yield grapes.
Why did it yield sour grapes instead?

5   Very well, I will tell you
what I am going to do to my vineyard:
I will take away its hedge for it to be grazed on,
and knock down its wall for it to be trampled on.
6   I will lay it waste, unpruned, undug;
overgrown by the briar and the thorn.
I will command the clouds
to rain no rain on it.
7   Yes, the vineyard of Yahweh Sabaoth
is the House of Israel,
and the men of Judah
that chosen plant.
He expected justice, but found bloodshed,
integrity, but only a cry of distress.

5:8   Woe to those who add house to house
and join field to field
until everywhere belongs to them
and they are the sole inhabitants of the land.

9   Yahweh Sabaoth has sworn this in my hearing,
"Many houses shall be brought to ruin,
great and fine, but left untenanted;

10   ten acres of vineyard will yield only one barrel,
ten bushel of seed will yield only one bushel."

11   Woe to those who from early morning
chase after strong drink,
and stay up late at night
inflamed with wine.

12   Nothing but harp and lyre,
tambourine and flute,
and wine for their drinking bouts.

Never a thought for the works of Yahweh,
never a glance for what his hands have done.

13   My people will go into exile,
for want of perception;
her dignitaries dying of hunger,
her populace parched with thirst.

14   . . . Yes, Sheol opens wide his throat
and gapes with measureless jaw
to swallow up her thronging nobility
as they are shouting for joy.

15   The mortal humbled, man brought low,
proud eyes will be cast down.

16   Yahweh Sabaoth will increase his glory by his
sentence,
the holy God will display his holiness by his
integrity.

17   Lambs will graze as at pasture,
fatlings and kids browse in the ruins.

18   Woe to those who draw down punishment on
themselves
with an ox's halter,
and sin
as with a chariot's traces:

5:19   and to those who say, "Quick! Let him hurry his
           work
        so that we can see it;
     these plans of the Holy One of Israel,
     let them happen and come true
     so that we can know what they are."

  20   Woe to those who call evil good, and good evil,
     who substitutes darkness for light
     and light for darkness,
     who substitute bitter for sweet
     and sweet for bitter.

  21   Woe to those who think themselves wise
     and believe themselves cunning.
  22   Woe to the heroes of drinking bouts,
     to the champions at preparing strong drinks.
  23   Woe to those who for a bribe acquit the guilty
     and cheat the good man of his due.
  24   For this, as stubble is prey for the flames
     and as straw vanishes in the fire,
     so their root will rot,
     their blossom be carried off like dust,
     for rejecting the Law of Yahweh Sabaoth,
     and despising the word of the Holy One of Israel.

  25   So, Yahweh aflame with anger against his people
     has raised his hand to strike them;
     he has killed the princes, their corpses lie
     like dung in the streets.
     Yet his anger is not spent,
     still his hand is raised to strike.

  26   He hoists a signal for a distant nation,
     he whistles it up from the ends of the earth;
     and look, it comes, swiftly, promptly.

  27   None of them faint or weary,
     none sleeping or drowsy,
     none of them with belt loose,
     none with sandal-straps broken.

  28   Its arrows are sharpened,

its bows all bent,
the hoofs of its horses are like flint,
its chariot-wheels like tornadoes.

5:29   Its roar is the roar of a lioness,
like a lion cub it roars,
it growls and seizes its prey,
it bears it off, and no one can snatch it back.

30   Growling against it, that day,
like the growling of the sea.
Only look at the country: darkness and distress,
and the light flickers out in shadows.

6:1-2   In the year of King Uzziah's death I saw the
Lord Yahweh seated on a high throne; his train
filled the sanctuary; ● above him stood seraphs,
each one with six wings: two to cover its face, two
to cover its feet and two for flying.

3   And they cried out one to another in this way,
"Holy, holy, holy is Yahweh Sabaoth.
His glory fills the whole earth."

4-5   The foundations of the threshold shook with
the voice of the one who cried out, and the
Temple was filled with smoke. ● I said:
"What a wretched state I am in! I am lost,
for I am a man of unclean lips
and I live among a people of unclean lips,
and my eyes have looked at the King, Yahweh
    Sabaoth."

6-7   Then one of the seraphs flew to me, holding
in his hand a live coal which he had taken from
the altar with a pair of tongs. ● With this he
touched my mouth and said:
"See now, this has touched your lips,
your sin is taken away,
your iniquity is purged."

8   Then I heard the voice of the Lord saying:
"Whom shall I send? Who will be our messenger?"

6:9   I answered, "Here I am, send me." • He said:
"Go, and say to this people,
'Hear and hear again, but do not understand;
see and see again, but do not perceive.'

10   Make the heart of this people gross,
its ears dull;
shut its eyes,
so that it will not see with its eyes,
hear with its ears,
understand with its heart,
and be converted and healed."

11   Then I said, "Until when, Lord?" He answered:
"Until towns have been laid waste and deserted,
houses left untenanted,
countryside made desolate,

12   and Yahweh drives the people out.
There will be a great emptiness in the country

13   and, though a tenth of the people remain,
it will be stripped like a terebinth
of which, once felled, only the stock remains.
The stock is a holy seed."

7:1-4   In the reign of Ahaz son of Jotham, son of
Uzziah, king of Judah, Razon the king of Aram
went up against Jerusalem with Pekah son of
Remaliah, king of Israel, to lay siege to it; but he
was unable to capture it. • The news was brought
to the House of David. "Aram" they said, "has
reached Ephraim." Then the heart of the king
and the hearts of the people shuddered as the
trees of the forest shudder in front of the wind.
• Yahweh said to Isaiah, "Go with your son Shear-
jashub, and meet Ahaz at the end of the conduit
of the upper pool on the Fuller's Field road, •
and say to him:
'Pay attention, keep calm, have no fear,
do not let your heart sink
because of these two smouldering stumps of firebrands,

5   or because Aram, Ephraim and the son of Remaliah

         have plotted to ruin you, and have said:

7:6   Let us invade Judah and terrorise it
         and seize it for ourselves,
         and set up a king there,
         the son of Tabeel.

7   The Lord Yahweh says this:
         It shall not come true; it shall not be.

8a   The capital of Aram is Damascus,
         the head of Damascus, Razon;

9a   the capital of Ephraim, Samaria,
         the head of Samaria, the son of Remaliah.

8b   Six or five years more
         and a shattered Ephraim shall no longer be a
            people.

9b   But if you do not stand by me,
         you will not stand at all.' "

10-12   Once again Yahweh spoke to Ahaz and said, ●
Ask Yahweh your God for a sign for yourself
coming either from the depths of Sheol or from
the heights above." ● "No," Ahaz answered "I will
not put Yahweh to the test."

13   Then he said:
         Listen now, House of David:
         are you not satisfied with trying the patience of
            men
         without trying the patience of my God, too?

14   The Lord himself, therefore,
         will give you a sign.
         It is this: the maiden is with child
         and will soon give birth to a son
         whom she will call Immanuel.

15   On curds and honey will he feed
         until he knows how to refuse evil
         and choose good.

16   For before this child knows how to refuse evil
         and choose good,
         the land whose two kings terrify you
         will be deserted.

17   Yahweh will bring times for you
         and your people and your father's House,

such as have not come
since Ephraim broke away from Judah
(the king of Assyria).

7:18　That day Yahweh will whistle up mosquitoes
from the Delta of the Egyptian Niles,
and bees from the land of Assyria,

19　to come and settle
on the steep ravine, on the rocky cleft,
on the thorn bush and on every pasture.

20　On that day the Lord will shave
with a blade hired from beyond the River
(the king of Assyria),
the head and hairs of the body,
and take off the beard, too.

21　That day each man will raise
one heifer and two sheep,

22　and because of the abundance of milk they give,
all who are left in the country
will feed on curds and honey.

23　That day, where a thousand vines used to be,
worth one thousand pieces of silver,
all will be briar and thorn.

24　Men will enter it with arrows and bow,
since the whole country will revert to briar and
thorn.

25　On any hillside hoed with the hoe
no one will come
for fear of briars and thorns;
it will be pasture for cattle and grazing for sheep.

8:1-2　Yahweh said to me, "Take a large seal and
scratch on it in ordinary writing MAHER-SHALAL-
HASH-BAZ. ● Then find me reliable witnesses,
Uriah the priest and Zechariah son of Jeberechiah."

3-4　I went to the prophetess, she conceived and
gave birth to a son. Yahweh said to me, "Call him
Maher-shalal-hash-baz, ● for before the child
knows how to say father or mother, the wealth of
Damascus and the booty of Samaria will be carried
off before the king of Assyria."

5　Yahweh spoke to me again and said:

8:6   Because this people has refused the waters of
           Shiloah
        which flow in tranquillity,
        and trembles before Razon
        and the son of Remaliah,
7   the Lord will bring up against you
        the mighty and deep waters of the River
        (the king of Assyria and all his glory),
        and it will overflow out of its bed
        bursting all its banks;
8   it will inundate Judah, flow over, pour out,
        flooding it up to the neck,
        and its wings will be spread
        over the whole breadth of your country, O Im-
           manuel.

9   Know this, peoples, you will be crushed;
        listen, far-off nations,
        arm yourselves, yet you will be crushed;
10   Devise a plan, it is thwarted;
        put forward an argument, there is no substance in
           it,
        for God is with us.

11   Yes, Yahweh spoke to me like this
        when his hand seized hold of me
        to turn me from walking in the path
        that this people follows.
12   Do not call conspiracy
        all that this people calls conspiracy;
        do not fear what they fear,
        do not be afraid of them.
13   It is Yahweh Sabaoth,
        whom you must hold in veneration,
        him you must fear,
        him you must dread.
14   He is the sanctuary and the stumbling-stone
        and the rock that brings down
        the two Houses of Israel;
        a trap and a snare
        for the inhabitants of Jerusalem.

8:15   By it many wlil be brought down,
        many fall and be broken,
        be trapped and made captive.

16   I bind up this testimony,
        I seal this revelation,
        in the heart of my disciples.

17   I wait for Yahweh
        who hides his face from the House of Jacob;
        in him I hope.

18   I and the children whom Yahweh has given me
        are signs and portents in Israel
        from Yahweh Sabaoth
        who dwells on Mount Zion.

19   And should men say to you, "Consult ghosts
        and wizards that whisper and mutter"—
        by all means a people must consult its gods
        and, on behalf of the living, consult the dead.

20   To obtain a revelation and a testimony,
        without doubt this is how they will talk,
        since there is no dawn for them.

21   Distressed and starving he will wander through
          the country
        and, starving, he will become frenzied,
        blaspheming his king and his God;

22   turning his gaze upward,
        then down to the earth,
        he will find only distress and darkness,
        the blackness of anguish,
        and will see nothing but night.

23   Is not all blackness where anguish is?

        In days past he humbled the land of Zebulun
and the land of Naphtali, but in days to come he
will confer glory on the Way of the Sea on the far
side of Jordan, province of the nations.

9:1   The people that walked in darkness
        has seen a great light;
        on those who live in a land of deep shadow

a light has shone.
9:2 You have made their gladness greater,
you have made their joy increase;
they rejoice in your presence
as men rejoice at harvest time,
as men are happy when they are dividing the
    spoils.

3   For the yoke that was weighing on him,
the bar across his shoulders,
the rod of his oppressor,
these you break as on the day of Midian.

4   For all the footgear of battle,
every cloak rolled in blood,
is burnt,
and consumed by fire.

5   For there is a child born for us,
a son given to us
and dominion is laid on his shoulders;
and this is the name they give him:
Wonder-Counsellor, Mighty-God,
Eternal-Father, Prince-of-Peace.

6   Wide is his dominion
in a peace that has no end,
for the throne of David
and for his royal power,
which he establishes and makes secure
in justice and integrity.
From this time onwards and for ever,
the jealous love of Yahweh Sabaoth will do this.

7   The Lord hurls a word against Jacob,
it falls on Israel.

8   All the people of Ephraim and all the inhabitants of
    Samaria know it.
In their pride they have said,
speaking in the arrogance of their heart,

9   "The bricks have fallen down, then we will build
    with dressed stone;
the sycamores have been cut down, we will put
    cedars in their place."

9:10   But Yahweh is marshalling his people's enemies
           against them,
       he is stirring up their foes:
11   to the east, Aram, to the west, the Philistines
       devour Israel with gaping jaw.
       Yet his anger is not spent,
       still his hand is raised to strike.

12   But the people have not come back to him who
           struck them,
       they have not come looking for Yahweh Sabaoth;
13   hence Yahweh has cut head and tail from Israel,
       palm branch and reed in a single day.
14   (The "head" is the elder and the man of rank;
       the "tail," the prophet with lying vision.)
15   This people's leaders have taken the wrong turning,
       and those who are led are lost.
16   And so the Lord will not spare their young men,
       will have no pity for their orphans and widows.
       Since the whole people is godless and evil,
       its speech is madness.
       Yet his anger is not spent,
       still his hand is raised to strike.

17   Yes, wickedness burns like a fire:
       it consumes briar and thorn,
       it sets the forest thickets alight
       and columns of smoke go rolling upwards.
18   The land is set aflame by the wrath of Yahweh
           Sabaoth
       and the people are food for the fire.
       Not one spares his brother,
19b   each devours the flesh of his neighbour.
       On the right side they carve and still are hungry,
       on the left they devour and are not satisfied.
19a   Manasseh devours Ephraim, Ephraim Manasseh,
       and both hurl themselves on Judah.
       Yet his anger is not spent,
       still his hand is raised to strike.

10:1   Woe to the legislators of infamous laws,
       to those who issue tyrannical decrees,

10:2   who refuse justice to the unfortunate
and cheat the poor among my people of their
    rights,
who make widows their prey
and rob the orphan.

3   What will you do on the day of punishment,
when, from far off, destruction comes?
To whom will you run for help?
where will you leave your riches?

4   Nothing for it but to crouch with the captives
and to fall with the slain.
Yet his anger is not spent,
still his hand is raised to strike.

5   Woe to Assyria, the rod of my anger,
the club brandished by me in my fury!

6   I sent him against a godless nation;
I gave him commission against a people that
    provokes me,
to pillage and to plunder freely
and to stamp down like the mud in the streets.

7   But he did not intend this,
his heart did not plan it so.
No, in his heart was to destroy,
to go on cutting nations to pieces without limit.

8   He said, "Are not my officers all kings?

9   Is not Calno like Carchemish,
Hamath like Arpad,
Samaria like Damascus?

10   As my hand has reached out to the kingdoms of
    the idols,
richer in sculptured images than Jerusalem and
    Samaria,

11   as I have dealt with Samaria and her idols,
shall I not treat Jerusalem and her images the
    same?"

12   When the Lord has completed all his work
on Mount Zion and in Jerusalem, he will punish
what comes from the king of Assyria's boastful
heart, and his arrogant insolence.

13   For he has said:

"By the strength of my own arm I have done this
and by my own intelligence, for understanding is
    mine;
I have pushed back the frontiers of peoples
and plundered their treasures.
I have brought their inhabitants down to the dust.

10:14 As if they were a bird's nest, my hand has seized
the riches of the peoples.
As people pick up deserted eggs
I have picked up the whole earth,
with not a wing fluttering,
not a beak opening, not a chirp."

15   Does the axe claim more credit than the man who
        wields it,
or the saw more strength than the man who
        handles it?
It would be like the cudgel controlling the man
        who raises it,
or the club moving what is not made of wood!

16   And so Yahweh Sabaoth is going to send
a wasting sickness on his stout warriors;
beneath his plenty, a burning will burn
like a consuming fire.

17   The light of Israel will become a fire
and its Holy One a flame
burning and devouring thorns
and briars in a single day.

18   He will destroy the luxuriance of his forest
and his orchard, soul and body too;
that will be like a sick man passing away;

19   the remnant of his forest trees will be so easy to
        count
that a child could make the list.

20   That day,
the remnant of Israel and the survivors of the
        House of Jacob
will stop relying on the man who strikes them
and will truly rely on Yahweh,
the Holy One of Israel.

10:21   A remnant will return, the remnant of Jacob,
        to the mighty God.

22-23   Israel, your people may be like the sand on the
        seashore, but only a remnant will return. A de-
        struction has been decreed that will bring inex-
        haustible integrity. ● Yes, throughout the country
        the Lord Yahweh Sabaoth will carry out the
        destruction he has decreed.

24   And so Yahweh Sabaoth says this:
        My people who live in Zion,
        do not be afraid of Assyria who strikes you with
                the club
        and lifts up the rod against you.
25   A little longer, a very little,
        and fury will come to an end,
        my anger will destroy them.
26   Yahweh Sabaoth will whirl the whip against him,
        like the time he struck Midian at the Rock of Oreb,
        like the time he stretched out his rod against the
                sea
        and raised it over the road from Egypt.
27   That day,
        his burden will fall from your shoulder,
        his yoke will cease to weigh on your neck.

        He advances from the district of Rimmon,
28   he reaches Aiath,
        he passes through Migron,
        he leaves his baggage train at Michmash.
29   They file through the defile,
        they bivouac at Geba.
        Ramah quakes,
        Gibeah of Saul takes flight.
30   Bath-gallim, cry aloud!
        Laishah, hear her!

        Anathoth, answer her!
31   Madmenah is running away,
        the inhabitants of Gebim are fleeing.
32   This very day he will halt at Nob.

He will shake his fist against the mount of the
    daughter of Zion,
against the hill of Jerusalem.

10:33   See, the Lord Yahweh Sabaoth
hews down the boughs with a crash.
The topmost heights are cut off,
the proudest are brought down.

34   The forest thickets fall beneath the axe.
Lebanon and its splendours collapse.

11:1   A shoot springs from the stock of Jesse,
a scion thrusts from his roots:

2   on him the spirit of Yahweh rests,
a spirit of wisdom and insight,
a spirit of counsel and power,
a spirit of knowledge and of the fear of Yahweh.
(The fear of Yahweh is his breath.)

3   He does not judge by appearances,
he gives no verdict on hearsay,

4   but judges the wretched with integrity,
and with equity gives a verdict for the poor of the
    land.
His word is a rod that strikes the ruthless,
his sentences bring death to the wicked.

5   Integrity is the loincloth round his waist,
faithfulness the belt about his hips.

6   The wolf lives with the lamb,
the panther lies down with the kid,
calf and lion cub feed together
with a little boy to lead them.

7   The cow and the bear make friends,
their young lie down together.
The lion eats straw like the ox.

8   The infant plays over the cobra's hole;
into the viper's lair
the young child puts his hand.

9   They do no hurt, no harm,
on all my holy mountain,
for the country is filled with the knowledge of
    Yahweh

as the waters swell the sea.

11:10   That day, the root of Jesse
        shall stand as a signal to the peoples.
        It will be sought out by the nations
        and its home will be glorious.

   11   That day, the Lord will raise his hand once more
        to ransom the remnant of his people,
        left over from the exile of Assyria, of Egypt,
        of Pathros, of Cush, of Elam,
        of Shinar, of Hamath, of the islands of the sea.

   12   He will hoist a signal for the nations
        and assemble the outcasts of Israel;
        he will bring back the scattered people of Judah
        from the four corners of the earth.

   13   Then Ephraim's jealousy will come to an end
        and Judah's enemies be put down;
        Ephraim will no longer be jealous of Judah
        nor Judah any longer the enemy of Ephraim.

   14   They will sweep down westwards on the Philistine
            slopes,
        together they will pillage the sons of the East,
        extend their sway over Edom and Moab,
        and make the Ammonites their subjects.

   15   And Yahweh will dry up the gulf of the Sea of
            Egypt
        with the heat of his breath,
        and stretch out his hand over the River,
        and divide it into seven streams,
        for men to cross dry-shod,

   16   to make a pathway for the remnant of his people
        left over from the exile of Assyria,
        as there was for Israel
        when it came up out of Egypt.

12:1   That day, you will say:
        I give thanks to you, Yahweh,
        you were angry with me
        but your anger is appeased
        and you have given me consolation.

    2   See now, he is the God of my salvation

> I have trust now and no fear,
> for Yahweh is my strength, my song,
> he is my salvation.

12:3   And you will draw water joyfully
> from the springs of salvation.

4   That day, you will say:
> Give thanks to Yahweh,
> call his name aloud.
> Proclaim his deeds to the people,
> declare his name sublime.

5   Sing of Yahweh, for he has done marvellous things,
> let them be made known to the whole world.

6   Cry out for joy and gladness,
> you dwellers in Zion,
> for great in the midst of you
> is the Holy One of Israel.

THE ACCUSATION

(1:1-4)

1:1   The vision of Isaiah son of Amoz concerning
        Judah and Jerusalem, which he saw in the reigns
        of Uzziah, Jotham, Ahaz and Hezekiah, kings of
        Judah.

2   Listen, you heavens; earth, attend
        for Yahweh is speaking,
        "I reared sons, I brought them up,
        but they have rebelled against me.

3   The ox knows its owner
        and the ass its master's crib,
        Israel knows nothing,
        my people understands nothing."

4   A sinful nation, a people weighed down with guilt,
        a breed of wrong-doers, perverted sons.
        They have abandoned Yahweh, despised the Holy
            One of Israel,
        they have turned away from him.

The book of Isaiah begins with a short comment, placed
as a kind of heading by later generations above the much
enlarged and emended edition of the prophecies of Isaiah:
"The vision of Isaiah . . . which he saw in the reigns of
Uzziah, Jotham, Ahaz and Hezekiah, kings of Judah." This
heading confronts us immediately with the annoying fact
that for many biblical names there are two sometimes
very different ways of spelling in circulation. Those who
regularly read Scripture and who know all the kings of
Judah by heart have perhaps never heard of the Uzziah

and Hezekiah mentioned here. They can be reassured: Uzziah is the same king as their familiar Ozias and Hezekiah is none other than Ezechia or Ezechias.

This annoying difference, however, should not evoke the question of right and wrong. This situation is not a recent development, but has its roots in the more remote past. It had already begun before Christ, when Greek-speaking Jews mutilated the Hebrew names, gradually changing the pronunciation from that of their Hebrew-speaking congeners and coreligionists. Meanwhile it is unfortunate that I cannot indicate the prophet and the book, which I will have to mention so often, with a name which is familiar to every reader. It is difficult to make a choice between Isaiah and Isaias. Isaias is the current pronunciation of the Hellenized name from the second or third century B.C. I believe that we can safely follow the Hebrew spelling: I will not refer to Isaia, nor to Isaias, but to Isaiah.

The reign of the kings mentioned in the heading can be dated accurately within just a few years. Since Isaiah was called in the year of the death of the first-mentioned king (6:1)—that is, around the year 738 B.C.—we can give forty years for the length of his public life, i.e., until shortly after 700 B.C. The book of Isaiah has everything to do with these forty years of preaching, but in a different way to what was held for a long time. For the book was not completed in forty years, but in four hundred years. Around the year 200 B.C. the book of Isaiah had the size and contents which it has in our Bibles, as we already knew from the Greek translation which dates from that time. This has also been confirmed rather splendidly by the complete Isaiah scroll, which was discovered near the Dead Sea in 1947. We can safely accept that the book dates back several more generations and had received its present form already in the fourth century B.C. This is still several centuries after the prophet died.

Much can be said in favor of the argument that Isaiah himself wrote portions of what we know as the book of Isaiah, or at least that they were written by disciples who noted down what he preached orally. Consequently, even during his lifetime the old kernel of the book, which later generations would rightly name after him, was formed. So it is not true to say that Isaiah simply has written the book as presently found in Scripture. But it is true that the most important part of the first major section of the book conveys a reliable impression of what the prophet really said. No one person sat down to write the book of Isaiah, least of all the prophet himself. But even during Isaiah's lifetime certain collections had been made from his many prophecies which were in circulation. After his death a steadily growing need must have been felt to possess a collection as complete as possible of everything that had survived.

Isaiah's powerful personality, however, has been at work for centuries since then. Disciples followed in the master's footsteps, passing on his message to the younger generation and adapting his great principles of faith to the new circumstances. Also the best or the most outstanding passages of their preaching were saved and recorded; in this way new collections of prophecies, which received their places partly in between, behind the already collected oracles of Isaiah himself, originated, so that the new totality could pass as an updated and annotated edition of what can be rightly called Isaiah's heritage.

The book of Isaiah is therefore not only a reflection of

the forty years of Isaiah's apostolate, but also of the activity of an anonymous group of faithful who lived by his inspiration. As Isaiah remarks himself, he seals his message in the hearts of his disciples (8:16). This pledge of faith was therefore no dead capital, but a living possession, conquered by a personal decision of faith and stimulating a personal testimony of faith. Passed on from hand to hand, from generation to generation, the word, which Isaiah "saw" (2:1), blossomed forth, unfolding all the richness contained in it. Therefore, the whole book rightfully bears the mark and name of the prophet. So much, then, with regard to the heading.

The following two verses, which actually form the beginning of the book, should be as familiar to us as the entrance of a cathedral upon which we have gazed since our youth. "Listen, you heavens, earth, attend / for Yahweh is speaking." Yahweh is the national God of the Israelites. Compared to him the national gods of the other peoples fade away, for he is the God of the world and humanity; the Creator of heaven and earth. The fact, then, that Yahweh speaks is already reason enough for heaven and earth to listen. But here, they are especially called forth to be witnesses of what Yahweh is going to say (cf. Deut. 32:1; Mic. 6:1ff.). Something heretofore unheard of is about to follow.

Unheard of is what Yaheweh has done for Israel. Of this people he can say: "I reared sons, I brought them up." This refers to the delivery from Egypt, through which Israel was formed into a people, and the further development of this group of roaming herdsmen into a prosperous kingdom under David, by which Israel indeed began to figure as an adult in the society of the ancient Eastern peoples.

"I reared sons." This historiographer inspired by the prophets later elaborated this short sentence by having Moses say to Israel: "Put this question, then, to the ages that are past, that went before you, from the time God created man on earth: Was there ever a word so majestic, from one end of heaven to the other? Was anything ever heard? . . . Has any god ventured to take to himself one nation from the midst of another . . . all this that Yahweh your God did for you before your eyes in Egypt" (Deut. 4:32-34).

A historian of the same school has David pray to Yahweh: "Is there another people on the earth like your people Israel, with a God setting out to redeem them and make them his people, make them renowned, work great and terrible things on their behalf, drive nations out and gods before his people? You have constituted your people Israel to be your own people for ever; and you, Yahweh, have become their God" (2 Sam. 7:23ff.).

What Yahweh has done for Israel is unheard of, but yet more unprecedented is Israel's reaction. For Yahweh remarks about these privileged children: "But they have rebelled against me. . . . They have abandoned Yahweh, despised the Holy One of Israel, they have turned away from him." Jeremiah shows how unprecedented this is by having Yahweh say to unfaithful Israel: "Now take ship for the islands of Kittim or send to Kedar to enquire. Take careful notice and observe if anything like this has happened. Does a nation change its gods?—and these are not gods at all! Yet my people have exchanged their Glory for what has no power in it." Israel, which has experienced the glory and the real divinity, seeks refuge from the powerless gods of its pagan surroundings. Jeremiah wants to say: Even if you search the whole world and its corners, even among the barbarian peoples, you will not find any people which would dare to treat its god as Israel has treated its God, and that while Israel's God is the only true One (Jer. 2:10ff.).

The closing verses of Vondel's **Joseph in Dothan** run like this:

> . . . geen mensch kan Vader troosten
Och d'ouders teelen't kint
> en maecken't groot met smart
Het kleene treet op't kleet,
> de groote treen op't hart.[1]

The "Song of Moses" describes how adult Israel crushes God's fatherly heart: Yahweh is Israel's Rock, a God of fidelity and without deceit. But his degenerated sons stood up against him. "Is this the return you make to Yahweh? O foolish, unwise people! Is not this your father, who gave you being, who made you, by whom you subsist?" Jeshurun (that charming, small Israel of long ago), having grown fat and bloated, turned restive and disowned the God who made him, thereby dishonoring the Rock of his salvation. "You forget the Rock, who begot you, unmindful now of the God who fathered you" (Deut. 32:4-6, 15, 18).

The art of reading Sacred Scripture rests on a holy conviction that what has happened between Yahweh and Israel in the past is a vital picture, even more, a revelation of what is still going on between God and man. On the

[1]Trans. note: *Joseph in Dothan* is a verse drama, written by Joost van de Vondel in 1640. A literal translation runs:
> no man can console Father.
Oh, the parents rear the child
> and bring it up with many a pain.
In its youth it steps on their garment,
> but, becoming adult, it steps on their heart.

one hand, there is God, who looks for man and tries to fashion him after the good and beautiful design that he, the Creator, has in mind of him; on the other hand, there is man, who clings to his own shortsighted design and consequently tears down what God wants to build within him. Isaiah underscores this eternally human tension by referring to brute creation: "The ox knows its owner, and the ass its master's crib, Israel knows nothing, my people understands nothing. A sinful nation, a people weighed down with guilt, a breed of wrong-doers, perverted sons."

Creation is well organized. The mechanics of the universe are well tuned. The earth is good and inexhaustibly rich. There is only one thing that is out of tune, as it were, and that is man. Everything obeys the Creator perfectly: it is an obedience necessitated by nature. The only one who can freely choose does not want to cooperate; the only one who can say wholeheartedly Yes, says No. Therefore, man is the only dissonant which disturbs the harmony of the whole of creation; as a result, the irrational animal puts the King of Creation to shame. Domestic animals are loyal and attached: they "know" their master and distinguish him from everyone else. But Israel does not "know." At issue here is not merely intellectual knowing, but that surrender of the whole person, which exactly conveys this special, emotional value of the biblical word "to know." Privileged Israel, which should know so much better, does not know Yahweh and does not even distinguish him from other gods. Jeremiah reproaches likewise: "Even the stork in the sky / knows the appropriate season; / turtle dove, swallow, crane, / observe their time of migration. / And my people do not know / the ruling of Yahweh! [that is, do not understand God's ruling with regard to man, nor how to behave toward him]" (Jer. 8:7).

Men of all times can take this to heart. He who knows himself recognizes that this accusation reveals something of an obscure abyss present in his own ego. It does not have to become a dominating experience; it may be a somber tone which gives depth to joy and gratitude for the fatherly love of God which restores everything. According to the counsel of a master in spiritual life, it can be healthy for me at times to experience an exclamation of wonder by viewing from this angle the creatures surrounding me: to wonder that they have borne with me and have left me in life; to wonder about the earth, that it did not open itself and swallow me; to wonder about sun, moon and stars, about fruits, birds and beasts, that they, instead of taking out their revenge against their Creator on me, keep assisting me (Ignatius of Loyola, **Spiritual Exercises,** 1st week, 2nd exercise, 5th point).

The ox knows his owner, the ass knows its master's crib, but Israel does not know. This reproach addressed to ancient Israel has been remembered by the Christian people down through the ages. The biblical account of Christmas narrates without any further details that Mary laid her firstborn in a manger, since there was no room for them at the inn. Christian devotion has put an ox and an ass near the crib. It is obvious that they draw this picture from the beginning of the book of Isaiah. The faulty and hence puzzling Greek (and Old Latin) translation of Habakkuk 3:2 facilitated this: "In the middle of two animals you will be recognized" (cf. Matins of January 1, 6th Responsory; Good Friday, Midday Rites, Tract after 1st Reading).

We sometimes hear that the ox and the ass are only a pious invention. But a sheer negative reaction such as this is here, and in similar cases, completely out of place.

What the earlier Scripture readers lacked in technical knowledge, they often made up for by an enviable feeling for the import of the texts. Without any annoying side reflection on the ox and the ass, therefore, we can let them keep their places in the nativity scene, as soon as we consider how purely the devotion which invented them was inspired, however less well-informed they might have been than we. Israel's attitude with regard to Yahweh is striking for a generally human attitude toward God, an attitude which is sharply brought out in the human reaction to Christ, of whom it is written that he came into the world as the true light, but the world did not know him—mind you, again that "not knowing"—and also, that he came to his own people, but they did not welcome him. The Jewish majority remained indifferent; Herod persecuted him; at the inn there was no room. But where man fails to show up, there the irrational animal is present.

The nativity scene, by portraying these introductory verses, literally touches the kernel of Isaiah's thought as well as the Christmas story. Where we are driven to critical, historical reconstructions by our scientific apparatus, ancient devotion—notwithstanding, and sometimes thanks to, all kinds of childish misunderstanding—had an open eye for the eternal quality of these texts. They recognized in the time and place-bound word of Isaiah the figure of God's Word which is for all ages and is spoken not only to the Israelite of long ago, but also to the Scripture reader of today in a personal manner.

The ox and the ass knew their Master and Creator in their instinctive way. To know God in a fully human manner, to see and to realize the hand of the Father in our personal circumstances today and tomorrow, such is the way to real life.

2

THE BEATEN MAN

(1:5-9)

1:5   Where shall I strike you next,
        since you heap one betrayal on another?
        The whole head is sick, the whole heart grown
           faint;
6   from the sole of the foot to the head there is not
           a sound spot:
        wounds, bruises, open sores
        not dressed, not bandaged,
        not soothed with oil.

7   Your land is desolate, your towns burnt down,
        your fields—strangers lay them waste before your
           eyes;
        all is desolation, as after the fall of Sodom.

8   The daughter of Zion is left
        like a shanty in a vineyard,
        like a shed in a melon patch,
        like a besieged city.
9   Had Yahweh not left us a few survivors,
        we should be like Sodom,
        we should now be like Gomorrah.

Since the reader of Scripture is always dealing with a book, he is inclined to forget that Isaiah was primarily a prophetic preacher, and only secondarily a prophetic writer. How could Isaiah, who had so many consoling and encouraging things to say, begin a book with a chapter in which he ridicules his readers by calling them all sorts of names? The people of God is called a sinful populace;

the family of Abraham, a guilty race; the children of Yahweh, degenerated sons. The climax is a comparison with Sodom and Gomorrah, which, according to the national tradition, is the classical example of complete perversion and depravity. Isaiah can hardly have approached his people for the first time with this. They sound far more like a severing of relations with the general public for the time being, comparable to the way Christ reproaches "his city" (Matt. 9:1): "And as for you Capernaum . . . if the miracles done in you had been done in Sodom, it would have been standing yet. And still, I tell you that it will not go as hard with the land of Sodom on judgment day as with you" (Matt. 11:23ff.). Still, Isaiah actually said these harsh words. He undoubtedly hurled these words passionately upon his listeners.

It is an established fact that Israel did not at all appreciate being addressed in this manner. This is quite understandable. There are, however, indications from which it is evident that such provocations were difficult to digest—even for the faithful posterity, with all its adoration of Isaiah. In this Scripture passage, for example, the name "Sodom" appears twice. But in the first place (vs. 7) the less hateful word "strangers" (ZRM instead of SDM) is used in the manuscript; in the second place (vs. 9) the softening "nearly" was later added: "nearly like Sodom."

This same posterity is responsible for the complete collection of Isaiah prophecies as they lie before us now. Two things follow from the location of this particular prophecy at the beginning. First, this address is definitely from Isaiah himself, since the compilers were surely not inclined to fabricate such remarks (so offensive to the national feeling) and place them on the lips of Isaiah. Second, it may be termed characteristic for the first period

of Isaiah's appearances. For the often still-observable
headings of the book—disconnected parts and collections
already formed—are arranged along broad lines according
to the times in which they belong. But it does not necessarily follow that this first chapter had to be Isaiah's first
address per se. The passionate tone leads one to suspect
that many unavailing addresses had gone before. Besides,
this chapter perhaps came about in a completely different
way from what the reader of a book would spontaneously
imagine.

Nothing forces us to believe that the prophet was able
to present a ready-made poem of sixty lines. It seems
equally unreal to have him at work first and then to call
upon him to speak. Our data recall a completely different
picture: an explosive man of God who speaks straight-
forwardly; he is possessed by some great thoughts which
recur regularly; he meets the same abuses over and over
again and encounters the same unwillingness everywhere.
In this way he gradually finds his form of expression, often
harping on the same subject. There is no carefully built
argumentation, but short, catching, almost disconnected
oracles: an aphorism, an accusation, a comparison, a threat,
a parable, a satire, a curse. The first chapter may have
grown in the prophet in the same way with regard to
content as well as form. It may be the final redaction as
edited by Isaiah himself, not just one of his many addresses.
The chapter, then, illustrates his public appearance during
his first years, more precisely.

The question of what was going on at the time the
prophet felt himself called upon to speak in this way
presses more and more. Israel's glory from the time of
David and Solomon had long vanished. It was almost two
centuries since their kingdom had been divided into two

unequal parts: the larger kingdom of the North (Ephraim or Israel) and the smaller kingdom of the South (Judah). Both kingdoms had just finished a long period of prosperity such as they had not known since the time of Solomon. An ominous storm was in the wind, but one carried on superficially and carelessly "as in Noah's day" (Matt. 24:37). We know that kind of feeling: people no longer knew what war was all about. But suddenly disaster strikes, even in small Judah. We hear it: "Your land is desolate, your towns burnt down, your fields—strangers lay them waste before your eyes; all is desolation, as after the fall of Sodom." Jerusalem, the capital, is still there, but packed with war refugees in want of the bare necessities of life.

When the crops ripen, huts of poles and branches are improvised in the vineyards and fields, for shade against the sun and as shelter for the night. The crop can be guarded day and night in this way and, when harvest comes, more work can be done, since there is no need to go back and forth to city and town, where everyone safely lives together. After the season, these huts remain, blighted, falling apart, and disheveled in the midst of the now desolately bare fields. Jerusalem is now like that, while only a short time ago it was the proud center of a prosperous country; or—it is not certain that the prophet was thinking only of the city—this vision is called forth by the remnant of Judah's population driven together: "The daughter of Zion is left / like a shanty in a vineyard, / like a shed in a melon patch."

Although scholars have a quite clear picture of the nightmare which descended on the world at that time, to understand Isaiah we do not have to unravel the international complications of which Judah became one of the victims. This is so much the better, for he is now under-

standable to everyone. The special aspect is not that
Judah was struck by a national disaster; Judah's neighbors
were struck by the same fate and sometimes were worse
off. The peculiarity is that only in Judah did a prophet
stand forth and give meaning, from his religious background, to the disasters of his time. In other words, the
book of Isaiah is not important merely because it depicts
what was going on politically and militarily at that time,
but because the world events of that time became transparent to a prophet: his eyes opened themselves to the
real factors which were at work in the mute facts. That is
the reason why Isaiah has so much to say to us: his
religious outlook affects the spiritual and eternal background of man's precarious existence.

The succession of facts become history only by the free
choice which determines human actions: history is made.
Hence, only man has history; the rest has history only due
to and by its relation with man. Furthermore, only man
can understand the language of facts and view them as
history. But man becomes a believer only when he surrenders to the truth that history is made by God and man
together, and develops itself as a dialogue with question
and counterquestion, with word and response. Israel's
prophetism in general and Isaiah's in particular are the
important expression of this belief. Long before the Greek
sensed the meaning of history, only Israel (otherwise insignificant) of all the ancient Eastern cultures had a feeling
for history. The explanation of this remarkable phenomenon lies in the fact that Israel was essentially a community of faith, which came about by the historical action
of God. Israel's faith saw this historical connection, because
it considered its national adventures as salvation history.
Israel saw and wrote history because it lived salvation
history.

Isaiah notably formulates here his vision of faith on the national disasters of Israel and thereby on his religious insight into human misery as such. He had to fight for his certainty of faith in a strenuous inner conflict. As a true-born citizen of Jerusalem, he was baffled when he understood that the existence of his city was at stake: without his city his life would not make sense. But now he had been prepared for the worst and had digested it religiously beforehand. Therefore, he had to speak out. He saw that only faith could still give any meaning to the fate of a nation and was her only possibility for life.

In the first instance the unrest and passion to rescue a beaten people speaks in Isaiah, but the kernel of his message is (even today) equally directed to the rescue of beaten man. The prophet himself occasions the extension of his vision of the nation to the individual, because he actually compares his people with a beaten man: "The whole head is sick, the whole heart grown faint; / from the sole of the foot to the head there is not a sound spot: / wounds, bruises, open sores / not dressed, not bandaged, / not soothed with oil."

The picture is complete: it portrays a man who has also been broken spiritually. Judah's wounds go deeper; the sourse of life has been hit, for this people can live only from the Word which comes forth from Yahweh's mouth (Deut. 8:3). "But if you do not obey the voice of Yahweh your God . . . Yahweh will strike you down with foul boils, for which you will find no cure, from the sole of your foot to the top of your head" (Deut. 28:15, 35). This is the extent to which Judah has gone—this son of David of whom man once was able to say: "In the whole of Israel there was no man who could be praised for his beauty as much . . . ; from the sole of his foot to the crown of his head there was not a blemish on him" (2 Sam. 14:25). By turning away from God, who is the source of national life, Judah as a people of God, as a community of faith, has been battered. This essentially spiritual situation reveals itself in the battered situation of city and country.

How a person faces God is, according to our modern feelings, the strict secret of that person's personal spiritual life. But the peculiarity of the Old Testament is that the faithful community of God has a mundane and national shape: the Kingdom of God has the shape of an ancient Eastern state. This involves the spiritual situations immediately coming into the open and, as it were, can be read from the national welfare. Likewise the man Job, who was struck "with malignant ulcers from the sole of his foot to the top of his head," is not so much the symbol of the sick or hard-hit man but, far more, of the man whose actual misery is due to his spiritual confusion.

To express it in another way: Sacred Scripture is always and everywhere concerned with the dialogue between God and man. But in the Old Testament the explicit subject of this dialogue is, for the time being, not the eternal salvation of the individual soul, but the prosperous life of the country. Israel's national adventures, therefore, portray precisely the goings-on between God and man. In the Old Testament the point ultimately is not that Judah is stricken in its national welfare, or Job in his bodiliness; it is concerned with man who is struck in his bodiliness because he has lost sight of God.

Isaiah uses Israel's prophetic style, of which he, after all, is the epitome and the classical representative. For this reason all those mundane and national affairs about which he speaks may sound strange to us at first. But at

the same time he speaks from a purely religious conviction
and so we need, eventually, to be able to understand him.
As a citizen of the ancient small state of Judah he is someone from another world; as a believer he is our contemporary and our companion—even a master who can form the
believer in us.

Isaiah speaks not so much because his city and his
people have suffered, but especially because they suffer
unprofitably and thus will perish spiritually. We know all
too well that the need of the times does not automatically
reform men. On the contrary, mankind seems sometimes
to evoke the question: "Where shall I strike you next, since
you heap one betrayal on another?" Suffering can purify,
but it can also embitter and harden; it can be a curse and
a blessing. A blessing, since there is something in man
which needs a counterbalance for suffering. If we ask
ourselves what that something actually is, then we are
delving into a mystery for which we cannot find any better
name than "sin"—or "sinfulness." In fact we need suffering
to keep growing interiorly, to come to a deeper, more
complete humanity. Those who have been purged by
suffering have the most to give and the most to tell us.
In suffering, man shows his real greatness, or he grows
toward it.

But the national disasters that strike Judah reveal a
spiritual barrenness, an inner desolation, which leads to
fear for the worst: Judah's political collapse, which has
almost become inescapable and threatens to become the
complete downfall of a whole people.

The turn, which the history of a man's life has once
taken, perhaps by a former choice, cannot be undone—
Judah has reached this point—yet, further developtment is

not automatic, but is always codetermined anew by free human factors. Thus there is always hope for the man who really wants to make the best of "circumstances."

For Judah this is the crossroads: the road of faith, which is one of purification, or the road of remnantless desolation, the road of Sodom. In Sodom there was no remnant—not even fifty, not even ten people. Hence the city could not be saved any longer (Gen. 18:24ff.). In Judah there is still a remnant of authentic believers; Isaiah is living proof of this. He feels himself connected with it ("we" in vs. 9). Their belief is creative and life-giving: it created Israel, which attributes to this faith its national character and its growth into a separate nation. If that faith fades away, Judah will disappear sooner or later without any trace among the ancient Eastern people from which it had separated itself by its faith at one time. However, where faith remains, new children of Abraham can always be begotten, who, despite all oppression, will grow into a new people of God.

Isaiah has not lived in vain. Politically, Judah fell, but from this death a new and better life originated. That Judaism could originate in Judah must be attributed to Isaiah and the movement of the authentic belief of which his preaching is the source.

Judaism, rightly named after Judah, feels again and again as a painful loss the lack of its own national living space and the whole ancient national framework. But through this suffering it became greater and better than it could have become by political independence.

It is this beaten and downtrodden Judaism which surpasses itself and the Old Testament in chapters 40 to 55 of the book of Isaiah. Is it not as if the faithful, among

whom the four hymns of Yahweh's Servant with their
sensitive framework originated, indicate how much they
owe to the prophet Isaiah by adding these hymns to the
book of Isaiah? In the Suffering Servant (especially chap.
53), "a man of sorrows and familiar with suffering . . . someone punished, struck by God and brought low" (53:3ff.),
unrecognizably disfigured from the sole of his foot to the
top of his head, so that he seemed no longer human and
his figure was not like that of man's children anymore
(52:14)—in this Suffering Servant of Yahweh the purified
Remnant of Israel finds its new meaning of existence, which
remains not only politically and nationally a failure, but in
which even the faithful man seemingly has to be the under-
dog. The community of authentic faith, in learning to
accept through the Servant its humble earthly shape, begins
to discover itself as the people of the "poor," already
pusillus grex ("little flock"; Luke 12:32) in the midst of a
corrupt world.

The national traces of the Servant are hidden behind
his spiritual mission—to be the personification of the light
and the covenant of the peoples and, like a new Moses, to
gather a new people of God. He does not pursue his task
of bringing true religion to the world by poltical success,
but by a complete earthly failure. Israel's miserable fate
seems to be a call. Only from human failure, from the
sacrifice of the most valuable thing, is a true believer born.
By belief in a resurrection, Abraham grew to the stature of
religious patriarch. So also, by this faith in the resurrection,
Israel can fertilize the loss of its national privilege. This
belief finally gives human existence its true dimension (cf.
Theologische Week over De Mens [Nijmegen, 1958],
pp. 73ff.).

By suffering faithfully, man, without perhaps realizing

it, enters into a vital communion with the Christian mystery of death and resurrection, as the spiritual elite of Judaism did in anticipation. That Judaism was allowed to see the tragic course of the Servant's life in this way, as is clear from the hymns, proves that faithful acting and living ultimately lead to a true realization of God's saving answer to the problem of suffering man: the Man and the Suffering Servant who pre-eminently made his saving act transparent for blind eyes by his saving word concerning the grain which has to die in order to become productive (John 12:24).

Judaism, therefore, preserved the prophetic heritage of ancient Israel and let it grow in depth, and even spread it throughout the world, so that it finally could overflow into the Christian world-church.

It is a mystery of the Lord of Hosts, who punishes his people unto death in order that they may live. Yahweh of Hosts is his name; that is, nothing is beyond his power. Even if man has made so many mistakes, even if everything seems lost, God loves to the end what was once his work, a remnant preserved, from which something new can grow. Fate has not yet been sealed. It is not yet Sodom. A new Jerusalem can still rise.

3

WORSHIP IN SPIRIT AND
IN TRUTH (1:10-17A)

1:10   Hear the word of Yahweh,
        you rulers of Sodom;
        listen to the command of our God,
        you people of Gomorrah.

11   "What are your endless sacrifices to me:
        says Yahweh.
        I am sick of holocausts of rams
        and the fat of calves.
        The blood of bulls and of goats revolts me.
12   When you come to present yourselves before me,
        who asked you to trample over my courts?
13   Bring me your worthless offerings no more,
        the smoke of them fills me with disgust.
        New Moons, sabbaths, assemblies—
        I cannot endure festival and solemnity.
14   Your New Moons and your pilgrimages
        I hate with all my soul.
        They lie heavy on me,
        I am tired of bearing them.
15   When you stretch out your hands
        I turn my eyes away.
        You may multiply your prayers,
        I shall not listen.
        Your hands are covered with blood,
16   wash, make yourselves clean.

        "Take your wrong-doing out of my sight.
        Cease to do evil.

The land of Judah had already been struck so severely that it resembled the land of Sodom in all its confusion. But Jerusalem, too, is like Sodom. The city remains erect, but she behaves like Sodom. If she does not change her way of life, she can expect the same fate as Sodom: Jerusalem turned upside down.

Such is the threat that is contained in the manner in which Isaiah addresses his listeners: "Hear the word of Yahweh, you rulers of Sodom; listen to the command of our God, you people of Gomorrah." Indeed, there follows a divine lesson, an instruction. On behalf of God the prophet is going to correct this situation. He will clearly distinguish what is usually dangerously confused by the people (and not only by the people of that time): religion and worship, religion and temple cult, religion and church service.

Jerusalem fancies itself as the holy city of Yahweh because of the glorious Temple which is named after Yahweh or—expressed in a biblical manner—where Yahweh made his Name to dwell. During the great yearly festivals the city is filled with pilgrims and the Temple is turned completely into a slaughterhouse. The blood of sacrificial animals flows from the colossal altar down the temple hill, coloring the Kidron with its red hue. Yahweh should be satisfied and Jerusalem can feel safe.

But Yahweh is not satisfied. "I hate and despise your feasts, / I take no pleasure in your solemn festivals. / Let me have no more of the din of your chanting, / no more of your strumming on harps. / But let justice flow like water, / and integrity like an unfailing stream" (Amos 5:21-24).

Yahweh is not a pagan god, a human caricature of the true Divine One. He claims the whole man for himself and accepts his gifts only insofar as man truly surrenders to God his own person in these gifts. However, this attitude is completely lacking. Jerusalem—in name, the city of Yahweh—is actually another Sodom. Therefore, a lesson about authentic religion by our God.

Religion and worship are integral to each other. But if, according to the example of the prophet, we separate them for a moment, we can say that religion is a question of philosophy of life and an attitude toward life—a question, especially, of a path and the conduct of life. Worship is consequently an expression of this as well as the source and inspiration.

As contrasted with the international word "religion," the Dutch word **godsdienst** points directly to the service of God. A servant serves his master by fulfilling his wishes; his service is action. He proves by deed that he recognizes his master as such. Yet human relations require that the servant in due time show his submissiveness by word, gesture, or otherwise, which in its turn benefits his actual services rendered.

Religion is a service of God which primarily consists in action: that of fulfilling God's will. But worship, too, is service and an action of which God is the immediate object. By word, gesture, and symbolic action, man professes and witnesses his readiness for service, and seeks communion and companionship with the Lord whom he serves. By the direct contact with God in worship the believer cleanses himself from his former disloyalty. He realizes again what God demands of him and there finds inspiration to act according to God's will in his daily and secular business.

But again there is always that inclination to keep religion separate from daily life, to push it out of the working week into the Sundays, from the world into the church building. Again, there is always the tendency to limit religion to worship, by which also worship itself looses its content and becomes a lie. It is a cheap way to get rid of God: at set times God receives the prescribed portion; after that, man once again goes his own way.

That was Israel's situation when Isaiah entered on the scene. As no one else, the prophet had experienced the nearness of Israel's God. In the vision of his call the nearness of Israel's Holy One had been a tangible, almost bodily experience. He realizes again the rudiments of Israel's religion, concisely expressed in the name of Israel's God, Yahweh—the Faithful One. Yahweh is a God who can really help, but who can also make equally real demands and expects an equally real answer from man. The religious desolation of the paganism surrounding Israel, however, has affected her and now, after some centuries, Israel's religion is losing its authenticity: Israel serves gods of her own choice and her own making—gods who are easily and spontaneously liked by Israel and hence do not make real demands. Israel readily swings over to this, since belief in Yahweh is no longer a belief, but merely superstition. One honors Yahweh in a pagan way. One places trust in shrines, altars, sacrifices, prayer formulae— in short, in all those externals which were once an expression of a genuine belief in Yahweh, but which now are connected with him only by name and official designation. This is superstition.

The best illumination of this is Jeremiah's remarks about the House of Yahweh, that is, the Temple of Jerusalem. How he must have teased his southern audience by drawing a parallel with the once famous shrine of Yahweh at Shiloh in the Northern Kingdom, which kingdom was extinct by Jeremiah's time.

"The word that was addressed to Jeremiah by Yahweh, 'Go and stand at the gate of the Temple of Yahweh and there proclaim this message. Say, Listen to the word of Yahweh, all you men of Judah who come in by these gates to worship Yahweh. Yahweh Sabaoth, the God of Israel, says this: Amend your behaviour and your action and I will stay with you here in this place. Put no trust in delusive words like these: This is the sanctuary of Yahweh, the sanctuary of Yahweh, the sanctuary of Yahweh! But if you do amend your behaviour and your actions, if you treat each other fairly, if you do not exploit the stranger, the orphan and the widow (if you do not shed innocent blood in this place) and if you do not follow alien gods, to your own ruin, then here in this place I will stay with you, in the land that long ago I gave to your fathers for ever. Yet here you are, trusting in delusive words, to no purpose! Steal, would you, murder, commit adultery, perjure yourselves, burn incense to Baal, follow alien gods that you do not know?—and then come presenting yourselves in this Temple that bears my name saying: Now we are safe—safe to go on committing all these abominations! Do you take this Temple that bears my name for a robber's den? I at any rate, am not blind—it is Yahweh who speaks.

" 'Now go to my place in Shiloh where at first I gave my name a home; see what I have done to it because of the wickedness of my people Israel! And now since you have committed all these sins—it is Yahweh who speaks—and have refused to listen when I spoke so urgently, so persistently, or to answer when I called you, I will treat this Temple that bears my name, and in which you put your trust, and the place I have given to you and your ancestors, just as I treated Shiloh, I will drive you out of my sight, as I drove all your kinsmen, the entire race of Ephraim. . . .

"For when I brought your ancestors out of the land of Egypt, I said nothing to them, gave them no orders about holocausts and sacrifices. These were my orders: Listen to my voice, then I will be your God and you shall be my people. Follow right to the end the way that I mark out for you, and you will prosper'" (Jer. 7:1-15; 22-23).

When we compare Isaiah with Jeremiah, it is strikingly evident that both prophets contrast actual religion with formalism and worship that has degenerated to sheer externalism. Semitic usage tends toward complete antithesis. They do not say: Yahweh desires good conduct and does not like this empty worship. No, they say it far more forcefully: Good conduct and no worship; Yahweh actually never wanted worship. Isaiah says: "Who asked you to trample over my courts?" Jeremiah says: "When I brought your ancestors out of the land of Egypt, I said nothing to them, gave them no orders, about holocausts and sacrifices."

If there is anything in the Old Testament that we dislike, then it is surely Israel's worship, and particularly the bloody character of it. Then there is the endlesss number of regulations prescribed even to the smallest detail, which were supposed to have been thought out by Yahweh himself and proclaimed through revelation. Every Scripture reader knows about them. This massive body of laws has been a stumbling block to the zeal of many a beginner. We easily misunderstand the prophets, when they agitate against the cult: we readily agree that all this ado should be abolished. Still these words are really not written to give the New Testament reader a feeling of superiority arising from the fact that this crude, material worship has become a vanquished point of view for them, as if they are finally "the true worshippers [who] will worship the Father in spirit and truth" (John 4:23ff.). These texts are not written that we might search another's heart, but our own. Then we will understand what the prophets actually mean. Wherever people worship God, they do it in a human way—that is to say, as children of their time and circumstances. Therefore, large differences exist between the past and the present, between the East and the West. Readers who are not used to cattle should be reminded that Israel's sacrificial practices originated in a society of herdsmen and farmers, to whom cattle belonged as part of the family. In the sacrifice man ultimately wants to offer himself. Hence he yields the best to his God, the best as a sign of himself and as a sign of all the possessions on which he lives. Where a whole society depends so much on cattle and land, worship is consequently characterized by bloody and unbloody sacrifices. These are, for that matter, sort of gifts in nature for the priests and sanctuary. Besides, they have to attribute a religious character to the daily meal at which one eats and drinks what is destined for private use.

In certain Dutch villages it is still a custom that when the farmer slaughters, the minister or parish priest is presented with a quarter, preferably a fat one. That is then "for the Church." Israel's legislation goes into so many details because it has also a social aspect: it is at the same time a legislative regulation which provides for the maintenance of the sanctuary and its attendants. But it also involves a religious aspect, because the life of an ancient Eastern farmer is wholly penetrated by religion. This would have remained paganism in Israel, if the religion of Yahweh had not incorporated by very definite regulations all the characteristic events peculiar to farming and herding cattle.

In other words, it is difficult to see that the prophets could have objections in principle to the fact that ancient Israel worshiped God according to the indispensable customs of the society of that time. We note as a matter of fact that Isaiah does not object to the bloodiness of the sacrifices. He speaks just as much against the unbloody meat offerings and incense offerings. Besides, he rejects all festivals, although these were mainly commemorations of Yahweh's saving deeds. Finally—and this is positive— prayer also receives the same prophetic death sentence.

We can no longer escape the conclusion that Isaiah by no means condemns external worship or prayer as such, but he stigmatizes both as useless, even as an abomination for God, unless they are accompanied by a corresponding conduct of which they are an expression. That is exactly the case in Israel, whose worship is degenerate and consequently to be rejected. The context is clear: the hands which Israel stretch out according to the ancient posture for prayer are still stained with the blood of his unjustly treated fellow man; that is the reason why Yahweh does not want to see them and to listen to Israel's prayer (Isa. 1:15).

What is a rejection out of principle in the prophets can be explained from a Semitic usage. Where Hosea has God say: "What I want is love, not sacrifice," the denial (not sacrifice) serves to stress the affirmation preceding it (love). The contradistinction between Yes and No expresses a difference in appreciation and importance, as the parallel sentence indicates: "Knowledge of God, not [=rather than] holocausts" (Hos. 6:6). The famous oracle of Samuel to Saul should be taken in the same vein: "Yes obedience is **better** than sacrifice, submissiveness **better** than the fat of rams" (1 Sam. 15:22). Such black-and-white statements recur also in the New Testament: "I showed my love for Jacob and my hatred for Esau" (Rom. 9:13=Mal. 1:3); "If any man comes to me without hating his father, mother . . ." (Luke 14:26) with the parallel text: "Anyone who prefers father or mother to me" (Matt. 10:37).

Jeremiah, himself of priestly descent—priest, law, and sacrifice belong together (Deut. 33:10)—knew very well that the biblical, sacrificial legislation is always introduced by the words: "Yahweh said to Moses: go and tell the sons of Israel." Yet Jeremiah puts into Yahweh's mouth: "When I brought your ancestors out of the land of Egypt, I said nothing to them, gave them no orders, about holocausts and sacrifices." By this strong denial, Jeremiah does not intend to contradict the Law—if it could not be taken as a figure of speech, he would have made himself ridiculous in the eyes of his audience—but he placed all stress on the deeper meaning of the Law: "These were my orders: 'Listen to my voice, then I will be your God and you shall be my people.' "

Like Paul, Stephen, and Christ himself, the prophets were not against the Temple and worship, but they thought so much of it that they fiercely reacted against the desacralization and ravishment of them. They were not eight centuries ahead of their time, but genuine believers who clearly saw that the exterior must bear out the inner disposition and conduct. Hence their words are still very current and adaptable to every worship.

Worship can be colorful and luxurious; it can also be sober, plain, and even puritanical. But the faithful, and especially the ministers and leaders of the communal celebration, should always be careful that it remains genuine with regard to what they do and pray—that it does not become mere routine or even an occasion to reach human aims. Christian worship is surely not protected against degeneration, as the letters of the apostles confirm and as we can learn from daily practice. Belief and superstition are extremes which can sometimes touch.

Isaiah took a position opposite to degeneration. Hence he saw so clearly and expressed so revolutionarily what God actually demands of man when he approaches the altar with a sacrifice: "Go and be reconciled with your brother first, and then come back and present your offering" (Matt. 5:24). One has to do one thing without forgetting about the other. We should not cheer prematurely when our churches are filled, even though it is still not a good sign when they are empty. Isaiah does not provide a biblical basis for such an emancipated belief which feels itself superior to the simple congregation that likes decorative services and whose daily life is surrounded by pious devotions. Religion can penetrate daily life exactly in this way.

It is not given to man to live completely and to his fullest extent in all his words and gestures of divine worship. The exteriority has also a task to lead to the interior and the soul. It is still good to teach children sound Christian practices. Practice means routine, but it gives them an anchorage. It is the bed on which the stream of inspiration flows safely through dry places to new sources. It is already a deed and an act, an act of worship; a loyal act by which, if the head cannot see clearly or the heart is ailing, a breach with a valuable past can be prevented; a loyal act which remains an exhortation to worship in daily life, and which is the obvious way to adoration in spirit and in truth.

4

THE REDEEMING JUDGMENT
OF GOD (1:17B-28)

1:17   Learn to do good,
search for justice,
help the oppressed,
be just to the orphan,
plead for the widow.

18   "Come now, let us talk this over,
says Yahweh.
Though your sins are like scarlet,
they shall be as white as snow;
though they are red as crimson,
they shall be like wool.

19   "If you are willing to obey,
you shall eat the good things of the earth.
20   But if you persist in rebellion,
the sword shall eat you instead."
The mouth of Yahweh has spoken.

21   What a harlot she has become,
the faithful city,
Zion, that was all justice!
Once integrity lived there,
but now assassins.

22   Your silver has turned into dross,
your wine is watered.
23   Your princes are rebels,
accomplices of thieves.
All are greedy for profit
and chase after bribes.
They show no justice to the orphan,
the cause of the widow is never heard.

1:24   Therefore—it is the Lord Yahweh Sabaoth who
           speaks,
      the Mighty One of Israel,
      "Ah, I will outdo my enemies,
      avenge myself on my foes.

25   "I will turn my hand against you,
      I will smelt away your dross in the furnace,
      I will remove all your base metal from you.

26   "I will restore your judges as of old,
      your counsellors as in bygone days.
      Then you will be called City of Integrity,
      Faithful City."

27   Zion will be redeemed by justice,
      and her penitents by integrity.
28   Rebels and sinners together will be shattered,
      and those who abandon Yahweh will perish.

This Scripture passage consists of two unequal parts.
The first part (vss. 17-20) is the close of the long address
to the people of Judah (1:1-20). A typical close to a
penitential sermon: Cease to do evil and learn to do good.
Yahweh is prepared to try it once again with us and to
erase our past. There is still a choice: if you will act
according to God's will, all may be well yet; but if you
persist, you are heading for destruction. The prophet can
say "amen" here. What should he add to it? He has had
his say. Now it is up to the people. They will decide their
fate by their deeds. The prophet says indeed "amen" by
the words: "The mouth of Yahweh has spoken." That is a
close. The address has ended.

The second part (vss. 21-28) deals, not with the people
of Judah, but very definitely with the city of Jerusalem.
It is another address, but with the same contents and
import, having the same structure and thought pattern.
This was undoubtedly preached also in the same period

of Isaiah's ministry, and therefore made much more sense together with the first address as prologue to the book of Isaiah. Besides, both addresses have this in common, that they, as it were, sketch at what stage the people and city have arrived at this time.

Now-a-days graphs are much in use. The newspaper has made everyone familiar with them. The rise or decline, the so-called curve, of a line indicates exactly how a certain phenomenon develops, whether it is the building of homes, theater visits, or a patient's fever. In this way Isaiah draws two lines, which run surprisingly parallel: they show the decrepit situation of both people and city. The line starts at the top, leading out from the healthy situation, and slackens off to decline faster. At the time the prophet speaks, the line has almost reached its lowest point. But the future will reveal how the curve will proceed. The line stops, but the prophet extends it by two dotted lines: the first one follows the direction of the curve heading for the zero point of death; the second one swings upward with a sharp angle to new, healthy life.

This curve has much to say to us. For it not only pictures the existence of Judah and Jerusalem, but at the same time indicates the whole history of man and even of each individual. This is so because the curve is the result of two forces, which are at work not only in Judah and Jerusalem, but also in the whole of mankind and in every man. These forces are (1) divine, salvific intention and (2) human sinfulness.

The situation of Judah and Jerusalem is a thoroughly human one: it is the human condition in its national form and as it is lived in the existence of a people. This existence of the people has now reached a critical stage.

Exactly during the critical moments it can be observed what the whole of existence is all about. Judah and Jerusalem therefore portray here precisely what the actual and eternal risk of man's life is and to what kind of an existential decision of faith man is exposed in his existence. We therefore read the first chapter well only if we discover from it where we stand and at what point we have arrived as man and believer. By juxtaposing these addresses it is possible to distinguish the line more clearly. What is primarily meant for the people of Judah and the city of Jerusalem, we will translate in general, though indicative, human terms. Every man has his personal secret and consequently his own line of life. We are concerned here with only the clarification of the way in which contemporary man is addressed by the Scriptures and how he can feel as the addressee. For the sake of clarity, numbers will indicate the prophetic thought pattern.

1. The line starts from the top. Both addresses begin with God's work, with the original divine plan. For us it is the short indication of the perfect beginning, of the unused capital with which the Creator has endowed man in his life or with which the young man, still pure, begins his fully conscious human life. Of the **people** Yahweh can say: "I reared sons, I brought them up" (vs. 2). Of the **city** he remarks: "Zion, that was all justice! Once integrity lived there" (vs. 21).

It is the reminiscent of the beginning of an existence of the Israelite people, which has become an idyll: "Yahweh says this: / I remember the affection of your youth, / the love of your bridal days: / you followed me through the wilderness, / through a land unsown. / Israel was sacred to Yahweh, / the first-fruits of his harvest" (Jer. 2:2-3).

It is the remembrance of David, the man after God's

heart, and of Zion, the city of David. It is Zion which Yahweh cannot forget: "Zion, does a woman forget her baby at the breast, / or fail to cherish the son of her womb? / Yet even if these forget, / I will never forget you. / See I have branded you on the palms of my hands, / your ramparts are always under my eyes" (Isa. 49:15-16).

It is the idyll of paradise. Israel's religious conscience has indeed this prophetic insight into Yahweh's real and original purpose, with Judah and Jerusalem copied in a generally human scale in the paradise story: the man of paradise expresses what God intends for man and what he still attempts to accomplish with him! All the more reason why the Scripture reader can understand the divine plan for his own life from the innocent beginning of Judah and Zion.

2. The same paradise story shows how man cuts through God's plan. Man is real man; he lives, by the Word which is uttered from God's mouth, by the actual listening to God's voice (Deut. 8:3; cf. 30:20). God's Word created man, and is at the same time the law of life which sustains him and allows him to grow in humanity by his personal and deliberate assent. But man deviates from this life-giving Word by dissenting from God, thus heading for his destruction. In this manner the paradise story is used to make apostate Israel realize by prophetic preaching the perilous road on which it is traveling.

Isaiah follows in the same vein. After having remembered the rather promising beginning, Yahweh speaks about the people, concerning those who are his children: But they have rebelled against me. Israel knows nothing, my people understands nothing. They have abandoned Yahweh, despised the Holy One of Israel, they have turned away from him (vss. 2-4). What are your endless sacrifices to me? Your hands are covered with blood (vss. 11-15). And about the city, his bride, Yahweh says: What a harlot she has become, a nest of assassins. Your silver has turned into dross, your wine is watered. Your princes are rebels, accomplices of thieves. All are greedy for profit and chase after bribes. They show no justice to the orphan, the cause of the widow is never heard (vss. 21-23).

The prophet has to make clear to the public exactly what sin is and that such things are sinful. Where, however, the awareness of God is not pure, one is unable to evaluate properly what is or is not serious in the field of sin. We saw in the preceding chapter that Israel did not know what genuine religion was nor what Yahweh actually demanded from his people. Consequently, this people then must have a wrong idea, also, of what is contrary to Yahweh's will. Naturally, superstition deforms the conscience too. To the superstitious trust in external worship corresponds superstitious scrupulosity in keeping the ritual, and superstitious qualms of conscience, if a mistake was made even accidentally. People, who are persistently restless concerning their soul and happiness due to certain futilities, while doing wrong in fundamental matters with an easy conscience, are a commonly recurring phenomenon in the history of religions.

That the relationship with God is that bad, is known by the prophet from the conduct with regard to neighbor. In both addresses blood and murder and social injustice by applying the right of the strongest one are at issue, so also the attitude toward widows and orphans as a norm of genuine religion. Genuine religion as well as real sin are only realized within human relations. For example, "Anyone who says 'I love God' and hates his brother, is a liar, since a man who does not love the brother that he can see cannot love God, whom he has never seen" (1 John 4:20).

3.   Sin is a loss of humanity and creates inhumanity. It affects man's being and therefore makes him unhappy. This brings the prophetic thought pattern to a third chain, which we meet once again in the paradise story and in personal human experience: sin is immediately followed by human misery. Man is left with the pieces which he himself has made, and consequently sin punishes itself. Such is the sentence of the paradise story and in the same vein the prophet speaks of a divine revenge.

What the people have brought unto themselves is first expressed in imagery by the prophet: The whole head is sick, the whole heart grown faint; from the sole of the foot to the head there is not a sound spot: wounds, bruises, open sores not dressed, not bandaged, not soothed with oil. This is followed by a sober description of the stern facts: Your land is desolate, your towns burnt down, your fields —strangers lay them waste before your eyes (vss. 5-7). The miserable fate of the city is sufficiently indicated by the pathetic threat of the formidable Yahweh of Hosts, Israel's Mighty One: "Ah, I will outdo my enemies, / avenge myself on my foes. / I will turn my hand against you" (vss. 24-25).

4.   But God punishes to heal. The misfortune which man inflicts upon himself is used by God to bring him to his senses and to purify him: the better parts of his ego are unshakled and provide a new nucleus: the lost son repents near the pig trough. The paradise promise opens up a perspective for the fallen and punished man. Isaiah does the same. With regard to the people: "Had Yahweh

not left us a few survivors, / we should be like Sodom, / we should now be like Gomorrah" (vs. 9). And the oracle about the city reads: "I will smelt away your dross in the furnace, / I will remove all your base metal from you" (vs. 25).

5. If man digests his purification faithfully and is prepared by deeds, he receives the chance to start again, with the full guarantee that God remains true to his original plan and will realize it. Concerning the people: "Though your sins are like scarlet, / they shall be as white as snow; / though they are red as crimson, / they shall be like wool. / . . . You shall eat the good things of the earth" (vss. 18-19). And concerning the city: "I will restore your judges as of old, / your counsellors as in by-gone days. / Then you will be called City of Integrity, / Faithful City" (vs. 26).

6. But if man does not repent, he definitely heads toward misfortune. To the people: "But if you persist in rebellion, / the sword shall eat you instead" (vs. 20). To the city: "Rebels and sinners together will be shattered, / and those who abandon Yahweh will perish" (vs. 28).

Scripture sees so clearly what life is all about, since it views it in the light of divine awareness, so consequently in the light of God's judgments over it. And that is a condensed final judgment. Biblical preaching, therefore, is called eschatological, according to the Greek word **eschatos,** which means "last, ultimate." God's judgment reveals itself only in the end, but it has already begun. Man lives under God's judgment and he enacts it unto himself. "The axe is laid to the roots of the trees" (Matt. 3:10). He who comes after John the Baptist has his winnow in his hand and he will clean his threshing floor and gather the wheat into

the barn, but the chaff he will burn in an inextinguishable
fire (Matt. 3:12). This sifting judgment is called in Greek,
krisis. Judah and Zion have arrived at such a point of
crisis. They live "their day" on which they must realize,
now or never, what will be beneficial to their peace (Luke
19:42, text variant). This divine trial is their last chance
(**kairos,** Luke 19:44). Now they have to make their choice
which will decide whether "the last day" will be a judgment of rejection or redemption.

In the Kingdom of God action is important. What
Judah and Zion have to do now is, very simply: "Be just
to the orphan, plead for the widow." It is the old safe
norm of all genuine religion, and according to this norm
the sifting of the final judgment will take place. For the
King will say: "Insofar as you did this to one of the least
of these brothers of mine, you did it to me; insofar as you
neglected to do this to one of the least of these, you
neglected to do it to me" (Matt. 25:40, 45). The Old
Testament, therefore, speaks often about the widow, the
orphan, and the stranger: those were the poorest people in
the society of that time. Whoever afflicts them, tampers
with the apple of Yahweh's eye.

Here a road is opened up for many willing people, who
are at a loss with the God of their youth and, in the
intricacies of a human life with good and bad and all inter-
mediary stages, cannot have a clear idea of their relations
with the supernatural and the afterlife. Religion can then
look like the most complicated thing of all. "Widow and
orphan," however, point them to the shortest road. Where
there is a service to man, there we are already far on our
road to genuine religion. By doing what is true, as expressed in the New Testament (John 3:21; 1 John 1:6), man
will find the truth which will make him free (John 8:32).

With unforgettable words Isaiah points to this short road which directly leads from chaos to God's heart: "Come now, let us talk this over, / says Yahweh. Though your sins are like scarlet, / they shall be as white as snow; / though they are red as crimson, / they shall be like wool." The angry God does not place himself as a punishing judge face to face with man, but next to him as an equal, guaranteeing that man does not have to be the losing party because of the past. The Hebrew language uses a term borrowed from jurisdiction: God will enter a case with man, as it were, against a third party (cf. Mic. 6 in the hearing of the mountains, the hills and the foundations of the earth), not to crush him with his divine right but to give him another chance.

Isaiah, who knows and realizes the sin of his people (6:5), witnesses that Yahweh is prepared to execute a miracle of pardon to man, as he had experienced in the flesh (6:7). Crimson and purple are indelible colors and, as such, are not easily removed. But God is prepared to do for man what man himself is unable to do: washed in the blood of the Lamb (Rev. 7:14), the cloth, crimson with sin, becomes white as snow and wool. Even if a man has pursued the wrong course so far, God will put him back at the cross-road where man himself can choose anew: If you are willing to obey, you shall eat the good things of the earth. But if you persist in rebellion, the sword shall eat you instead.

"The good things of the earth." This is a reference to the old Promised Land and is the summarized indication of the new happiness which God will allow to arise from the faithfully digested loss of the old happiness that was discarded for sin. It already points to the land which will be possessed by the meek (Matt. 5:5). The sword which will

eat those who persist in rebellion already indicates the
ultimate fall. The old choice between national welfare
and national destruction (cf. the Sinaitic legislation) begins
to develop, in the prophets, on a basis of strictly personal
choice between eternal life and eternal death.

In the light of this development, when biblical historiography presents Israel's national existence as an existential
decision of faith, then I can apply this to myself personally.
Israel places in Moses' mouth the following farewell words
at the moment when Israel starts on its way through
history: "See, today I set before you life and prosperity,
death and disaster. If you obey the commandments of
Yahweh your God that I enjoin on you today, if you love
Yahweh your God and follow his ways, if you keep his
commandments, his laws, his customs, you will live and
increase, and Yahweh your God will bless you in the
land which you are entering to make your own. But if
your heart strays, if you refuse to listen, if you let yourself
be drawn into worshipping other gods and serving them,
I tell you today, you will most certainly perish; you will
not live long in the land you are crossing the Jordan to
enter and possess. I call heaven and earth to witness
against you today: I set before you life or death, blessing
or curse. Choose life, then, so that you and your descendants may live in the love of Yahweh your God, obeying
his voice, clinging to him; for in this your life consists,
and on this depends your long stay in the land which
Yahweh swore to your fathers Abraham, Isaac and Jacob
he would give them."

With this text we are back at the beginning of Israel's
history. The prophetic thought pattern proceeds indeed in
a circle, but without continuously revolving in it: it is a
return to the perfect beginning, but not in order to repeat

history in its old way; no, rather, now as a starting point of a linear course which breaks through the national and earthly cycles, finding its completion in the infinite.

The worldly course of life ends in a "land without return"; but as long as we are still a people on the march, a return, a change, a conversion is still possible. Where sin is, a divine judgment must follow, but Zion's better ego will be redeemed in that judgment: for those who are converted, it will be a divine judgment of redemption.

5

THE CITY ON THE
MOUNTAIN (2:2-4)

2:2   In the days to come
the mountain of the Temple of Yahweh
shall tower above the mountains
and be lifted higher than the hills.
All the nations will stream to it,

3   peoples without number will come to it; and they
         will say:
"Come, let us go up to the mountain of Yahweh,
to the Temple of the God of Jacob
that he may teach us his ways
so that we may walk in his paths;
since the Law will go out from Zion,
and the oracle of Yahweh from Jerusalem."

4   He will wield authority over the nations
and adjudicate between many peoples;
these will hammer their swords into ploughshares,
their spears into sickles.
Nation will not lift sword against nation,
there will be no more training for war.

So far, except for three verses, we have gone through the entire first chapter of the book of Isaiah. This seems to be a well-rounded unit; only those last three verses appear as an addition. They form a separate oracle of doom, a fragment accidentally preserved, which seems to have been put in the book rather accidentally. It is directed against the many shrines spread all over the country.

As a heritage of the ancient native religion, these have been hearths of superstitious practices and Baal cult throughout the whole history. Invariably it must have been a sort of nature shrine, formed by an isolated tree or a bush, preferably on a mountain. By their enclosure they look like gardens. Those are the famous "heights" mentioned so often in the books of Kings. The prophets vehemently object to them. Yahweh said to Jeremiah: "Have you seen what disloyal Israel has done? How she made her way up every high hill and to every spreading tree, and has prostituted herself there?" (3:6). "They offer sacrifice on the mountain tops, burn their offerings on the hills, under oak and poplar and terebinth, so pleasant is their shade" (Hos. 4:13).

It is worthwhile to read the only oracle concerning this from Isaiah. The first verse runs: "Yes, you will be ashamed of the terebinths / which give you such pleasure; / you will blush for the gardens / that charm you."

In Hebrew the word for "terebinth" is homonymous to "gods." Such a thing is hardly casual in Isaiah. He uses this to refer to the Baal cult which is often associated with those heights and which constitutes a violation of the covenant with Yahweh, adultery in the religious realm, as Jeremiah expresses rather crudely: "Yet on every hill and under every spreading tree you have lain down like a harlot" (2:20). We may also think of this as an allusion to the paradise story. The "terebinths which give you such pleasure" remind us of the tree in paradise of which the fruit looked "desirable." Paradise is Yahweh's garden (Gen. 13:10; Isa. 51:3). Man scorns God's garden and chooses his own. Israel has done that literally: "You will blush for the gardens that charm you."

The idols which man has selected and from which he expects salvation bring him disaster, since they can only let him share in their worthlessness: the worth of a people depends on the worth of its god. This is expressed in the second verse: "Since you will be like a terebinth / with faded leaves, / like a garden / without water." Again we are reminded of Jeremiah: "They have abandoned me, the fountain of living water, only to dig cisterns for themselves, leaky cisterns that hold no water" (2:13).

Separated from the living God, man falls back on his own insignificance. He who imagines himself to be "strong" and attempts to make it on his own will find out and notice that he has caused his own destruction by his "work," by his action. This is reflected in the third and last verse: "The man of high estate will be tinder, / his handiwork a spark. / Both will burn together / and no one put them out."

All together, an oracle worthy of Isaiah the penitential preacher. In its entirety it runs as follows:

> Yes, you will be ashamed of the terebinths
> which give you such pleasure;
> you will blush for the gardens
> that charm you.
> Since you will be like a terebinth
> with faded leaves,
> like a garden
> without water.
> The man of high estate will be tinder,
> his handiwork a spark.
> Both will burn together
> and no one put them out.
>   Isaiah 1:29-31

Although this oracle is an addition, literarywise it is not annoying in its context. On the contrary, it has the effect of an echo, since it is the resounding of the verse with which the actual prologue closes: "Rebels and sinners together will be shattered, / and those who abandon Yahweh will perish" (vs. 28). Amplified, it reads: "Both will burn together / and no one put them out."

The prophets have not yet a conception of heaven and hell in the well-defined sense in which we apply it so thoughtlessly. Though their knowledge is lacking, yet their realization of the ultimate happiness or disaster of man is much deeper. A definite being-with-God and consequently truly human life, or a definite break with God by which man irrevocably perishes. They did not know hell, but they realized the astonishing mystery of it. To express this mystery in words, they employed the images from which eventually the biblical hell-image grew. Hell is in line with the prophetic preaching of doom and it derives its original ominous ring from it. The biblical message of doom is one coherent entirety; it is preaching about hell, the reverse of the salvific message that God is and wants to be our redemption, and that there is no redemption outside God.

This profound coherence between Old Testament and New Testament disaster, between the woes of Isaiah and the woes of Christ, shows itself in the language used. Christ does not speak in terms of Isaiah merely by accident.

The last sentence of Isaiah's first chapter runs: "Both will burn together / and no one put them out." The last sentence of the whole book of Isaiah reads: "Their worm will not die / nor their fire go out; / they will be loathsome to all mankind" (66:24). Probably a few centuries have elapsed between these two sentences. We can, therefore, detect a growth: a certain religious conviction concerning a miserable afterlife begins to grow here and, accordingly, the human language in which that belief expresses itself.

In the religious conviction concerning a happy hereafter, a similar growth can also be observed. Namely, heaven is in line with the prophetic preaching of salvation and reveals only the full extent of it. The biblical message of salvation, too, is one coherent entity; it is preaching concerning heaven, preaching, namely, that God wants to be for us and with us.

That God guarantees our salvation, that he will bring us salvation, seems to find ground ultimately in that God himself is our salvation. Thus not only a salvific God which endows us with various means to salvation, but who is himself in his own person the highest of these means of salvation (Exod. 33:15). That is something which the genuine believers of the Old Testament have clearly realized (Psalms). However earthly and nationally the Old Testament salvation may sound to our ears, the New Testament preaching of salvation adds on strange elements to it but develops further and gives clearer expression to what is contained in it.

This religious growth, too, shows itself in our language: the New Testament speaks about our eternal salvation in words and images which are borrowed from the Old Testament without exception (cf., for example, the expressions in the second half of the verses in Matt. 5:3-10). In our present-day Christendom, heaven threatens to become a trite commonplace; we hear the hazardous leap of faith resound in it even though it may be weak. As we have to go back to the prophetic message of doom for authentic belief in hell, so too we have to go back for living belief in heaven to the prophetic message of salvation which once and for all shaped the salvation proclaimed by the Bible.

It is therefore very nice that in this Scripture reading, immediately after the oracle of doom about the inextinguishable fire, we come to an oracle of salvation, and one which has also played an important role in the development of the biblical imagery of heaven. Presently the question can rest as to how this oracle of salvation has been placed in such an unexpected position in the book of Isaiah. For the time being it will suffice to say this passage concerning the City of God forms a rounded "literary unit," a separate oracle, which has at one time enjoyed an independent existence. This is also evident from the fact that we find it literally included in the prophet Micah (Mic. 4:1-4). This has consequently been called a "loose leaf." First a consideration of the text in detail. What the prophet predicts will happen in the near or distant future; whether the future is near or distant is not indicated. It is in any case a definite future, not just a disconnected future event. As a result of a decisive intervention, for which the believer must keep watching with an unshakable trust, Yahweh once more will create order in the human society, which has become chaos through sin; a new order which will be indestructible. The biblical term for the fulfillment of this future is "the end of the days" or "the time of the end." Through the whole history, which precedes this, the people still have "their days," but then it will be "the Day of Yahweh." "In the days to come the mountain of the Temple of Yahweh shall tower above the mountains and be lifted higher than the hills. All nations will stream to it."

When Isaiah utters these words, the Temple of Jerusalem is still standing. But the intimate circle of faithful disciples to which Isaiah speaks, knows that this Temple is doomed and will be destroyed. That is one of the regular subjects of prophetic preaching of doom. Here, however, Isaiah shares with his disciples his religious certainty that the judgment over this degenerated temple will lead to the construction of a new Temple of a completely different and imperishable character. It will be firmly anchored and, towering over all, will dominate not only the national surroundings but also the whole world. This should not be taken in the geographical sense, of course, but as a characteristic of the New Jerusalem: the Temple of the future is no longer a national affair: "All the nations will stream to it, / peoples without number will come to it; and they will say: / 'Come, let us go up to the mountain of Yahweh, / to the Temple of the God of Jacob / that he may teach us his ways / so that we may walk in his paths.'"

Referring to the faith of a pagan soldier, Jesus turns to the crowd following him. When he says, "Many will come from east and west to take their places with Abraham and Isaac and Jacob . . . in the kingdom of heaven," this is a new and unheard of idea which has to be stressed with an "I tell you solemnly" (Matt. 8:10-11; Luke 7:9). Jesus wonders about the faith of a pagan, but we have more reason to wonder about the faith of Isaiah, who seven centuries before broke through the narrow national outlook in which even Jesus' contemporaries were completely caught.

To evaluate this breakthrough it is necessary to penetrate beyond the skin of the ancient Israelites. We have to realize what it means that the religion of revelation has evolved from being first the national religion of a certain people, namely, of Israel. God has revealed himself as Yahweh, that is to say, as a national god of people. Yahweh is Israel's God, and Israel is Yahweh's people. That is the Old Testament, the old covenant: the bond between a certain people and its God, with whom other people have nothing to do; besides, they each have their own god; they are the "strange gods" which the Bible mentions. "For all the people go forward, each in the name of its god; but we, we go forward in the name of Yahweh, our God, for ever and ever more" (Mic. 4:5). Israel is established as a nation by belief in Yahweh. Israel stands or falls with Yahweh. Still Israel infringes on its covenant. That is its destruction. It is Isaiah's message of doom.

But Yahweh does not stand or fall with Israel. He has in his power even to create children of Abraham from stones; how much more, then, can he build up a new people of God from Israel's faithful remnant. Isaiah and the disciples to which he speaks form the poor remnant amidst an unfaithful mass at this moment. Their faith will be their salvation in the catastrophe that will wipe out ancient Israel. To encourage them, Isaiah opens to them his own religious visions of the new people of God which goes up to the Temple of Jacob's God, that is, of Israel from all corners of the world.

By Israel's destruction the true religion is no longer a national religion. Israel's faithful remnant is called upon to preserve the essential values of the national past and to think about them and to learn to live without giving them a national perspective. That is a crisis of belief; that is a struggle of faith, where those of little faith can go under, but the genuine believer learns to breathe freely in a brand-new world of belief. That is a struggle of faith which the prophet has experienced himself, at the time of his conclusion that the old dispensation had passed. Since his call he has learned to rethink the old familiar belief of his youth: without the Temple as Yahweh's house, without a king as Yahweh's anointed one, without Canaan as Yahweh's land, yes, without Israel as Yahweh's people. He knows now where he stands with Yahweh, regardless of what may come.

He wants to convey this religious certainty to his disciples by this oracle. Hence he speaks of a new temple, technically as impossible as Ezekiel's, since the prophet does not mean material religion can be learned. Jacob's God will instruct them in his ways, so that they will be able to follow his paths. "Since the Law will go out from Zion, and the Oracle of Yahweh from Jerusalem."

The prophet has religious certainty concerning a future, new, divine reality among men, but how this reality will reveal itself is not expressed by his faith. As an Israelite speaks to the Israelites, he can only fall back on the old national data in which God expressed his presence: the mountain of the Temple, house of Yahweh, Zion, Jerusalem. In this way he can formulate and somewhat furnish his vision of the future. He speaks therefore about Law and Word as an indication of the new revelation, since the ancient revelation is contained in the Law of Moses and the Word which comes to the prophets: the Law and the Prophets, that is the entire Old Testament.

This oracle not only breaks through national boundaries but also heralds another equally essential point. There is no mention of political domination. This prophecy does not give any reason to think that David's kingdom will return in glorified form and that all peoples will be part of it only as vanquished persons or as slaves. The breakthrough to the worldwide perspective is simultaneously a breakthrough to the spiritual dimension. The New Jerusalem will be the center of the world, since the peoples will surrender to the divine truth spontaneously. The Kingdom of God is indeed in the world, but not of the world.

This oracle of salvation forms a contrast with the current ideas of Jesus' contemporaries, by which his mission was so misunderstood, thereby becoming such a national disappointment. But the real counterpart of this oracle is the story of the Tower of Babel, eternal type of the kingdom of this world: a high tower which reached to the clouds, visible to all peoples, signifying that the city of Babel exercised power over the whole world. Babel's tower in the Bible is the expression of national pride which tramples on the rights of other peoples and unites all in one complete state by arms.

Babel, and the national self-idolization of which it is a personification, is in this way the cause of all hate and enmity among the peoples, and in this way Babel ruins the original divine world-design of **one** God and consequently one large family of men, one in speech and mind (Gen. 11:1). Opposed to this Babel is the New Jerusalem of Isaiah as the City of God where only truth reigns. Only by the free human acceptance of the truth is one incorporated into this Kingdom and registered as a citizen of Jerusalem (Ps. 87).

Only in the Kingdom will God realize the goal that he had always intended for man and which is expressed in the paradise story. That is why the prophets regularly go back to the time of paradise to illustrate the future: the peace of paradise recurs (cf. Isa. 11:6-8), the curse of Babel has been undone: "He will yield authority over the nations /

and adjudicate between many peoples; / these will hammer their swords into ploughshares, / their spears into sickles. / Nation will not lift sword against nation, / there will be no more training for war."

Flesh and blood did not reveal this salvific vision to Isaiah, for it goes against everything which an Israelite would be able to imagine. This vision can only have grown from a very special experience of God. We know which one, we do not need to guess it. Anyone can see that this vision directly results from Isaiah's vision of his call. For, this is a temple vision, too, but in such a way that the temple takes on cosmic dimensions: earth and heavenly temple merge. Isaiah views the national God of the Israelite people as King of heaven and earth, whose glory no longer remains enclosed within the ancient temple but permeates all the earth. The time of national privilege has passed; just as in Ezekiel's vision, Yahweh's glory moves out of the temple defiled by Israel to found a new sanctuary in the world of pagans.

In Isaiah's time God's work of salvation on earth has only recently started, but heaven sees that work of salvation in its perfection through God's eye. It is praised by a double choir of seraphim, which fills the whole heaven with its majestic sound but which will also fill the earth at a future time. A people with unclean lips cannot participate in that new song. This vision is the source of inspiration of Isaiah's message of damnation for the old national people of God, and of his message of salvation for the new international people of God.

The Christian Church, gathered from pagans of the four winds, sings in all her liturgies the trisagion, the threefold "holy" of the heavenly liturgy. The faithful profess with this that they are pilgrims on earth but possess citizenship in heaven. The Christian is already vitalized by the new life of him who sits at the right hand of the Father. He is convinced that in him and in the whole of mankind the heavenly Jerusalem is under construction and growing. Thus he faithfully celebrates his citizenship in an earthly liturgy till the City of God will reveal itself at the second coming of the Lord.

The book of Revelation is the pure source of this earthly liturgy, since John wants to witness by his lengthy description of the heavenly liturgy what the Church's existence on earth is. In this description the apostle summarizes everything that his prophetic predecessors have seen, together in one grand vision. Essentially one and the same vision was revealed to Isaiah and John. The religious awareness of the prophet went much deeper than his words which, in order to concretely grasp what he sees, look for an anchorage in the earthly and national symbols of Yahweh's presence among his old people. John declares himself to be of the same faith as Isaiah by quoting his words and filling them with what his eyes have seen, his ears have heard, and his hands have touched with regard to the Word of life (1 John 1:1-4). His book, therefore, is also a pure source for the Christian understanding of the ancient prophecy.

The future temple about which Isaiah speaks is already more than and different from Solomon's Temple, but this faithful searching of the prophet has become a clearer and more explicit concept with the apostle, who declares that he no longer sees a temple.

Another example: It is clear that John's description of the New Jerusalem cannot refer to a material city. But how much the prophets already realized of what the actual existence of the future City of God would consist of can be shown in the word with which Ezekiel concludes his seemingly topographical description of city, country, and temple (chaps. 40-48): "The name of the city in future is to be: Yahweh-is-there" (48:35).

The religious development from the prophetic to the apostolic witness conclusively shows an inner religious affinity in the book of Revelation. The following quotation closely links the apostolic witness with the Scripture reading of this chapter, and thus clearly reflects its deepest meaning:

"In the spirit, he took me to the top of an enormous high mountain, and showed me Jerusalem, the holy city, coming down from God out of heaven. It had all the radiant glory of God and glittered like some precious jewel of crystal clear diamond" (Rev. 21:10-11). "I saw that there was no temple in the city since the Lord God Almighty and the Lamb were themselves the temple, and the city did not need the sun or the moon for light, since it was lit by the radiant glory of God and the Lamb was a lighted torch for it" (Rev. 21:22-23).

Isaiah was allowed to catch something of this light in the filmy mirror of human faith. He has spoken so that we too may believe and may find our way back to the city of our birth with the torch of this light of faith (2 Pet. 1:19), through the darkness of the earthly exile.

THAT WILL BE
GOD'S DAY (2:6-22)

2:6 Yes, you have cast off your people,
the House of Jacob;
the land is full of soothsayers,
full of sorcerers like the Philistines;
they clap foreigners by the hand.

7 His land is full of silver and gold
and treasures beyond counting;
his land is full of horses
and chariots without number;

8 his land is full of idols . . .
They bow down before the work of their hands,
before the thing their fingers have made.

9 The mortal will be humbled, man brought low;
do not forgive them.

10 Get among the rocks,
hide in the dust,
at the sight of the terror of Yahweh,
at the brilliance of his majesty,
when he arises
to make the earth quake.

11 Human pride will lower its eyes,
the arrogance of men will be humbled.
Yahweh alone shall be exalted,
on that day.

12 Yes, that will be the day of Yahweh Sabaoth
against all pride and arrogance,
against all that is great, to bring it down,

13 against all the cedars of Lebanon
and all the oaks of Bashan,

2:14   against all the high mountains
       and all the soaring hills,
15   against all the lofty towers
       and all the sheer walls,
16   against all the ships of Tarshish
       and all things of price . . .

17   Human pride will be humbled,
       the arrogance of men will be brought low.
       Yahweh alone will be exalted,
       on that day,
18   and all idols thrown down.

19   Go into the hollows of the rocks,
       into the caverns of the earth,
       at the sight of the terror of Yahweh,
       at the brilliance of his majesty,
       when he arises
       to make the earth quake.

20   That day man will fling to moles and bats the
    idols of silver and the idols of gold that he made
    for worship,
21   and go into the crevices of the rocks
       and the rifts of the crag,
       at the sight of the terror of Yahweh,
       at the brilliance of his majesty,
       when he arises
       to make the earth quake.

22   Trust no more in man,
       he has but a breath in his nostrils.
       How much is he worth?

A well-preserved ruin is sometimes more impressive than a brand-new building, if it is seen in the proper perspective. One should not examine every detail of a ruin in full daylight, nor attempt to restore it at any cost as it perhaps might have been originally. To get the proper impression of the original building it is far better to look at it from a distance in order to assimilate the whole as it rises up from the landscape, or to wander around the weather-beaten walls and lopsided towers in the twilight.

This comparison may be helpful to convey the right attitude toward a Scripture reading like that with which we are dealing: an attitude of complete acceptance, of openness with regard to the actual shape which a scriptural passage has.

The Old Testament documents are just the preserved and collected literature of a people. One does find forceful as well as weak literature in it, masterpieces as well as rhetorical works. Similarly, there are well and badly preserved fragments. God's Word has indeed taken on a human form in Scripture. The question is not whether this form is perfect and attractive. It is a question, rather, of what the sacred author intended to say, and of what the faithful community saw in these words, as they were lived and preserved in their midst (in their original form or not). In any case, concerning this Scripture passage, it should be such that we would not exchange these powerful fragments of biblical poetry at any price for a perfect and impeccable poem.

Poetry is more difficult than prose regardless of the language. This is caused both by the contents and by the form. The poetic thought transcends the vulgar realm and goes deeper than the daily superficiality: it is somewhat like a discovery and a surprise. The poetic form must exploit the utmost possibilities of the language: rare words and construction fallen into disuse appear in poetry. This, together with the proverbially poetic freedom, causes poetry to relinquish its secret less readily than prose and therefore to relinquish it less easily.

The poetic biblical texts have therefore come to us generally less perfect than stories in prose. Those who handed down and copied the texts, did not always read what was there, but what they understood or what in their opinion should be there. Likewise, many textual corruptions originated. Since there are, however, certain fixed ways in which relators and scribes used to make mistakes, the biblical text can be restored to its original form in many cases by so-called textual criticism. There are, however, always cases about which one can only speculate as to what the original text was like.

Textual "corruption" is actually a strong word. The "corrupted" text can sometimes be more profound and richer than the original text. By way of clarification, an example with a far-reaching effect will follow.

Technically speaking, the Greek translators of the Old Testament, in the third century B.C., have not completely rendered the original text, where they misunderstood or misinterpreted the Hebrew text. But they hardly wrote nonsense. Rightly or wrongly they expressed their own faith from the text which they meant to translate. This confession of faith, reflection of what existed among the true believers during the last centuries before Christ, has value, perhaps even scriptural value, even separate from the Hebrew original. The Greek Bible can therefore be considered as an enlarged edition of the Hebrew Bible, updated according to the latest understanding of faith. The Greek Bible often expressed an advanced and more explicated understanding of faith. How seriously we should take this is conclusive from the fact that the New Testament continues to build on this. The heritage of the Hebrew Bible is taken up in its Greek translation in the New Testament.

Such a "textual corruption," such a faithful re-reading, interpreting, and updating of the text has not only occurred in the transition period from the Hebrew to the Greek Bible, but also, and probably much more severely, during the many centuries which preceded this, so in the framework of the transmission of the Hebrew text itself.

The actual form of the book of Isaiah, therefore, has always something worthwhile to say to us, independent of the question of how accurately the original words of the prophet are recorded in it. Even supposing that a text in this or that form does not go back to the historical Isaiah, then we are still concerned with real Scripture. For it is sure that posterity, completely living on Isaiah's message of salvation, wanted to express its own holy conviction.

The faithful community of the Old Testament did not intend to present a textual critical edition of Isaiah; they wanted to preserve and hand down the faith which Isaiah preached in a living form. Scripture owes its existence, its value, and its present form to this inspired transmission of faith, of which prophets, priests, and wise men were the most important exponents.

With a somewhat greater degree of confidence we can now return to the "literary ruin" which we will evaluate in this chapter.

Isaiah is an outstanding poet. He has command of a rich vocabulary and has a sensitive ear for the sound-effects of words. He is fluent and playful at will, passionate and harsh, heavy and lofty. Much of this is lost in a translation. Only the rhythm, in which his thoughts succeed, complement, or repeat each other, is clearly tangible even in a translation—in this book it is also typographically visible—while this naturally can also convey the impression of Isaiah's imagery.

Although the book of Isaiah consist mainly of poetry, it has been preserved in very good condition. The best proof for this is the passage which we are about to consider. It represents the most poorly preserved fragment. Still there is much left, as it is printed here, so much that we get a very reliable impression of the import of the whole. If we can speak of a ruin, then it shall be one from which the main lines of the architecture are still recognizable. That is important, for the prophet's main theme (which dominates the entirety) converges with the biblical message, so that we can say that this entirety has come to us perfectly, yes, perhaps even in this crumbly form it is seen to its full advantage and makes a greater impression. Besides, many a fragment has been well preserved; how all these fragments were once connected, we do not know.

After a closer look, this Scripture passage is not as disorderly as it appears at first sight. This is evident after an examination. Two major pieces stand out at once: a poem concerning something "of which the House of Jacob is full" and a poem concerning "the Day of Yahweh." The rest seems to be composed of various insertions; but if we sort out these insertions, each one appears to recur three times. We discover, therefore, that they form a composed refrain which is thrice repeated, but each time in a slightly changed form. Now we can go to work in an orderly fashion. First we will deal with the two poems and then with the refrain; in this manner we will have recaptured a beautiful fragment of Scripture.

We begin to see in greater detail those two major and perfect fragments. Perhaps they were once separate oracles that were combined in the greater whole. The first oracle forms the beginning of our Scripture reading; it is a poetic fragment concerning the overcrowded House of Jacob.

The House of Jacob! The second chapter opens with a vision of the future, of numerous peoples who are marching to the holy mountain of Jacob's God, to be instructed there in true religion by Yahweh himself. That will be Israel's richness. Jacob's House possesses Yahweh's Law and Word. All peoples will share in this richness. But that is in the future. How different is the present reality! All too pointedly, later generations add the admonition to this prophecy of salvation: "O House of Jacob, come, let us walk in the light of Yahweh." What a force emanates from this admonition: Israel does possess the light of Yahweh; let Israel now finally do what even the pagans will do at a future date: walk in the light of Yahweh. This verse (vs. 5) forms in the book the link with which the oracle of salvation, which was placed here later, is connected with that of doom, which now follows. Compare Romans 11:13. St. Paul hopes to arouse the jealousy of his Jewish congeners by his success among the pagans. We have something similar here. What an unforgivable foolishness it would be if Israel, which possesses the light that will enlighten the whole world, would just go to the pagan for information.

And yet such is the reality: "The House of Jacob; / the land is full of soothsayers, / full of sorcerers like the Philistines; / they clasp foreigners by the hand." Disloyal Jerusalem sought its salvation in foreign superstition of East and West instead of in Yahweh's Law and Word, of which Jerusalem was the cradle. Instead of Yahweh it chose the foreign idols.

Instead of its imperishable riches, it accumulated for

itself deceitful ones: "His land is full of silver and gold
and treasures beyond counting; his land is full of horses /
and chariots without number." Silver and gold, horses and
chariots: they are the biblical and eternally human symbols
of man's greed and lust for power; they are the typical
means of the kingdom of this world, the typical means for
man to save himself and to be self-sufficient; the typical
means of the man who has no use for God and does not
dream of relying on him, since he wants to be humanly
assured by earthly possessions.

That is actually superstition. Man wants to do it his
way, tolerating no restraint; he sets himself up as God:
inventing gods made of his gold and his silver after his
own choice and taste. The explicit idolatry is only the
religious sealing of an essentially godless attitude. The
prophet closes his enumeration very profoundly: "His land
is full of idols. / They bow down before the work of their
hands, / before the thing their fingers have made."

This shows a fragment of the true ancient prophetic
style. Besides, it has received a place in the book which
is completely in Isaiah's line. As the prophet understands
through the vision of his call that his own people, unclean
of lips as it is, cannot partake in the glorification of which
the world will be full in the future, so this Israel which
has defiled itself by going to the pagans and imitating
their religion, will never participate in the religion of
the future, when the peoples of the earth will find Yahweh
on the place where he has lived from of old, but is now
neglected by the people to whom he has originally revealed
himself.

What becomes a message of salvation for the whole
world is, therefore, at the same time one of doom for

Israel. The New Testament rises from the destruction of the Old Testament. The salvation of the new people of God has an ominous reverse for the old people of God.

This paradoxical course of salvation history is contained in the vision of Isaiah's call. This is also stressed by an almost accidental circumstance, i.e., posterity gave a counterbalance to this harsh, prophetical oracle against Israel's religious degeneration by preceding it with the oracle of Jerusalem's salvation as a center of world religion.

The second chapter of Isaiah contains, therefore, a lasting warning for all who count themselves among the oldest children of God's home, to return to the youthful freshness and fervor of converts, if they do not want to become gradually estranged from the true religion and ultimately be excluded.

So much, then, with regard to the first poem. It is indeed a valuable fragment, which pointedly emphasizes the preceding oracles of salvation by a contrast effect to which the connecting verse calls our attention.

The second poem can be approached as follows. Yahweh reigns in heaven. From his lofty throne he watches the human situation. The prophet has experienced God's magnitude and has learned to see the sublunary world through God's eye. He reads into man's pretensions; it is the deceptive glimmer of the idols themselves, which are pre-eminently of human making. Yahweh alone is the divine reality and he alone is great. Yahweh sits on his throne, high and elevated, but Yahweh will one day rise from that throne. Then this sublunar existence will suddenly have had its time, and the day of men will pass for good. At that time it will be clear what all human actions are worth.

The prophet proclaims this religious certainty in his oracle concerning the Day of Yahweh. The Day of Yahweh is a question of belief. The believer must long for it with perseverance, Yahweh's silence being a difficult test of faith. For the time being, earthly man seems to be right. Isaiah's message concerning the Day of Yahweh is received with scornful ridicule, as is evident from a later oracle: "Woe to those who say, 'Quick! Let him hurry his work so that we can see it; these plans of the Holy One of Israel let them happen and come true so that we can know what they are'" (5:19).

A very old fragment of poetry echoes in the unwavering testimony of the prophet: "Yes, that day will be the day of Yahweh Sabaoth / against all pride and arrogance, / against all that is great . . . ."

This general statement is now elaborated, first with images taken from nature. "Against all the cedars of Lebanon / and all the oaks of Bashan; / against all the high mountains / and all the soaring hills."

Finally, the prophet mentions some remarkable human accomplishments: "Against all the lofty towers / and all the sheer walls, / against all the ships of Tarshish / and all things of price."

The phrases of the prophet are adapted to his time and surroundings. He mentions what the people of his time considered as great and as imperishable, and what was admired as summits of technical skill. It is easy for us to substitute the technical miracles of the twentieth century for them. The faith of the prophet is of all times and with images which are still relevant to us; he has positively had his say, also for our time. It has become clearer since Isaiah, that there is an earthly and human greatness, but also, that this can turn against the earth and mankind, if man does not bow before the superiority of a higher order.

Every age has its dangers of megalomania and our time is no exception. Hence, not only every age needs this message of faith, but also every man. Whoever feels the vigor of life in him, having success and a brilliant career, will have to gird himself with this faith in order not to lose himself in earthly matters, and to live a life in surroundings in which God does not mean anything real.

On the other hand, the sick, the severely tried, the humbled—in short, everyone who painfully drags himself through this earthly existence—must strengthen himself with this message of salvation in order not to fall into unleashed greed for earthly goods which he does not possess and in order to learn to discover man's source of life from their very lack.

Here it holds good: happy you, the poor, and woe to you, the rich. Richness is a danger, and poverty is a chance. But it always remains a difficult art to be rich in a faithful way and to be poor in a faithful way. Human happiness is ultimately not an economic question.

The two poems with which we have now dealt are set off advantageously by the ever-recurring elements of the refrain running through it. This refrain creates the atmosphere and gives an irresistible force to the whole prophecy. It will be worthwhile, therefore, to examine the motifs of the refrain with all their variations.

Immediately after the first poem we hear in verse 9: "The mortal will be humbled, man brought low." "Man" serves as parallel to "mortal"; the word can have the emotional value of "respected," important master, but also of "fragile being"; Isaiah is probably making a play on words here. There are two variants of this verse, which differ slightly, verses 11 and 17: "Human pride will lower its eyes, / the arrogance of men will be humbled. Yahweh alone shall be exalted, / on that day." The second poem is linked up with this: "Yes, that will be the day of Yahweh Sabaoth against all pride and arrogance, etc."

Note that here we have always the reverse side of the oracle of salvation concerning the mountain of Yahweh's temple, which stands as the highest of the mountains. The Tower of Babel was mentioned as its biblical counter-balance. It is clearly that Babelic mentality of self-idolatry which expresses itself in all those proud and high elements that are enumerated in the second poem. Indeed, com-pared to Yahweh's mountain, all earthly mountains and hills are humbled; compared to the future temple, high towers and sheer walls pale into insignificance.

We feel, therefore, also a contradiction between the peaceful candle procession of the peoples to Yahweh's mountain and the terrified and hasty hiding of the idolaters in dark holes. Verse 10: "Get among the rocks, / hide in the dust / at the sight of the terror of Yahweh, / at the brilliance of his majesty, / when he arises / to make the earth quake."

The first variant of verse 10 is verse 19: "Go into the hollows of the rocks, / into the caverns of the earth, / at the sight of the terror of Yahweh, / at the brilliance of his majesty, / when he arises / to make the earth quake." The second variant is linked with this one and provides us at the same time with the clue to the whole chapter that makes it into a balanced entirety. The prophecy immed-iately came to the radical accusation: "his land is full of idols . . . / They bow down before the work of their hands, / before the thing their fingers have made" (vs. 8). On Yahweh's Day the worthlessness of all human works will be obvious; the idols, however, are only mentioned in passing. Verse 18 says laconically: "And all idols [will be] thrown down." The manner remains a surprise for the end: the worst humiliation of man is the humiliation of his idols. "That day man will fling to moles and bats the idols of silver and the idols of gold that he made for worship, / and go into the crevices of the rocks / and the rifts of the crag, / at the sight of the terror of Yahweh, / at the brilliance of his majesty, / when he arises / to make the earth quake."

By leaving God, man leaves himself. By proclaiming his ego as absolute, man makes himself to be the idol which ultimately fades into nothingness together with man himself.

In this very nationalistic, penitential sermon, the national aspect is submerged in the general human aspect. Consequently, this prophecy is intimately related to the ancient story of the man who wanted to be like God— independent in the knowledge and practice of good and evil—but who ultimately came to the conclusion that he was naked and had to hide himself when God's majesty approached him.

What looked like a confusing prophecy has become a strong unity by patient investigation. Near a ruin a few loose stones can still lie around. Likewise in verse 6: "Yes, you have cast off your people." And in verse 9: "Do not forgive them." These are clear and therefore misleading translations of very dubious elements, which we consequently have left aside.

The closing verse is a moralizing review from a later date. If this is not from Isaiah himself, it is still the word of Scripture and, as such, has much value. This vision of man, which—though not exhaustive—still cannot be forgotten without impunity, should be remembered by us for a long time: "Trust no more in man, / he has but a breath in his nostrils. / How much is he worth?"

7

BETWEEN GOD
AND CHAOS (3:1-15)

3:1   Yes, see how the Lord Yahweh Sabaoth
is taking from Jerusalem and Judah
support of every kind
(support of bread and support of water):

2   hero, man-at-arms, judge, prophet,
3   diviner, elder, ● captain, noble,
counsellor, sorcerer, soothsayer.
4   "I give them boys for princes,
raw lads to rule over them."

5   The people bully each other,
neighbour and neighbour;
a youth can insult his elder,
a lout abuse a noble,
6   so that everyone tries to catch his brother
in their father's house, to say,
"You have a cloak, so you be leader,
and rule this heap of ruins."

7   When that day comes the other will protest,
"I am no doctor,
in my house is neither bread nor cloak;
do not make me leader of the people."
8   Yes, Jerusalem is falling into ruins
and Judah is in collapse,
since their words and their deeds affront the Lord,
insulting his glory.

9   Their insolent airs bear witness against them,
they parade their sin like Sodom.
To their own undoing, they do not hide it,
they are preparing their own downfall.

3:10   Tell them, "Happy is the virtuous man,
          for he will feed on the fruit of his deeds;
   11   woe to the wicked, evil is on him,
          he will be treated as his actions deserve."

   12   O my people, oppressed by a lad,
          ruled by women.
          O my people, your rulers mislead you
          and destroy the road you walk on.

   13   Yahweh rises from his judgement seat,
          he stands up to arraign his people.
   14   Yahweh calls to judgement
          the elders and the princes of his people:

          "You are the ones who destroy the vineyard
          and conceal what you have stolen from the poor.
   15   By what right do you crush my people
          and grind the faces of the poor?"
          It is the Lord Yahweh Sabaoth who speaks.

So far we have dealt with the first two chapters of the
book of Isaiah, except for one verse, namely, the short
heading above chapter 2, saying: "The vision of Isaiah
son of Amoz, concerning Judah and Jerusalem" (2:1).

This heading seems redundant after the more elaborate
heading with which the first chapter, and consequently
the whole book, begins. Still, this is no reason to leave
it out as has been done in some instances. The translator
not only exceeds his field of competence but also renders
the Scripture reader a poor service by smoothing out an
inequality, which shows something of the growth and
composition of the book.

This heading is an indication that at this point we are
to read oracles which were already collected when the
book was composed in its present order. The editors
placed at the beginning an old prophecy as prologue—
the present first chapter—and provided this with an

elaborate heading with which they attempted to cover the contents of the whole collection. However, due to this process they left the authentic heading of the compiled collections unimpaired. With the second chapter there actually begins a distinctive collection, although it is difficult to say how far this extends; certainly up to chapter 5, but perhaps even up to chapter 12.

In any case, chapters 2-5 belong to each other again in a special way and it is understandable that they have been transmitted together from very early times. They contain similar oracles of doom always directed against Judah and Jerusalem; furthermore, they were uttered in the first period of Isaiah's ministry, that is to say, before Assyria became directly concerned with Israel.

Chapters 6-12 form again another distinctive group; among other similarities they have the same threatening background, namely, the Assyrian invasion. The threat of chapters 2-5 is more general and more vague: it is a nameless and obscure threat which increases from oracle to oracle. Ever darker clouds are building up on the horizon; it is clear to him who sees and is not blind that the long period of peace and welfare in which one still lives will soon belong to the past. It is certain that a catastrophe threatens, but no one knows what form this disaster will take, or precisely where and when the ax will fall.

The first five chapters of the book of Isaiah are therefore pregnant with a coming judgment without describing time and place—which makes it easier to apply them to the whole of humanity. Only the last verses of the fifth chapter seem clearly to allude to the Assyrians. They take care of an apotheosis of disaster in this damnation collection, while they announce the collection that follows. While the

curtain falls over the first part, we hear in the distance
the rumbling step of the irresistible, advancing armies that
will be on stage throughout the second part.

To prevent the overfreighting of our further Scripture
reading and unnecessary repetitions, we can use these
closing verses of the fifth chapter for explanation.

5:25   So, Yahweh aflame with anger against his people
        has raised his hand to strike them;
        he has killed the princes, their corpses lie
        like dung in the streets.
        Yet his anger is not spent,
        still his hand is raised to strike.

26   He hoists a signal for a distant nation
        he whistles it up from the ends of the earth;
        and look, it comes swiftly, promptly.

27   None of them faint or weary,
        none sleeping or drowsy,
        none of them with belt loose,
        none with sandal-straps broken.

28   Its arrows are sharpened,
        its bow all bent,
        the hoofs of its horses are like flint,
        its chariot-wheels like tornadoes.

29   Its roar is the roar of a lioness,
        like a lion cub it roars,
        it growls and seizes its prey,
        it bears it off, and no one can snatch it back.

30   Growling against it, that day,
        like the growling of the sea.
        Only look at the country: darkness and distress,
        and the light flickers out in shadows.

It is not enough to say that this is a beautiful passage.
After our acquaintance with individually beautiful passages from Isaiah, there still remains enough to be discovered. We will particularly develop a feeling for the

dramatic tension and the development among the fragments themselves, by the reading and re-reading of them. The very coherent chapters 2-5 offer a fine opportunity for this purpose.

To prevent us from failing to see the forest for the trees, we would like to recapitulate.

We limit ourselves in this book to the first twelve chapters of Isaiah. These twelve chapters are divided into two sections: the first consists of chapters 1-5; chapter 1—which is at the same time the prologue to the whole book—forms the natural introduction to this first section; chapter 6—the vision of Isaiah's call—can be considered as the monumental introduction to the second part, which closes fittingly with the psalm of praise in chapter 12.

Although it is clearly one and the same Isaiah, whose preaching we hear in both these sections, still there are important differences. One difference has been mentioned: the oracles of the first part have been pronounced before the Assyrian invasion, while the second part always presupposes that this is taking place or is already an accomplished fact.

Another difference is coherent to the first: the first part contains especially prophecies of doom, since the prophet is speaking to a people which is well off, feels safe, and lives lightheartedly. The prophecy of salvation plays a major role in the second section; a great national disaster is taking place: the destruction is a fact, the prophet has every reason to point to the possibilities of a new future.

Still, the unity of both sections transcends their differences: in both, the prophet of the nearness of God speaks; it is his message that God will come. Well, then, God's coming means both salvation and damnation, since his coming is a divine judgment, which will be a judgment of redemption or of destruction, according to the attitude which man adopts. Because the first chapter poses the very choice between these two possibilities—such is the dilemma—so clearly, therefore, it can serve eminently as prologue of the whole book.

Then the real collection of oracles of doom, chapters 2-5, begins: God's coming as the source of disaster; the Day of Yahweh as a day of calamity, as a **Dies Irae,** a day of anger and of wrath! They are oracles, spoken in a prosperous, unbelieving, and spoiled society, consequently so harsh and apparently so one-sided. Yahweh appears to be exclusively a God of doom and wrath.

This, however, is all too harsh and one-sided for later readers who belong to a humbled and well-tried people. In and for their circle the apparent one-sidedness and harshness of this whole collection was balanced by the oracle of salvation with which the second chapter opens. This prophecy of salvation sets off the following oracles of doom to their full advantage: we see disaster as part of a greater entity, the entirety of God's dealings with man.

God becomes near to man to make him happy, to bring him divine salvation. It is man's attitude which, as it were, forces God to be a God of doom in the first instance, but even this doom is directed toward ultimate salvation. This structure of God's acting is also the structure of all prophecies, especially in the case of chapters 2-5 of the book of Isaiah. This collection of oracles of doom begins meaningfully with a prophecy of salvation, and returns to a prophecy concerning salvation in chapter 4.

The passage which we now read puts us into the midst

of the preaching of doom. In the last presentation we
became acquainted with a powerful prophecy of doom
against all human greatness, "greatness" which will vanish
when Yahweh appears in all his majesty. It is a general
and fundamental prophecy of doom, which any man can
take to heart: Israel's greatness will fall like sheer human,
hollow greatness. It is the magnificent overture to this
whole damnation collection. It is followed by three great
oracles of doom which go into greater detail and make
certain applications to the situation in Judah and Jerusalem.
Now we read the first one of these.

In the last Scripture reading the general position that
all human greatness will vanish on the Day of Yahweh
was at issue; now we hear what specific consequences the
Day of Yahweh will have for Jerusalem and Judah.

Everything which seems there to be great and strong,
and by which man feels his existence assured, is enumerated. But Yahweh will remove all these pillars: "Yes,
see how the Lord Yahweh Sabaoth / is taking from
Jerusalem and Judah / support of every kind . . . hero,
man-at-arms, judge, prophet, / diviner, elder, captain,
noble, / counsellor, sorcerer, soothsayer."

Where the pillars break down, a collapse is bound to
follow. The description of this gains in vividness by the
sudden change to the first person. "I give them boys for
princes, / raw lads to rule over them" (vs. 4). There is only
a choice between God's will and wantonness, between God
and chaos. Where God is no longer the source of authority,
the road which leads to tyranny and chaos is open.
Tyranny: "O my people, oppressed by a lad, / ruled by
women" (vs. 12). Chaos: by force everyone provides himself with what he desires: "The people bully each other, /

neighbour and neighbour; / a youth can insult his elder, / a lout abuse his noble" (vs. 5).

How far it will go is sketched by the prophet with biting irony in a dramatic close-up: ". . . everyone tries to catch his brother / in their father's house, to say, / 'You have a cloak, so you be leader, / and rule this heap of ruins.' / When that day comes the other will protest, / 'I am no doctor, in my house is neither bread nor cloak; / do not make me a leader of the people'" (vss. 6-7).

It happens rather often that one is at the end of one's wits with regard to the revenging God of doom of the Old Testament. Many take offnese from it. Perhaps this oracle of doom can help to make the biblical usage more understandable. It is rather obvious that the anarchy and disorder to which Yahweh's people are delivered are the logical consequence of the general degeneration.

At issue is a people which from origin and by essence can exist only as a people of God. If this is so, Jerusalem and Judah have denied their very existence as city and people of God; the whole building still stands, but the structure no longer rests on the cornerstone of faith in God: the functions of service in the Kingdom of God have degenerated to human power position; in this way those who are called to retain the national society contribute to its decay. What can be left, for example, of Israel's authentic character and consequently of Israel's reason for existence, if its prophets degenerate to ordinary, ancient Near Eastern, hired prophets, who do not interpret God's will but attempt to make a good business by pretending that the things the people want to hear are, in truth, the Word of God. That it had come to this with the prophets is evident from many data, among them the fact that Isaiah sums up,

in one breath, prophets, counsellors, sorcerers, and soothsayers (vs. 3). Just as the prophets have facilitated paganism, so jurisdiction has become a source of injustice. And
it is the same everywhere. By his enumeration of the leading classes, Isaiah pictures a complete, decadent society
for us. It is thus logical that all this disaster is bound to
come one day.

The prophet points to this logic by quoting a proverb
of Israel's national wisdom: "Happy is the virtuous man, /
for he will feed on the fruit of his deeds; / woe to the
wicked, evil is on him, / he will be treated as his actions
deserve" (vss. 10-11).

This is, however, only one side of the picture. By sin,
man not only attacks his own humanity but also attacks
God: Judah and Jerusalem have already stumbled and
are now fallen, since their tongue and their deeds challenge Yahweh's glory; as shameless as Sodom they openly
proclaim their sin; they are proud of it (vss. 8-9).

Sin challenges God and he takes revenge. The prophet
attributes, therefore, an active role to Yahweh in the
destruction of Judah: Yahweh takes away the pillars. He
appoints children as kings, so that chaos is bound to
follow. So far as we are annoyed by this divine "revenge-
fulness," it is only a question of language, as is clear from
the previous pages; but this is at the same time the
proclamation of a truth of faith, namely, that human
misery is not only a naturally necessary extension of faulty,
human action, but at the same time also divine punishment.
And that is a very important truth, which is also stressed
in the paradise story by the literary form of a divine
judgment.

It remains true, therefore, that sin recoils on itself.

But man would be lost beyond redemption if, with this
everything concerning human disaster had been said
There would be no way out if the process of sin and
punishment were to proceed with the iron logic of a
mechanism. It is, therefore, not an obnoxious, but an
extraordinarily consoling, truth, which the Bible constantly
teaches, that it is also and ultimately God who takes re
venge, who punishes, who judges, who sentences.

The prophetic usage has a very positive meaning. It is
perhaps still possible for the twentieth-century Christian
to appreciate the **Dies irae.** In the disaster which is caused
by sin God reveals his anger. That is his very salvation. As
soon as man, who experiences the disastrous consequence
of his deeds, comes to the belief that it is God's hand
which strikes, which strikes with justice, which is forced
to strike, then he has discovered the hand which strikes
to heal. Through this faithful realization the iron mechan
ism is already broken and there is always something of a
change in the human attitude, through which man becomes
accessible again for divine redemption. Then what was
a curse becomes a blessing; then disaster can be salvific
With the unrepentant sinner God continues his dialogue
in the only possible way, namely, by using the consequences
of the sin as punishment. But it still is a dialogue, and
God hopes for an answer. In the prophecy of Isaiah
nothing can be found in the spirit of "Just wait; who
laughs first, laughs last"; nothing in the vein of "Revenge
is sweet." Just as the prophet is compelled by what we
presently would call pastoral zeal, so his God Yahweh
is driven by love. This, too, repeatedly breaks through in
the prophecy of doom. It is the love of an angry father
whose tears well up in his eyes, seeing what has become
of his child. Yahweh is angered. He threatens to strik

his people. But this threatening oracle betrays itself in that he strikes this people just because he still believes in what he loves and what he wants to save:

"O my people, your rulers mislead you / and destroy the road you walk on. / . . . Yahweh calls to judgement / the elders and the princes of his people: / 'You are the ones who destroy the vineyard / and conceal what you have stolen from the poor. / By what right do you crush my people / and grind the faces of the poor?' " (vss. 12-15).

This is not a judgment which crushes ruthlessly like a roller, but a moving judgment of God, which can be reacted to in a human way and is followed by a new divine response.

It is always God's glory, which Isaiah saw. If man continues to challenge it, he will be crushed under this divine gaze. But if he faithfully surrenders, he will be purged and healed.

Just as God came in this fashion, so also will he come today and tomorrow. Now as God of salvation, now as God of disaster, but always to be, for as many people as possible, a God of salvation on the day of his second coming.

8

ZION AND ZION'S

DAUGHTERS (3:16-4:6)

3:16   Yahweh said: Because of the haughtiness
of the daughters of Zion,
the way they walk with their heads held high
and enticing eyes,
the way they mince along,
tinkling the bangles on their feet,
17   the Lord will give the daughters of Zion itching
heads
and uncover their nakedness.

18-23   That day the Lord will take away the ankle
ornaments, tiaras, pendants ● and bracelets, the
veils, ● headbands, foot chains and belts, the scent
bottles and amulets, signet rings and nose rings, ●
the expensive dresses, mantles, cloaks and purses,
● the mirrors, linen garments, turbans and mantillas.
24   Instead of scent, a stink;
instead of belt, a rope;
instead of hair elaborately done, a shaven scalp,
and instead of gorgeous dress, a sack;
and brand marks instead of beauty.

25   Your men will fall by the sword,
your heroes in the fight.
26   The gates will moan and mourn;
you will sit on the ground desolate.
4:1   And seven women will fight
over a single man that day:
"We will eat our own food,

> and wear our own clothing," they will say
> "let us bear your name;
> take our disgrace away."

4:2   That day, the branch of Yahweh
> shall be beauty and glory,
> and the fruit of the earth
> shall be the pride and adornment
> of Israel's survivors.

3   Those who are left of Zion
> and remain of Jerusalem
> shall be called holy
> and those left in Jerusalem, noted down for
>   survival.

4   When the Lord has washed away
> the filth of the daughter of Zion
> and cleansed Jerusalem of the blood shed in her
> with the blast of judgement and the blast of
>   destruction,

5   Yahweh will come and rest
> on the whole stretch of Mount Zion
> and on those who are gathered there,
> a cloud by day, and smoke,
> and by night the brightness of a flaring fire.
> For, over all, the glory of Yahweh

6   will be a canopy ● and a tent
> to give shade by day from the heat,
> refuge and shelter from the storm and the rain.

The first part of this Scripture reading touches on a welcome subject, about which preachers of all times have had their say. We will not attempt to improve on them. One cannot dismiss Isaiah with the crushing argument that he does not know what he is talking about, since he shows a thorough knowledge concerning the female wardrobe, which makes a Scripture translator despair but which is a gold mine for an investigator into the history of fashions.

The twenty-one articles which the prophet has seen

hanging on or around the daughters of Zion have set many scholarly pens in motion. Rather serious books have been written about them. Some of these articles can be illustrated by images on monuments and especially by what has been found in digs on or in the neighborhood of withered bones excavated during the last century. In all probability, these things did not always belong to the aforementioned daughters of Zion, but nevertheless they surely belonged to no less coquettish representatives of the ancient fair sex.

It is outside our scope to go into detail about this, since we do not use Scripture, here, as a source of peculiarities— with which it is filled—but as a source of faith. We seek, therefore, what the prophet as authoritative witness of faith has really to say to us. We should not take him lightly. It is quite possible that the prophet was influenced by male irony as well as being inspired by the Spirit of God in formulating his message. The male Scripture readers should not cheer too early, neither should the female readers be annoyed too soon.

What the prophet means will be clarified by the collection concerning the damnation, in the framework of which he deals with female make-up, and by the two oracles which immediately follow and which form a unity with them in the book. This is the reason for combining them in one Scripture reading.

The collection of prophecies of doom, chapters 2-5, has as its main theme the Day of Yahweh. On that day it will be clear that God alone is really great. Then all pseudo-greatness will collapse. It reverses to the contrary: that on which man had built his success will now be the cause of his destruction; that, of which he was so proud, will humble him and will put him to shame.

Chapter 2 outlined it in general terms. But in the three great oracles, which follow, the prophet makes applications. In the first of these—the last Scripture reading—especially the men have to suffer: hero, man-at-arms, judge, prophet, elder, captain, noble, counsellor. They are important men who think themselves indispensable pillars of society. But when the Day of Yahweh comes, male snobbery will end suddenly. Yahweh will take away all the pillars. When women are mentioned here, it is done to give a clearer picture as to how low men should be brought. Others will take their high positions. And who are they? "O my people, oppressed by a lad, ruled by women" (3:12). That is the summit of destruction to men, at least to the ancient Near Eastern men.

But now the women have their turn. They abundantly get their share. The prophet reminds them of their real nobility: daughters of Zion, called to be mothers of God's people, mothers of faith, who have to keep up their famous tradition of a Sarah, a Rebekah, and a Rachel. It is difficult to recognize them in the fashionable Jerusalem matrons, the greater part of the dignified partners in life of the important pillars which Yahweh will remove. Well then, on his day, Yahweh will also take away something from the ladies; their glimmering delusive greatness, too, will pale before the splendor of Yahweh's coming and will bring disgrace. "That day the Lord will take away the ankle ornaments, tiaras, pendants and bracelets, the veils, headbands, foot chains and belts, etc." (vss. 18-23).

Scripture has nothing against female ornaments. On the contrary, it appreciates female grace as stressed by the attire of a bride or a queen, and it likes to see in it the beautiful human picture of radiant happiness which God will grant to men. But here there is nothing of that fairy-tale. When Yahweh takes away the ornaments, nothing is left. Zion's daughters lack integrity and personal value, and seek it therefore in externals. With this tinsel they disguise their meaningless existence and, once dolled up, they feel great. This parade of pride is bound to collapse. This prophecy affirms the suspicion that Isaiah himself descended from higher circles and freely moved around within this social level. He is a man who knows his world and sees through it completely. In his enumeration he upsets the whole boudoir. Yet, much order cannot be detected in the prophecy, and surely not in its translation. The prophet, due to his feeling for language, must have allowed himself to be influenced by the sound of Hebrew terms. By reading aloud the following example, always with the main stress on the last syllable, we can perhaps get an impression of this:

18. haakasim wehashshevisim wehassaharonim
19. hannetiphoth wehashsheroth wehalealoth

These are the first six ornaments mentioned, placed in a formation of three following three. The last eight are arranged by fours.

22. hammahalaçoth wehammaataphoth wehammitpahoth wehaharitim
23. wehaggilyonim wehassedinim wehaççeniphoth weharedidim

("We" is the conjunction "and"; "ha" is the article which generally demands a doubling of the following consonant; "oth" is the feminine plural, "im" the masculine plural form.)

The details here are of no importance; it is the enumeration which does the trick and immediately evokes a picture that is timeless: the image of a strutting lady, a rather flashy and gaudy fashion plate, bedecked with trinkets, who demands the whole sidewalk, at least insofar as the cloud of perfume enveloping her is concerned.

This dull enumeration, however, forms a loose, interrupting fragment inserted later into this powerful poem. It is worth the effort to read the three verses in one piece: "Because of the haughtiness of the daughters of Zion, the way they walk with their heads held high and enticing eyes, the way they mince along, tinkling the bangles on their feet, the Lord will give the daughters of Zion itching heads and uncover their nakedness. Instead of scent, a stink; instead of belt, a rope; instead of hair elaborately done, a shaven scalp, and instead of gorgeous dress, a sack; and brand marks instead of beauty" (vss. 16, 17, 24).

With this, the oracle concerning the women is finished. This is contradictory, for in the next three verses there is mention of women. Yet it is certain that we are dealing with another oracle, which is consequently not directed against the women, but against the city. The men and the heroes of the city will perish in the war by the sword. The gates of the cities will moan and mourn. Deprived of its manpower, the city will sit on the ground, desolate (vss. 25ff.).

How extensive the slaughter among the fighting men will be is tangibly portrayed by the prophet through his insertion of another dramatic scene (like the device he used earlier when just any member of a family was caught with the words: "You have a cloak, so you be leader and rule this heap of ruins" (3:6). This time seven women will fight simultaneously over a single man. Compare the corresponding phrase in the book of Leviticus, used there to portray the shortage of food: "One oven shall suffice for ten women to bake your bread" (26:26).

The shortage of men is so extensive that the roles are reversed: the women have to sue for the hand of the men, even seven women for one single man; they will support themselves; the only thing they ask for is that he take away what is, according to their ideas, the greatest disgrace to a woman: the unmarried state and childlessness (4:1). In no uncertain terms the prophet expresses a threat which repeatedly recurs in the prophecy of damnation: the elite of men will fall, the wives will become widows, the children orphans.

That the text was adapted to make this oracle a direct continuation of the oracles against the women is immaterial. These women have already been threatened with their due punishment for the haughtiness for which they are blamed: instead of scent, a stink, instead of gorgeous dress, a sack, etc. So, the text does not say that they will sit down moaning near the gates of the city as lonely widows!

We have, then, two separate oracles without mutual literary connection. But objectively there is a connection. This has been felt traditionally and these oracles have justifiably been put together. This also puts the oracle against the ladies in the proper perspective. It is this that the prophet wants ultimately to hurt in the daughters of Zion: the whole city, which is pre-eminently the daughter of Zion. Exactly by maintaining the difference between both oracles they receive their full impact.

The decadent beauty of the Jerusalem ladies is a significant expression of the decadence of the whole city. As the wife, beside the husband as head, is the heart of the family, so she is also the heart of society. When the women are good for nothing, there will also be something wrong with the men. The conduct of the women is a scale denoting the level of the whole society to which they belong.

The first oracle says, therefore, that the ladies will be affected in the very things in which they look for delusive greatness. The second oracle says that the entire disloyal city will have to pay for it: the men will die in battle, the women will be left behind, alone.

The first oracle contrasted the haughtiness of the dolled-up daughters of Zion with its humiliation, as those with a shaven scalp they will walk around wearing a sack. The editors of the book do complete justice to the thought of the prophet by contrasting the proud ladies with the disgrace of the women of the hard-hit city that is left without men and children.

By connecting these two oracles the knife cuts both ways. The feminine frivolousness is completely condemned, since it has deeper repercussions in this case: it is a symptom of the general decay, which is revealed by ladies in a typical, womanlike manner, but for which the city in her totality will have to pay as well.

They are then not only punished in their vanity; the greatest disgrace thinkable for women will happen to them. The second oracle complements the first one in this way, while it recalls at the same time that the prophet passes judgment on the entire urban society by sentencing the ladies. The pride of the women runs parallel to the pride of men. Only the women (as decadent daughters of Zion) are an effective typification of the disloyal city, **the** decadent daughter of Zion.

The coherence between both oracles is confirmed and explicated by a third oracle, which in its turn concerns the

whole city, but in such a way that the daughters of Zion
are called by name. It is an oracle of salvation, which
has been very meaningfully placed here, since it is a clear
counterbalance of the two damnation oracles with which
we have dealt. This Scripture reading forms in this way
a powerful entity, which always sticks to the same subject:
Zion and the daughters of Zion.

Therefore, we can follow here in a nutshell (an opportunity we seldom have) the prophetic train of thought.
This is always present in a larger context, but is never
easily seen at a glance. The main links are: reproach of
sin, threat of punishment, punishment as purification, for-
giveness of sin, restoration, and new economy of salvation.

The prophecy presupposes the existing order and that
is a situation of national and mundane welfare, which is
ultimately the result of the covenant with Yahweh through
which Israel gradually became a people and could figure
as such. But this principle of life of the nation is affected.
That is the sin which must lead in the long run to a national
disaster. The prophetic preaching of doom must be placed
in this setting: various reproaches for sin, all kinds of
threats with punishments. That is the case in this collection
of oracles of doom: the universal pride must be succeeded
by a universal humiliation (chap. 2), the special expressions
of pride, both of men and of women, will be succeeded
by special, fatal consequences (chap. 3).

Still, this is not the end. The prophecy of doom is
immediately succeeded by a prophecy concerning salvation.
The creative, salvific will, which called Israel into life,
remains in force. Yahweh of Hosts will retain a remnant.
The fate of Jerusalem does not need to become similar to
that of Sodom, which remained without a remnant.

In one or another form the idea of a remnant is always the link between disaster and salvation. The concept has its origin in the prophecy of doom: remnant is a poor remainder; of this numerous and prosperous Israel, only a remnant will be left. But this poor remnant is offered a chance to be the insignificant starting point of a new economy of salvation.

The further prophetic train of thought can now be followed step by step from the third oracle, in which the notion of remnant immediately stands out: "That day, the branch of Yahweh / shall be beauty and glory, / and the fruit of the earth / shall be the pride and adornment of Israel's survivors" (vs. 2).

Yahweh gives the true human salvation, indicated here as generally as possible—Israel's expectation of salvation is no expectation of certain "things," it is an expectation of Yahweh; there are no earthly factors which bring this salvation; it is a complete, new salvation, a creation of Yahweh; therefore: Yahweh will allow "the branch of Yahweh" to bud. It is further indicated with a term that summarizes what Yahweh has done for the fathers and that already begins to become the classical term for "what Yahweh holds in the future for his sons," namely, "the fruit of the [promised] earth."

This salvation from God is in sharp contrast to the false salvation sought by peoples themselves. The preceding damnation prophecy directs itself against this false salvation, against human self-sufficiency and, with regard to the ladies, against their proud attire. This kind of salvation, namely, this pride and this attire, will lead them to the contrary: damnation, that is, humiliation and disgrace.

Contrasted, the salvation which comes from God will

be an ornament and beauty, pride and attire; now a true pride and a true attire, so also true salvation for the faithful remnant.

As usual the unfaithful mass stand here contrasted with the faithful remnant, both with their own ornament and their own attire, in which the profound contrast between both becomes deadly visible: on the one hand, human tinsel which disguises the inner emptiness and human decadence, which nevertheless will mercilessly be exposed to view; on the other hand, the ornament of perfect humanity which comes from Yahweh; the masses do not have an eye for this and pass by disdainfully, but when the Day of Yahweh is at hand, only this ornament will endure and reveal its full splendor.

Isaiah elaborates on a contradistinction which is very similar to this—including the notion of remnant—in an oracle against the capital city of Samaria, which, due to its position and its buildings is literally the crown of the Northern Kingdom. The text is too beautiful and too much to the point not to quote it in part:

> Woe to the haughty crown of Ephraim's drunkards
> to the fading flower of its proud splendour
> overlooking the lush valley. . . .

> There will be trampled underfoot
> the haughty crown of Ephraim's drunkards,
> and the faded flower of its proud splendour
> overlooking the lush valley.
> Just like a fig before summer comes:
> whoever notices it, picks it,
> no sooner in the hand than swallowed.

> That day, Yahweh Sabaoth
> will be a crown of glory
> and a diadem of splendour
> for the remnant of his people.
> Isaiah 28:1-6

The similarity in thought pattern and even in the choice of words between this oracle and that concerning the daughters of Zion speaks for itself. Particularly the new salvation is in the oracle concerning Zion just as "beauty and adornment of Israel's survivors," that is, for those who will survive the national catastrophe; literally: for the group of people, who escaped and got away.

Those are not lucky ones by coincidence, but those who have maintained themselves spiritually in this catastrophe by saving or regaining the faith: their faith is their salvation (Hab. 2:4; Rom. 1:17). Precisely in order to arouse this faith and exhort to faithful loyalty, the prophet opens this salvific perspective, even before the disaster has completely broken loose.

The prophet continues: "Those who are left of Zion / and remain of Jerusalem / [once more two technical terms for the notion of remnant] shall be called holy." The holy ones are in principle already present in the sinful city: ". . . those left in Jerusalem, / noted down for survival" (vs. 3). God knows his people. He knows whom he has elected. The catastrophe will not destroy them but will purify and temper them. Through the disaster they will atone for their sin. As new people, as a seed of a new people of saints, they will come forth from the judgment "when the Lord has washed away / the filth of the daughter[s]* of Zion / and cleansed Jerusalem of the blood shed in her / with the blast of judgement and the blast of destruction" (vs. 4).

There they are again the daughters of Zion. Their old

*Editor's Note: Some translations use the singular form, others the plural. The Jerusalem Bible uses the singular and adds the note: " 'daughter' corr.; 'daughters' Hebr."

attire is lost, terrible disgrace has afflicted them, but insofar as they repent, Yahweh will cleanse them from their filth and provide them with a new attire and new ornaments. This whole prophecy of salvation is concerned with the city, with **the** daughter of Zion and may well have been placed here originally! That there is a plural is all the more an indication that this prophecy of salvation has been connected with the prophecy against the women. We will attempt to include them in the following text.

After the purifying judgment follows a complete restoration and more than that: "Yahweh will come and rest / on the whole stretch of Mount Zion / and on those who are gathered there, / a cloud by day, and smoke, / and by night the brightness of a flaring fire. / For, over all, the glory of Yahweh / will be a canopy and a tent / to give shade by day from the heat, / refuge and shelter from the storm and the rain" (vss. 5-6).

In this rich text the prophet recalls the time when Yahweh made Israel his bride, the trip through the desert which has become an idyll, the honeymoon, the time of the first tender love. Yahweh cannot forget his first love and is prepared for a grand repetition—but one which goes deeper spiritually—of the miracles of the exodus from Egypt, to fashion himself a new people as he created the old people at one time.

The text again makes mention of the city, not the women. But now the modern Scripture reader is allowed to do what we have seen the ancients do before in this prophecy: he is allowed to link this text to the disgrace of widowhood and childlessness which will afflict the proud women. Not only the bearing of the whole, but also the text in question points in that direction. The word which is translated here by "canopy" points in two other instances in which it is mentioned in the Bible always to a bridal room (Joel 2:16; Ps. 19:6).

We can therefore interpret it as follows: Yahweh will take away the disgrace of Zion's daughter by dressing her in a new bridal gown, and she who was known to be barren will be mother of many children again (54; 62:4-5; 66:7-13; cf. 61:10). We can also see a contrast here: the disgrace of the childless widows versus the fertile bridehood of the new Zion. The canopy of Yahweh's glory changes the cleansed mountain of Zion again into the bridal room in which the covenant between Yahweh and Israel is celebrated.

And concerning the daughters of Zion, they, cleansed, will be the living sign of the bridal character which will be pre-eminently proper to Zion's daughter: they will again be genuine mothers of faith like the ancestresses of the ancient people of God. Like Sarah, Rebekah, and Rachel, whose wombs were barren, Yahweh will offer them physical, but especially spiritual, fertility, so that they will become the highly adored mothers of many faithful generations, mothers of the new people of God.

This will be her inperishable fame, her real feminine ornament which cannot be taken away by anyone.

9

THE SONG OF
THE VINEYARD (5:1-24)

5:1   Let me sing to my friend
the song of his love for his vineyard.
My friend had a vineyard
on a fertile hillside.

2   He dug the soil, cleared it of stones,
and planted choice vines in it.
In the middle he built a tower,
he dug a press there too.
He expected it to yield grapes,
but sour grapes were all that it gave.

3   And now, inhabitants of Jerusalem
and men of Judah,
I ask you to judge
between my vineyard and me.

4   What could I have done for my vineyard
that I have not done?
I expected it to yield grapes.
Why did it yield sour grapes instead?

5   Very well, I will tell you
what I am going to do to my vineyard:
I will take away its hedge for it to be grazed on,
and knock down its wall for it to be trampled on.

6   I will lay it waste, unpruned, undug;
overgrown by the briar and the thorn.
I will command the clouds
to rain no rain on it.

7   Yes, the vineyard of Yahweh Sabaoth
is the House of Israel,
and the men of Judah
that chosen plant.

He expected justice, but found bloodshed,
integrity, but only a cry of distress.

5:8   Woe to those who add house to house
and join field to field
until everywhere belongs to them
and they are the sole inhabitants of the land.

9   Yahweh Sabaoth has sworn this in my hearing,
"Many houses shall be brought to ruin,
great and fine, but left untenanted;

10   ten acres of vineyard will yield only one barrel,
ten bushel of seed will yield only one bushel."

11   Woe to those who from early morning
chase after strong drink,
and stay up late at night
inflamed with wine.

12   Nothing but harp and lyre,
tambourine and flute,
and wine for their drinking bouts.

Never a thought for the works of Yahweh,
never a glance for what his hands have done.

13   My people will go into exile,
for want of perception;
her dignitaries dying of hunger,
her populace parched with thirst.

14   . . . Yes, Sheol opens wide his throat
and gapes with measureless jaw
to swallow up her thronging nobility
as they are shouting for joy.

15   The mortal humbled, man brought low,
proud eyes will be cast down.

16   Yahweh Sabaoth will increase his glory by his
sentence,
the holy God will display his holiness by his
integrity.

17   Lambs will graze as at pasture,
fatlings and kids browse in the ruins.

5:18 Woe to those who draw down punishment on themselves
  with an ox's halter,
  and sin
  as with a chariot's traces:

19 and to those who say, "Quick! Let him hurry his work
  so that we can see it;
  these plans of the Holy One of Israel,
  let them happen and come true
  so that we can know what they are."

20 Woe to those who call evil good, and good evil,
  who substitutes darkness for light
  and light for darkness,
  who substitute bitter for sweet
  and sweet for bitter.

21 Woe to those who think themselves wise
  and believe themselves cunning.

22 Woe to the heroes of drinking bouts,
  to the champions at preparing strong drinks.

23 Woe to those who for a bribe acquit the guilty
  and cheat the good man of his due.

24 For this, as stubble is prey for the flames
  and as straw vanishes in the fire,
  so their root will rot,
  their blossom be carried off like dust,
  for rejecting the Law of Yahweh Sabaoth,
  and despising the word of the Holy One of Israel.

The prophet can, of course, make use of the image of the vineyard throughout the whole year, if he so desires. But everything favors allowing him to do this during the time when the vineyard songs were heard everywhere and the highways and byways were sprinkled profusely with wine. There were such annual days.

Israel's calendar celebrates three great yearly festivals, generally known under the names of Passover, Pentecost, and the Feast of Tabernacles. All three feasts have their roots in very ancient rustic customs. They are the celebration of the great seasonal events in the lives of herdsmen and farmers.

Passover is the feast of the firstborn. It is spring. The first lambs gambol in the pastures. The barley has ripened to the extent that one can begin to cut it with the sickle (Deut. 16:19; Lev. 23:10). The firstborn are offered. One eats of the new grain taken right from the threshing floor, roasting it or making unleavened bread.

Pentecost comes fifty days later. Now the wheat, too, is ripe. One is already busily gathering it. Pentecost is the great feast of the grain harvest, of the produce of the field.

Finally, at the beginning of the fall there follows, as a closing of the year, the harvest of the produce of the trees, the harvest of fruit. Among them is the harvest of the vines, the most extensive and elaborate of them. During this time the vine-dresser lives in the vineyard with his whole family in a hut made of leaves. This is for the purpose of guarding the crop and having as many hands as possible for the work. Hence the name "Feast of Tabernacles." It is the most popular and exuberant of the feasts.

It was celebrated before the year 1000 B.C. in its ancient pagan form, as the book of Judges tells us: The citizens of Shechem "went out into the countryside to harvest their vineyards; they trod the grapes and held rejoicings and went into the temple of their god" (9:27). At the same time and in the same book we can already detect the Israelitic form of this feast in "Yahweh's feast which is held every year at Shiloh." The Benjaminites would hide themselves in ambush in the vineyard and carry off the daughters of Shiloh during their dances (21:19-21). These feasts, which stem from the culture of that day, have been "baptized" into the culture of Israel. This has happened also to a certain degree in Christendom. The religious tendency which these feasts already possessed, though it was pagan, became a pure Yahwistic tendency. They are and remain feasts of herdsmen and farmers, but they are an expression of Israel's belief in Yahweh. She experiences the benefits of the harvest as a gift of Yahweh, who crowned his great deeds of the exodus from Egypt by giving this land to her forefathers. He grants it fertility to this day.

The peasant custom receives a new meaning. It becomes a remembrance of what Yahweh did for the fathers. It is a profession of faith that he who manifested himself as God of the fathers also hovers over their posterity with the same redeeming love and grants them the enjoyment of the fruits of the Promised Land.

"When you have harvested the produce of the land . . . you shall take choice fruits, palm branches, boughs of leafy trees, and willows from the river bank, and for seven days you shall rejoice in the presence of Yahweh your God. . . . For seven days you are to live in shelters: all natives of Israel must live in shelters, so that your descendants may know that I made the sons of Israel live in shelters when I brought them out of the land of Egypt" (Lev. 23:39-43). The huts, which have their purpose in the circumstances of the harvest, are given a religious meaning: they are reminiscent of the tents used during the journey in the desert.

Pagan feasts became Yahwistic in this manner. Yahwism is a historical religion of revelation. The feasts which were permeated with pagan natural religion are related to Yahweh because they receive a historical meaning.

During Isaiah's day, Jerusalem was no longer a rural settlement. The prophet stood in the midst of a degenerate urban society. Not much was left of the good old days. But the exterior of things had been maintained, especially in regard to the feasts. Likewise the ancient wine feast. The tabernacles were still there. They served as a liturgical exterior on the temple square, and it was a popular custom to erect them on the flat roofs of houses. The feast, however, lacked any real religious convictions and had become nothing more than a wine festival.

We feel the tangible background in the prophet's woe against "those who from early morning / chase after strong drink, / and stay up late at night inflamed with wine. / Nothing but harp and lyre, / tambourine and flute, / and wine for their drinking bouts" (vss. 11-12). People who are not worth a button can now show off: "Woe to the heroes of drinking bouts, / to the champions at preparing strong drink" (vs. 22).

The picturesque and popular feast during the Eastern autumn, the idyll of the merry dances in the midst of the vineyards, cannot be found in the dissolute shouting on the streets and in the nightly feasting in bars and palaces. One gets to know a people very well from the style of its feasts, and it is particularly in its feasts that the decadence of Jerusalem can be seen by all.

The prophet sees through all this camouflage. He sees what merrymakers do not see: the nearness of God, which must become crushing for such a city. But literally and metaphorically fuddled, they pay "never a thought for the works of Yahweh, / never a glance for what his hands have done. / My people will go into exile, / for want of perception." This immoderate eating-and-drinking people will perish, "her dignitaries dying of hunger, her populace parched with thirst. Yes, Sheol, opens wide his throat / and gapes with measureless jaw / to swallow up her thronging nobility / as they are shouting for joy" (vss. 12-14).

The prophet senses here again the abyss of doom which will be more precisely defined in the Christian teaching concerning hell. In parenthesis, a clear example of "synthetic parallelism" can be found here; the thought is that both the masses and the nobles (dignitaries) will suffer from hunger and thirst.

This clamorous feast, therefore, will be followed by the silence of death. Where the brawling city presently is, there will be the silence of desolation: "Lambs will graze as at pasture, / fatling and kids browse in the ruins" (vs. 17).

This is the last great prophecy from the damnation collection. It concerns the Day of Yahweh as a day which will wipe out all hollow human reality, since on that day the only true reality will reveal himself. The coherence with the preceding prophecies is underscored in a happy manner by the insertion at this point of the borrowed fragment of chapter 2: "The mortal humbled, man brought low, / proud eyes will be cast down. / Yahweh Sabaoth will increase his glory by his sentence, / the holy God will display his holiness by his integrity" (vss. 15-16).

This very special damnation sermon, attuned to the wine feast, is reduced by these verses to the general damnation theme, in which perspective it receives its full import. The prophet is no more against celebration than against feminine ornaments. He turns himself against the self-assured, godless mentality which manifests itself in the celebrations of Jerusalem. The feast bears all the characteristics of a society in which rights and justice are lacking. It is a merciless feast. Therefore, it will turn to its own disadvantage when, on Yahweh's Day, his power and justice will manifest themselves.

Yahweh himself comes to establish right and justice in the city for whose right and justice he has waited so long and in vain. The right which he brings, therefore, will be revenging justice and destructive judgment. The prophet states this throughout the whole prophecy, but especially in the oracle with which it begins: the Song of the Vineyard.

As the woe oracles, some of which we have already mentioned, begin to speak more against the background of the wine feast, so much the more does this apply to the Song of the Vineyard, of which the woe oracles are nothing more than the practical adaptation.

The Song is famous, and according to style and contents it is a jewel. It is world literature. A deeply human situation suddenly takes shape in a very locally colored, occasional poem.

Jerusalem has never heard Isaiah speak in this way: instead of being a killjoy and spoil-sport, he seems to participate in the wine feast. He poses as a minstrel and asks them to listen to his vineyard song. He evidently commands the genre completely. The first lines show clearly that this singer will take home the first prize.

> Let me sing to my friend
> the song of his love for his vineyard.
> My friend had a vineyard
> on a fertile hillside.
>
> ('ashiranna lididi / shirath dodi lᵉkarmo
> kerem haya lididi / bᵉqeren ben-shamen)

After this melodious beginning the rhythm suddenly changes: "He dug the soil, cleared it of stones, and planted choice vines in it" (way⁼azz⁼qehu way⁼saqq⁼lehu wayyittaehu soreq): **soreq,** a choice type of vine which produces a favorite, clear red wine. The friend forgets nothing. He builds a watchtower and undertakes the difficult task of digging a press in the rocky bottom. All he has to do now is to wait for the fruits. But the vineyard yields only poor produce, rubbish, wild and withered sour berries.

A pregnant silence follows. In small emphatic traces the picture is complete. It does the trick. The prophet captivates his breathless audience. Where does he want to go from here? Suddenly the prophet speaks to everyone personally: "And now, inhabitants of Jerusalem / and men of Judah, / I ask you to judge / between my vineyard and me. What could I have done for my vineyard / that I have not done? I expected it to yield grapes. / Why did it yield sour grapes instead?"

The silence becomes more charged. Why? Say it! The prophet has completely caught the attention of his audience. There is no way out. What started out as a harmless idyll turns out to be a crushing accusation; the tense silence becomes a guilty one.

Against the dark background of this silence the prophet writes in searing letters his second merciless accusation: "Very well, I will tell you / what I am going to do to my vineyard: / I will take away its hedge for it to be grazed on, / and knock down its wall for it to be trampled on. / I will lay it waste, unpruned, undug; / overgrown by the briar and the thorn."

The prophet is inflamed, but he does not spoil the play. The bare truth is not yet told. It is still imagery.

But then they hear it: "I will command the clouds to rain no rain on it." That is familiar language (Ps. 78:23; Job 37:11, 15); what man can command the clouds so that they obey?

That is the bolt of lightning which immediately is followed by the thunderclap: "Yes, the vineyard of Yahweh Sabaoth / is the House of Israel, and the men of Judah / that chosen plant. / He expected justice, but found bloodshed, / integrity, but only a cry of distress."

In a short, biting play on words the prophet translates his imagery of grapes and refuse into human realities: he expected **mishpat,** but sees **mishpah;** he expected s^edaqa, but beholds s^eaqa,. He expected right, but Judah brought nothing but riot. In the midst of the merciless desert of paganism, it is not the oasis of social justice as dreamed of by Yahweh. Rather, everywhere around the country the suppression of the poor cries to heaven for vengeance.

The imagery has been broken: in Judah there is injustice and suppression. This thunderbolt, with which the idyllic Song of the Vineyard ends, rumbles through in a sixfold Woe, and in a threefold threat. "Woe to those who add house to house / and join field to field / until everywhere belongs to them / and they are the sole inhabitants of the land" (vs. 8).

"Woe to those who for a bribe acquit the guilty / and cheat the good man of his due" (vs. 23).

Summarizing, the prophet hits this evil in its deepest and eternal core: "Woe to those who call evil good, and good evil, / who substitute darkness for light / and light for darkness, / who substitute bitter for sweet / and sweet for bitter" (vs. 20). The prophecy of damnation consists of reproaches because of sin and of threats with punishment. The sixfold Woe formulates the sin; the threefold threat formulates the punishment.

"My people will go into exile. . . . Sheol opens wide his throat. . . ." And summarizing again for the third time: "For this, as stubble is prey for the flames / and as straw vanishes in the fire, / so their root will rot, / their blossom be carried off like dust" (vss. 13, 14, 24).

This sixfold Woe is not the result of an anticipated intention of the prophet himself—consequently one should not attempt to stretch it to seven Woe's—but is the result of the fact that some original Woe oracles were conducive to others. But, in the form in which this prophecy presents itself, with all its interruptions and enlargements, it is a powerful whole which raises the tension of the damnation collection to the apotheosis of disaster, personified by the Assyrian invasion to which the closing oracle of the collection alludes (5:25-30, quoted on p. 104).

The Song of the Vineyard is the most graphic explanation of the verse with which the book of Isaiah begins: "I reared sons, I brought them up, / but they have rebelled against me." It is the short summary of the prophetic preaching of doom. But the proclamation of salvation will also use this imagery. Isaiah takes the lead in this in a somewhat corrupted oracle:

> That day,
> sing of the delightful vineyard!
> I, Yahweh, am its keeper;
> every moment I water it
> for fear its leaves should fall;
> night and day I watch over it.
>
> I am angry no longer.
> If thorns and briars come

> I will declare war on them,
> I will burn them every one.
> Or if they would shelter under my protection,
> let them make their peace with me,
> let them make their peace with me.
>
> In the days to come, Jacob will put out shoots
> Israel will bud and blossom
> and fill the whole world with fruit.
> Isaiah 27:2-6

Hosea had already made some use of the image of the vineyard (10:1) shortly before Isaiah's time. However, it becomes classical and recurs regularly only after Isaiah (Ezek. 15:1-8; 17:3-10; 19:10-14). Jeremiah summarizes the whole Song in one sentence: "Yet I had planted you, a choice vine, / a shoot of soundest stock. / How is it you have become a degenerate plant, / you bastard Vine?" (2:21; cf. 5:10; 6:9; 12:10).

Damnation has come; the vineyard has been destroyed. The prayer of Israel's faithful remnant to restore Yahweh's vineyard is then a moving one:

> There was a vine: you uprooted it from Egypt;
> to plant it, you drove out other nations,
> you cleared a space where it could grow,
> it took root and filled the whole country.
>
> It covered the mountains with its shade,
> the cedars of God with its branches,
> its tendrils extended to the sea,
> its offshoots all the way to the river.
>
> Why have you destroyed its fences?
> Now anyone can go and steal its grapes,
> the forest boar can ravage it
> and wild animals eat it.
>
> Please, Yahweh Sabaoth, relent!
> Look down from heaven, look at this vine,
> visit it, protect

what your own right hand has planted.
                        Psalm 80:8-15

Although no one realized it, this prayer had already been answered in Judaism. Its devotion was attuned in its best elements to the interior and personal aspects of man. By this devotion and by its worldwide diaspora, it became the fruitful soil in which the Christian vineyard could prosper.

However, insofar as official Judaism assumed the same irreligious attitude against Christ as Judah in its own time against Isaiah, it is again the infertile vineyard about which Christ remarks, clearly joining Isaiah: "There was a man, a landowner, who planted a vineyard; he fenced it round, dug a winepress in it and built a tower; then he leased it to tenants and went abroad" (Matt. 21:33-43). But the prayer of all people of good will, who realize how little they can achieve by their own resources and who live up to the expectations of their divine vine-dresser, has been really answered in the redeeming word of the Master:

> I am the true vine
> and my Father is the vinedresser.
> As a branch cannot bear fruit all by itself,
> but must remain part of the vine,
> neither can you unless you remain in me.
> I am the vine,
> you are the branches.
> Whoever remains in me, with me in him,
> bears fruit in plenty;
> for cut off from me you can do nothing.
>   John 15:1-5

As he is the Good Shepherd, in contradistinction to Israel's bad shepherds, so also is he the True Vine, in contradistinction to those to which Isaiah speaks.

Bound by their life to the Master, who is pre-eminently

God's "choice plant," man is drawn into the eternal love of the Father for the Son and experiences the skilled hand which regularly cuts away his weak humanity to make him fruit-bearing.

THE EXPERIENCE

OF HOLINESS (6:1-13)

6:1-2   In the year of King Uzziah's death I saw the Lord Yahweh seated on a high throne; his train filled the sanctuary; ● above him stood seraphs, each one with six wings: two to cover its face, two to cover its feet and two for flying.

3   And they cried out one to another in this way,
"Holy, holy, holy is Yahweh Sabaoth.
His glory fills the whole earth."

4-5   The foundations of the threshold shook with the voice of the one who cried out, and the Temple was filled with smoke. ● I said:
"What a wretched state I am in! I am lost,
for I am a man of unclean lips
and I live among a people of unclean lips,
and my eyes have looked at the King, Yahweh
    Sabaoth."

6-7   Then one of the seraphs flew to me, holding in his hand a live coal which he had taken from the altar with a pair of tongs. ● With this he touched my mouth and said:
"See now, this has touched your lips,
your sin is taken away,
your iniquity is purged."

8   Then I heard the voice of the Lord saying:
"Whom shall I send? Who will be our messenger?"

9   I answered, "Here I am, send me." ● He said:
"Go, and say to this people,
'Hear and hear again, but do not understand;

see and see again, but do not perceive.'
6:10   Make the heart of this people gross,
its ears dull;
shut its eyes,
so that it will not see with its eyes,
hear with its ears,
understand with its heart,
and be converted and healed."

11   Then I said, "Until when, Lord?" He answered:
"Until towns have been laid waste and deserted,
houses left untenanted,
countryside made desolate,
12   and Yahweh drives the people out.
There will be a great emptiness in the country
13   and, though a tenth of the people remain,
it will be stripped like a terebinth
of which, once felled, only the stock remains.
The stock is a holy seed."

Under the fresh impression of this Scripture reading,
one may feel that the current idea of what a prophet is
hardly measures up to the historical reality. He will devote
some thought to it and formulate some impressions in
order, as it were, to make hay while the sun shines. Rather
than starting immediately with exegetical details, we will
first consider this important question which will enable
us to have a better understanding of this passage.

According to a current idea, the prophet is someone
who predicts the future. The five chapters of Isaiah which
we have read thus far lead us to suspect that a biblical
prophet is something completely different. In any case, he
is something more than a prophesier of the future. The
Bible itself calls him precisely and concisely, "Man of
God." He is a man whom God has called to lead a life
bound to him. He is filled with God and speaks out of
this fullness. All genuine prophecy is rooted in a special

experience of God. That is the essential element. It does not matter whether the prophet is speaking about past, present, or future.

This conforms to the data. In the Scriptures there are not only prophetic visions concerning the future, but biblical history, too, is thoroughly prophetic. Not only the future, but also the past, opens itself to the prophet. We even get the impression that the prophets say something about the future only because they see the past (and the present) through God's eyes. The facts become transparent for them. They penetrate God's real intentions and, likewise, a religious certainty arises in them about what Yahweh intends for Israel, what God intends for man. In the same way, they know what history will bring.

He who looks for "predictions of the future" easily loses sight of the fact that biblical prophecy is a religious message with which he primarily wants to reach his own generation. On the other hand, one must be aware that biblical historiography does not limit itself to the reproduction of past events, but often speaks about a religious certitude concerning the future in the light of the past. Scripture frequently expresses what should and will be in the same manner by which it relates what once was. This is true for many features in the biblical stories concerning the Mosaic theocracy and the Davidic monarchy. The book of Genesis offers the most illustrative examples. The story of Babel is a real prophecy concerning Babel, only not in the literary form of a prophecy, but of a story about the past. The paradise story, too, can be called a prophecy concerning man in a very true sense.

The current idea is based, therefore, on a correct observation: the prophets do see the perspective of things.

But can this not be explained from their seeing the dimension of depth? There is always a danger that a consequence of something is mistaken for its essential part. In this case, therefore, we run the risk of lowering the prophetic charism to a human caricature of it (viz., fortune-telling), with the difference, of course, that it would be a fortune-telling in the name of God and, consequently, one which is reliable and always correct.

Prophecy is more a miracle of insight than one of knowledge. Misled by the current idea, we imagine all too easily that the prophets were already informed of certain New Testament facts which we know concretely as history. This may or may not be so. Historical knowledge is knowledge of the past; prophetic knowledge is knowledge of the future. We are not allowed to equate the two. The prophets know the same facts that we do, but in a completely different manner: they recognize, as it were, the divine dimension of these facts. They understand the salvific structure and the essential bearing of it. Above all they have the assurance that the essential part will one day take place. But the facts themselves will have to show what the human dimension is: where, when, and how that essential will come true concretely and historically.

There are certain classical prophecies which, after a closer look, prove to be inadequate. The reason for this inadequacy is evident when we try to verify the prophets, using the later historical data at hand. We look for too many material data in the prophets. Sometimes these are present, but they usually play a secondary part. In light of these data, the prophet seems hardly or not at all to outline the material facts of the future, or even to have any intention of doing so. He simply expresses his religious certainty concerning the future in words and images at his disposal. He often uses words analogous to, or in contrast with, certain events and situations of his own time. The miracle of prophecy consists for the most part in its realization. The facts often realize the prophecy more literally than could be attributed to the intention of the prophet. For example, Zechariah 9:9 describes the Messiah as the humble King of Peace whose kingdom is not built on proud tyranny and force of arms (usually symbolized by war chariots and horses; cf. vs. 10 and Hos. 1:7). The peaceful intentions of this humble Prince are now illustrated by an image: the King comes to Jerusalem "humble and riding on a donkey, on a colt, the foal of a donkey." Former exegetes have already noticed that this prophecy, in its essential contents, would be completely realized in Christ, even if he had never entered Jerusalem on a donkey. He corresponds completely to the ideal of a Prince of Peace which Zechariah and other prophets had in mind. From the New Testament it is clear, however, that this prophecy was realized in Christ not only according to the spirit, but also according to the letter.

Similar instances also occur in Isaiah. The divine origin of prophecy seems to betray itself further unexpectedly in the peculiar phenomenon that the prophetic words often describe the future more literally than the prophet seems to have been able to intend in the given circumstances, provided we still want to let him speak meaningfully. The fostering of our current and too-narrow concept lies partly in this phenomenon, which is underscored by the New Testament practice of relating its historical data in Old Testament terms.

Although these considerations are not a direct explanation of the Scripture fragment which we have read, nevertheless they are confirmed by it. With the prophecies in front of us, we can say that, in order to proclaim them, the prophet did not need more inspiration than he had received in the vision of his call. It really does not seem that the prophet needed, as it were, additional divine information to be able to say what he said during his prophetic career after his call. Isaiah's vision of the future can be especially traced to this.

Of course, we should not isolate this vision from Isaiah's life. We should consider it as a fundamental experience which permeates all his further actions and continues to deepen itself in blessed companionship with his Lord. We do not intend to exclude at all the fact that Isaiah spoke under direct divine inspiration. It is clear that this inspiration naturally builds on a point of departure of a more fundamental character, which we signify by vocation.

The vocation of a man is not something that happens once and for all at the beginning of a man's life. It is the divine plan of a man's whole life. Vocation is a creative, divine, salvific will which, as a never-failing power, makes man grow according to God's plan for him. So Isaiah was in God's service throughout his prophetic life.

The prophet realizes this in the story of his call. This story undoubtedly goes back to a certain experience in the year of King Uzziah's death, but that does not exclude Isaiah's concentrating and summarizing his whole experience of God in the story which he relates. This is obvious in a story that is simultaneously prophetic preaching, as is very clear from its second half in which the prophet concentrates and summarizes his whole message.

Therefore, we say that Isaiah was a great prophet not

so much because he made predictions more or less accurately than other prophets, but because of his incomparable experience of God. By this experience, and as a great believer, he could see the shocking events through God's eyes. He recognized God's intentions and arrived at the assurance of faith concerning the future: God will realize his intentions. And the future fate of the people and of mankind will essentially be like this or like that, according to the attitude which they adopt.

Isaiah's special experience of God can be felt in all of his prophecies which we have read thus far. Even where we have difficulty in understanding what he says, we are impressed by a great man and a great believer. He takes hold of us by his holy conviction. In spite of all the strangeness and obscurity, he touches somewhere on the deepest core of our humanity. All frills and side issues disappear. He rips away all masks behind which I could hide myself, driving me into a situation which I would prefer to avoid, namely, coming face to face with God on my own, alone.

Isaiah can do this only because he himself has stood face to face with God. In reading him we suspect a great secret behind his life. He attempts to let us share in that secret in the sixth chapter, which we are reading. This immortal story of his call is the source of his whole activity and the key to all his prophecies. He states why and with what right he has spoken in this manner up to this point. It is a special justification of his improbable message of doom and, as such, the most important and most radical damnation prophecy of the entire book.

This passage, like the preceding chapters, bears all the traces of this vision. Take, for example, the authentic terms which he uses to indicate God: Adonai (here always translated as "Lord"), Yahweh of Hosts, and especially the Holy One of Israel.

The bearing of this vision cannot be seen all at once and can make sense only in the context of this whole series of Scripture readings. There are passages of Scripture which are so loaded that they are weakened rather than strengthened by analysis and exegesis. This passage mentions undefined and ineffable things "that no eye has seen and no ear has heard, things beyond the mind of man" (1 Cor. 2:9).

More than explanation, the reader needs this: these pages of Scripture should accompany him all his life as a sacred secret of which he never tires and in which new depths are ever opening for him.

In reading the book of Isaiah, we continually feel that a great believer is speaking. The prophet now literally hands over his credentials. He attempts to formulate the kernel of his religious experience and, in doing so, touches upon the kernel of the Church and each of us. His testimony of faith is one of the pillars upon which the religious awareness of the historical Church rests. It is even one of the sources from which the Church originated and by which she stays alive.

Perhaps we still live as believers by unknowingly experiencing God in this testimony of the faith. Our belief sometimes craves authentic food, and it would be less complicated and more genuine if we were more familiar with Isaiah. Experience proves that it is an irreplaceable privilege to meet a truly religious man, to be able to understand and to discover the mystery and inspiration of a noble and dedicated human life. Our indebtedness to a deeply religious father and mother is immeasurable; neither pastor nor minister can surpass them. As we possess in Paul's letters the living Paul, so we possess the living Isaiah in the book of Isaiah. They are irreplaceable. We suffer by not knowing them.

One does not get to know a man after one meeting. There is only one good method—regular social intercourse. True contact does not allow itself to be forced; it has to grow. The best way to grow up is in the presence of some worthy person. We now read a biblical chapter with which we should have grown up, as the Church has grown up with it. The Trisagion, the thrice-repeated "holy" that takes a special place in all the liturgies of East and West, surely dates back to this formulation of religious experience, which we may term the very threshold of apostolic faith.

We will understand Isaiah better if we clearly see how the "seraphic hymn" was rightly integrated into the liturgy. A sample explanation of this will follow. Through special grace, the nearness of God became a tangible reality for Isaiah, not just a matter of faith, as it is for us. It was also a case of human perception as we perceive of sublunar things. As an earthly creature, he could not look into God's inaccessible being, but he received an indelible impression of it, so that God allowed himself to be experienced in a veiled form adapted to man. Isaiah attempts to formulate this experience in his story.

The incarnation of God in Christ is the culmination and climax of all former divine revelations. It is the fulfillment and climax of this continuous adaptation of God to man. The humanly adapted manner, in which God's glory became visible to Isaiah, has its deepest meaning and finds its culmination in the form in which God's glory has appeared in Christ, a form pre-eminently adapted to human beings.

When Isaiah saw the world filled with God's glory, he understood more of the Christian mystery than did Jesus' contemporaries who did not want to surrender themselves to God, who was so near to them in the person of Jesus. John the evangelist meditates on the unbelief of his fellow countrymen, who saw without seeing and heard without understanding. He saw that Isaiah's prophecy, which he quotes literally, was fulfilled in this unbelief: "Isaiah said this when he saw his glory, and his words referred to Jesus" (John 12:41).

John surveys the whole of God's way to man and dares to say, therefore, that Isaiah has seen Jesus' glory; clearly a reference to the vision of his call.

When the Church, according to the command given to her by Christ on his departure to his Father, celebrates the commemoration of this under the signs of bread and wine, she knows that her Lord resides in her midst. He is the same Lord who lives in the glory of his Father and who is celebrated there in song by the seraphim. She cannot confess in faith an experience of the ever-present Lord more meaningfully than by the Sanctus, the threefold "holy."

She is at one with Isaiah's belief. Isaiah believed in the Lord who was yet to come, but whose ever-present work of redemption he could tangibly feel and personally experience in the miraculous sign of the vision which opened itself before him. The Church believes in the Lord who has already come, and attempts to realize in the glorious sign of her liturgy that he will be with her until the end of the world.

In summary: Yahweh is the God who is near. Faith in Yahweh therefore implies faith in Christ who is God-with-us. Implicit faith in Christ means that it touches the essence of the Christian mystery without knowing how it will happen concretely and historically. Isaiah's vision is a summit of that belief in Yahweh and of that implicit belief in Christ.

We know and see what kings and prophets have longed to see. But in finding a true religious attitude with regard to what we know and experience, in discovering the essential part of it, we can still learn from Isaiah, whose belief was exclusively dependent on the essential kernel. For, by stopping at the historical externals of the salvific events, we always run the risk of knowing Christ only "according to the flesh" (2 Cor. 5:16).

We sing the Sanctus, therefore, as an indication, an evocation, of Isaiah's vision. This Sanctus, to be sure, has an effect on the faithful. But how much better it would be if they were familiar with Isaiah's vision and recalled it at this moment in the liturgy.

Isaiah does not give a definition of God. He gives much more: he presents a living impression of God. In our lives we profit more from awareness than from definitions and intellectual notions.

The irreplaceable value of this biblical chapter seems to be well typified. It presents a graphic sense perception. The senses, which are intuitive, have advantages over the intellect. They catch the whole concrete event; they give an over-all and primary impression.

In the psyche, in the interior of the blessed prophet, his directly spiritual experience expresses itself in sensory images. His spiritual sight permeates his entire humanness and finds its direct translation and adapted composition in expressive material which comes from his innermost self. The prophet can likewise make himself conscious of what he has seen, reflect on it, and convey it.

But his spiritual sight and his sensory visualization form one, living, inseparable entity. By getting acquainted with the picture which Isaiah portrays, by assimilating it, we can absorb something of the primary impression of the divinity which he experienced. Here then, Scripture is in some way the bread of life for the faithful and **Biblia Pauperum,** the illustrated Bible of the poor.

If we take a close look at the picture in this passage, we see that it is the scene of a royal vision: a king, clothed in his stately robes, sitting on his throne in the royal room of his palace, surrounded by his royal court.

It was a high throne with many steps. We can mention Solomon here who "made a great ivory throne, and plated it with refined gold. The throne had six steps, and bulls' heads at the back of it, and arms at either side of the seat; two lions stood beside the arms, and twelve lions stood on either side of the six steps. No throne like this was ever made in any other kingdom" (1 Kings 10:18-20).

Concerning the heavenly court, we find a fine comparison in the vision which Micaiah relates to Ahab: "I have seen Yahweh seated on his throne; all the array of heaven stood in his presence, on his right and on his left." Here, too, Yahweh speaks to his court: 'Who will trick Ahab into marching to his death?" (1 Kings 22:19-20).

The over-all impression which Isaiah obtained from what he saw is expressed in: "I am lost. My eyes have looked at the King."

But at the same time it is a Temple vision with all kinds of reminiscences of the Temple liturgy: song, incense, altar, holy fire.

The whole Temple floor is covered with the hem of Yahweh's splendid attire. This is a symbol of Yahweh's highest authentic presence, even though veiled. For the hem of a garment has a special meaning in the ancient East, as is obvious from many biblical quotations. In those days, the hem or train was as characteristic of a person as, for example, a fingerprint or a signature is for us. For we think of a fingerprint or a signature as being charged with the whole power of the person whose print or signature it is.

The prophet really experiences the nearness of God as he stands apart as a lonely, diminutive, moral man in the colossal portal, the threshold which he feels trembling under his feet. The sound of the seraphim is powerful and apparently rather different from the "sweet heavenly" song of angels.

These "radiant" beings do not stand on the floor, since it is completely covered. They surround Yahweh's high throne and "stand" as birds are able to hover in the air. Two of their wings are constantly moving; with two they cover their faces, since even they cannot bear to look at the Holy One of Israel; and with two they cover the lower part of the bodies, hiding their mortal creatureliness from God's holy sight.

The Temple vision is presented in such a way that the Temple of Jerusalem and the heavenly Temple merge. It is actually the Jerusalem Temple, which has taken on worldwide, cosmic proportions. The Holy One of Israel, Yahweh of Hosts, is seated upon the ark as King of Glory

(**Rex Gloriae**). This ark becomes, in the heavenly vision, the heavenly throne, upon which Yahweh resides as the thrice-holy God of the world, and not merely the national God of the people of Israel. He not only fills the ancient "Holy of holies" with his glory, but also heaven and earth.

This short description may serve as a first accounting of the imaginary material used by the prophet to express in words his ineffable experience of God. They are data taken from the Temple and the palace as Isaiah could have experienced them. They are combined in Isaiah's inner life and transformed to the winning and subservient expression of the greatest vision he saw.

This transformation is immediately striking. However unmistakably national and Jerusalemlike his imaginary material may be in origin, it has become here the expression of a reality which transcends nation and world. We will examine this closer in the next Scripture reading. For it can be understood only in the light of the fact that the prophet was able to receive such an awe-filled commission in such a beautiful vision.

11

THE DECREE AGAINST
HARDNESS OF HEART
(6:9-10; 29:9-12; 28:9-13)

6:9   He said:
"Go, and say to this people,
'Hear and hear again, but do not understand;
see and see again, but do not perceive.'

10   Make the heart of this people gross,
its ears dull;
shut its eyes,
so that it will not see with its eyes,
hear with its ears,
understand with its heart,
and be converted and healed."

29:9   Be stupefied and stunned,
go blind, unseeing,
drunk but not on wine,
staggering but not through liquor.

10   For on you has Yahweh poured
a spirit of lethargy,
he has closed your eyes (the prophets),
he has veiled your heads (the seers).

11-12   For you every vision has become like the words
of a sealed book. You give it to someone able to
read and say, "Read that." He replies, "I cannot,
because the book is sealed.' • Or else you give
the book to someone who cannot read, and say,
"Read that." He replies, "I cannot read."

28:9   "Who does he think he is lecturing?

who does he think his message is for?
Babies just weaned?
Babies just taken from the breast?
28:10   With his
sav lasav, sav lasav,
kav lakav, kav lakav,
zeer sham, zeer sham!"

11   Yes, certainly with stammering lips
and in a foreign language,
he will talk to this nation,
12   he who once told them: Here is rest;
let the weary rest.
Here is repose.
—But they would not listen.
13   That is why Yahweh now says:
kav lakav, kav lakav,
sav lasav, sav lasav,
zeer sham, zeer sham.
So that when they walk they may fall over back-
wards
and be broken, snared and made captive.

Isaiah receives a command against which our sense
of justice spontaneously revolts. Why should Israel be
reproached and punished for a blindness which God himself has inflicted? Anyone knows that such a thing is
impossible and definitely not an act of God. But why does
Isaiah say it then? Or does he place it in Yahweh's mouth?
In other words, we have here really a text which the reader
hardly knows how to handle. In such cases the Bible often
explains itself. It is just as well, although an explanation
which, however correct it may be, has a text say the
reverse of what it seems to mean, often leaves the impression that the correction was made to save the Bible—until
the explanation is analyzed.

The Scripture reading consists of three parts. We will
have the Bible itself elucidating the most difficult passage

of the above Scripture reading by two other closely related oracles of Isaiah. The last oracle makes it especially clear that it is really the attitude of man himself which is responsible for the disaster that strikes him. Still we also find there in the last verse (28:13), the surprising "so that," the term at which we take so much offense in 6:10. It is, therefore, obvious that we are not allowed to interpret this "so that" simply as if it were Yahweh's preconceived intention to destroy Israel.

The outstanding difficulty will completely vanish if the reader draws upon the second and third chapters of Ezekiel in his comparative study. He will come to the conclusion that Ezekiel and Isaiah say essentially the same thing and that the way in which Isaiah formulates his decree can be reduced to and translated into the manner of Ezekiel. This manner draws our attention to one of the biblical ways of expression and at the same time to the actual intention of that way of expression.

Still this prophetic way of expression has a very positive background. We miss something of the biblical message if we cannot draw any other conclusion than that we are dealing here with hyperbole, which is proper to the prophetic style. Surely, where a Semitic way of expression plays a part, which is unquestionably the case here, we are allowed to take the words of the prophet not too strictly (compare the "black-and-white" expressions of p. 60). But if we attempt to maintain, in this case, the text in its strictly literal sense, we discover an element of truth, of which the exaggeration mainly exists in a one-sided emphasis. Then to what extent is it true that Yahweh strikes Israel with spiritual blindness, so that she actually cannot see anymore?

This Scripture reading is concerned with a mystery. Human language cannot speak directly about mysteries, but only in contradistinctions which seem to exclude each other. The Bible is very strong in this. Every heretic can, therefore, advantageously use a verse to suit himself; the error often lies in the one-sided emphasis of a compound truth. It is traditionally known that knowledge about God can only be reached by man along "the road of affirmation" and "the road of negation." It is always Yes and No together. By the tense balance between both, man's cognitive power can be purely directed to the divine reality. The Bible, which ultimately always speaks about God, is full of this Yes and No, which is more familiar to the Eastern than to the Western way of thinking.

The mystery touched on here concerns the mysterious exchange between divine grace and human free will. Heaven and hell belong to that mystery: man has to earn heaven. But if he makes it, it will be purely because of grace. Man is lost due to his own guilt, but still it is God who damns him. These are truths about heaven and hell which seem to exclude each other. Faith is not mathematics. The believer puts his trust in God: he will hold two opposite ends of the chain without noticing how they are linked. The believer bows here before the mystery, as did Job in his struggle with the problem of suffering. The facts which he had could not be reconciled with each other. Theoretically the problem remained unsolved, but he found a surrender in faith, the efficacious and existential solution: God himself.

Heaven and hell have their preamble here on earth. Man can carry hell in his heart. We call that hardness of heart, which already has a connotation of the definitive fate of eternal damnation. Hardness of heart corresponds to damnation insofar as it involves a free human decision, no matter how much of a divine judgment it may be. It is no wonder, then, that the text of Isaiah is difficult, for he speaks here about the mystery of Israel's hardness of heart. He speaks about it, not from man's point of view, but from God's: God strikes his people with hardness of heart, God orders the hardness of heart.

Note here that in complete accordance with the collective and earthly character, which is proper to the Old Testament, a collective and national hardness of heart is at issue. Consequently, the existence of a nation is at stake. It is not concerned with the personal hardness of heart of every Israelite, whereby heaven and hell are at issue. Nevertheless, what has been said here concerning Israel's national hardness of heart is a revelation concerning God's action with man. We have already mentioned to what a degree hell is an extension of the national disaster with which the prophets threaten (pp. 77-79).

God hardens man. That is one side of the truth, a side which is strongly emphasized here. This strong emphasis already proves that there is also another side. Otherwise, why the emphasis? Naturally, in order to convert the people. This penitential sermon seeks to play the highest trump; it is an ultimate appeal to the free human choice, which it includes rather than excludes.

Hardness of heart does not minimize the guilt, but increases it. This can be easily shown from the biblical language. But it does not make much sense to force doors that are already wide open, although there are some peculiar texts. It is more fruitful to look for a formula which does justice to the active role attributed to Yahweh and his prophet. Then, not only are certain texts peculiar, but it appears that this peculiarity makes sense.

Man hardens himself. In what way does God harden him? In what sense does Yahweh harden the mind of Pharaoh? In what sense does John the evangelist say that the Jews cannot even believe? We should remark in passing that John surely does not mean this as an extenuation, but as a summit, of guilt (John 12:39).

To err is human. To forgive is divine. But brutal and persistent sinning is perilous. God does not stand for any nonsense. Sometimes and somewhere the cup of wrath can overflow.

And then something will happen in the free cooperation of man, not only from man's side, but also from the divine side in the dispensation of grace. Hardness of heart and divine rejection are the result of an inscrutable interplay between the man who closes himself off from God, and God, who closes himself off from the man. "Yahweh says this: You have abandoned me, now I have abandoned you" (2 Chron. 12:5). This interaction plays a part in all of God's dealing with man, regardless of whether it concerns salvation or disaster: "Yahweh is with you as long as you are with him. When you seek him, he lets you find him; when you desert him, he deserts you" (2 Chron. 15:2).

A very important truth corresponds to this prophetic way of expression, although it is not the whole truth. But yet it is exactly the truth which Israel needed at that time.

The biblical historiography stresses Israel's traditional hardness of heart. By persistent sinning, man brings himself into a situation which complicates conversion. It has gone this far with Israel. She rejects any further grace, and this adds to her greater condemnation, for example, Isaiah's preaching and, later, Christ's coming. It is the one

sin which is not forgiven, since it is a sin against the Holy
Spirit, that is, against the Light itself, so that it ultimately
makes "seeing" impossible.

In this sense Yahweh gives his people up to hardness
of heart. He abandons his people; they are no longer his.
He no longer says "my" people, but "that" people. Israel
constantly broke the covenant with Yahweh; now Yahweh
breaks the covenant with Israel. That means the end of
the "old" covenant, hence the end of the Old Testament.

Indeed, it is just that. Soon the entire national structure
disappears, which had been carefully built during so many
centuries. It is the logical consequence of Israel's sin,
and at the same time the impenetrable divine decree (cf.
pp. 108-109). The centuries after Isaiah, which we include
in the Old Testament, are actually nothing more than a
transition period between Old and New.

The prophetic mission of Isaiah is the short summary
of an enormous revolution in salvation history. Classic
prophetism—by this we mean the prophets whose documents we possess—is the voice of this revolution, the link
between both Testaments, the hinge on which the Old
Testament opens into the New Testament.

The national restriction which made the covenant the
"old covenant" has been broken in principle. Like a blow-
pipe flame, the light appeared to the prophets by the
stone-hard collision of two realities which they deeply
realized: Yahweh's holiness and Israel's sinfulness.

This sharp contrast is nowhere so telling and so profoundly portrayed as in the vision of Isaiah's call. Also,
nowhere in this phase of national history is the idea of
Israel's rejection so sharply and definitely uttered. This

is not accidental; Isaiah's mission is the direct consequence of his experience of God.

It is important to see the connection clearly, since it is the most important key to the understanding of the prophetic books. There follows, therefore, some illustration with the help of the ancient divine name, which we have heard Isaiah so often use.

The name "Yahweh of Hosts" seems to be of humble and local origin. It is a name which attached itself to the Ark when it stood at Shiloh and when the Philistines and Hebrews contested the possession of the land in which they both had recently obtained a firm foothold (the Philistines from the sea, the Hebrews from the desert). The parents of Samuel left their dwelling place yearly "to worship and to sacrifice to Yahweh Sabaoth in Shiloh" (1 Sam. 1:3). Hannah began her tearful prayer with the invocation: "Yahweh Sabaoth" (1:11).

What are these "hosts"? The answer seems to lie in the word which young David shouted to Goliath: "You come against me with sword and spear and javelin, but I come against you in the name of Yahweh Sabaoth, **the God of the armies of Israel** that you have dared to insult" (1 Sam. 17:45).

Yahweh is traditionally Israel's God. But now Israel has to fight for her existence as a people. Yahweh is, therefore, now especially a God of war, the leader of the holy war. Israel is actually "fighting the battles of Yahweh" (1 Sam. 25:28). The name "Yahweh of Hosts" says that Yahweh is the leader of Israel's armies.

Since the Ark is a tangible expression of Yahweh's alliance with his people, this name is especially attached to the Ark which, as a kind of last trump, is literally thrown into the battle, to the horror of the Philistines: "God has come to the camp!" (1 Sam. 4).

The warlike character of the Ark is ancient, as is clear from the Ark formula in the Book of Numbers: "And as the ark set out, Moses would say: Arise, Yahweh, may your enemies be scattered and those who hate you run for their lives before you" (Num. 10:35; cf. Ps. 68:2).

The magnificence or glory of Yahweh was also traditionally associated with the Ark. The Holy One of Israel lives as a consuming fire in Israel's midst. Holiness is a specifically divine attribute, the strict authenticity of God by which he is completely Other, elevated above everything, the Unapproachable One, the Infinite One. Still his holiness acts close to man, closer to him than man can get to himself. That is the essence of salvation history, which will reach its final goal in this, that God will be all in all.

In ancient Israel we see the beginning of this salvation history, the beginning of God's road to man. Yahweh's hidden holiness reveals itself to Israel externally through his magnificence or glory. No man can see that glory and live. It can only be seen in the bright glare which radiates from the cloud enveloping this glory.

Well then, as is well known, the Bible often tells us that this cloud would come to rest above the Ark between the winged cherubs placed on the Ark. With this, the Bible wants to make clear how truly the Holy God lived in the midst of Israel through his entering into the covenant. This, then, is "the ark of God which bears the name of Yahweh Sabaoth who is seated on the cherubs" (2 Sam. 6:2).

These brief data are mentioned here in order to provide a sample of the ancient national atmosphere of the terms used by Isaiah: holiness, glory or magnificence, the Ark as the throne of Yahweh of Hosts, his royal character as leader in national war. The name "Yahweh of Hosts" is used in this national and warlike meaning only twenty times, namely, in the books of Samuel and in some psalms concerning the Ark (e.g., Ps. 24:1), points of reference where we are seldom disappointed if we want to see the national life in action.

Shiloh was destroyed by the Philistines and David finally brought the Ark to Jerusalem. But in the Northern Kingdom the name "Yahweh of Hosts" was not forgotten. Elijah and Elisha, both from the north, testify that they as prophet serve Yahweh Sabaoth (1 Kings 18:15; 2 Kings 3:14), filled with zeal for him (1 Kings 19:10, 14). Amos, who prophesied in the Northern Kingdom some twenty years previous to Isaiah, is in their tradition. Where he speaks about Yahweh of Hosts—and he does nine times— we feel the beginning of a new emotional sense of the name: "For he [Israel's God] it was who formed the mountains, created the wine . . . makes both dawn and dark, and walks on the top of the heights of the world; Yahweh, God of Sabaoth, is his name" (Amos 4:13; cf. 9:6).

This new emotional sense is rounded off and made classic by Isaiah: henceforth Yahweh of Hosts is the God who rules the powers of heaven and earth, the God of the universe, the world God, and God the Creator (56 times in the oldest part of the book of Isaiah, 82 times in Jeremiah, 53 times in the rather small book of Zechariah, and 24 times in the very small book of Malachi).

We have lingered over the name "Yahweh of Hosts"

so long because what has been illustrated with the help of a small detail, namely, with the help of this name, has generally happened in the vision of Isaiah's call: the prophet uses the old national terms, but they have received a worldwide meaning in their preaching.

That worldwide aspect is shown to Isaiah in this vision. This vision, positively expressed, says that Yahweh is a universal God and will reveal himself as a universal God. What he has intended so far only for Israel, he will intend for the whole world and for the whole of mankind in the future. Negatively expressed: the privileged time of Israel has passed. Israel has had its chance and did not utilize it. Yahweh turns away from Israel and is going to undertake on a universal scale what did not succeed with Israel.

Isaiah experiences the ancient Yahweh of Hosts, who is now the God of the universe; the ancient Adonai, the national Master, becomes Lord. This vision occurs in the Jerusalem Temple, which now has cosmic proportions. Yahweh is seated on the covenant throne, which becomes the heavenly throne. The Holy One of Israel is now the thrice-holy God of the universe, whose holiness revealed itself in the cloud of glory in the midst of Israel, but whose glory now fills the world. The cherubim, with their limited task of throne-bearers and gate-keepers, seem to be elevated and spiritualized to seraphim by Isaiah, in virtue of what he had seen (cf. Rev. 4:6-8, where the cherubim sing the Trisagion; the Te Deum combines both choirs of angels, while Jerome mentions that some people in his day pray, contrary to biblical tradition, "enthroned above the cherubim and seraphim," Ps. 80:2). The ultimate purpose of God's whole work is the revelation of his holiness. The goal is that Yahweh's name should be honored on earth as well as in heaven, that the world should be filled with his glory. This ultimate aim is in God's mind from all ages in its perfect stage; this final goal is the inexhaustible object of the heavenly liturgy. Isaiah has been momentarily a witness of this.

All the more painful is his experience that he, as man, is in the middle of history, which still is in evolution toward this ultimate aim. The earth is not yet filled with Yahweh's glory, and the people in whose midst the King of Glory lives, that people is a sinful people, a people of Sodom. It is his own people.

This vision effects in this way a great revolution in Isaiah's mind: Yahweh's salvation will be for a new universal Israel. As its reverse side, this salvation will cause great disaster for ancient national Israel. When Isaiah speaks to a nation which is beyond salvation, it is because he has personally experienced that a man of good will can be saved, even though it is by fire. The national catastrophe will be the salvation and redemption of many. Yahweh speaks, therefore, through Isaiah in order to fashion for himself a remnant from which, as from holy seed, the new Israel can bud forth from his rejected people by his creative word (6:13).

Israel's rejection actually has a long history. The Bible locates and concentrates the essence of history at a certain moment, as it were. It appears as though God said on a particular day: Now it is over. One cannot say, therefore, that Isaiah's vision does not go beyond, let us say, Israel's exile, by which Yahweh indeed casts his people from his sight. They are removed from his sight, as the Bible expresses it.

Israel's history continues in Judaism and, with it, the history of a people which Yahweh fashions for himself, and finally rejects again, repeats itself. Israel's rejection is likewise a historical process, like a long breath which passes by in a certain rhythm and in which several phases can be distinguished. This process comes to a striking end in the year A.D. 70 upon the destruction of Jerusalem. This is indeed (for the time being? Rom. 9-11) the end of the national dispensation of salvation.

But the process of election and rejection, of mass disloyalty and realignment of a purified remnant, continues on a higher, universally human and spiritual level till the day of the definite selection, when the elected ones— Israel's own remnant—will be gathered from the four corners of the world (Matt. 24:31).

Undoubtedly through contemplation of the history of his people, Isaiah formulates in his "theology of hardness of heart" a mystery which reaches further than ancient Israel and even Judaism. In the history of the dialogue between Yahweh and Israel, he discerns the essential structure of the dialogue between God and man up to the denouement. The vision of the prophet encompasses nothing more nor less than "the Day of Yahweh."

Stephen said to the representatives of Judaism: "Can you name a single prophet your ancestors never persecuted? In the past they killed those who foretold the coming of the Just One, and now you have become his betrayers, his murderers" (Acts 7:52). Christ alludes to them in his parable of the unjust tenants, who assault the servants of their lord and, eventually, his son (Matt. 21:33ff.). With this, Christ puts himself on the same line as Isaiah, and his audience on the same line as Isaiah's audience. In this parallel situation the rhythm of salvation history reveals itself. The existential decision concerning faith, with which every man will eventually be confronted, has received an exemplary shape in several complementary situations of the biblical history of salvation. Together they reveal literally how man stands in his life.

The New Testament confirms this in an impressive way by appropriating this difficult Isaiah text in a special manner.

After repeated, unavailing preaching, Christ turns away from the Jewish masses to concentrate on his disciples, who are the remnant of Judaism from which the Church will grow. At this turning point of Jesus' public life, all four Gospels mention the divine decree against the hardness of heart as Isaiah formulated it (Matt. 13:14; Mark 4:12; Luke 8:10; John 12:39). We find it mentioned in the Letter to the Romans, in which Paul tortured himself about the mystery of why the faith of the pagan should succeed Israel's unbelief (Rom. 11:8).

It was apparently difficult for the Jewish Christians, and even the apostles, to see that the Kingdom of God, as Christ had brought it, was no longer a national and Jewish affair. Only through the facts did the words become clear: "I tell you then, that the kingdom of God will be taken from you and given to a people who will produce its fruits" (Matt. 21:43).

Only then did they fully realize the significance of Isaiah's prophetic mission, as is witnessed by the frequent appeal which the New Testament makes to it. In this way the young Church overcame her first crisis: she becomes the Church of the Pagans.

After having quoted Isaiah's oracle concerning Israel's blindness and deafness, the book of the Acts concludes with a sentence which sounds like a shout of rejoicing: "Understand, then, that this salvation of God has been sent to the pagans; they will listen to it!" (Acts 28:28).

12

THE SIGN OF

IMMANUEL (7:1-17)

7:1-4   In the reign of Ahaz son of Jotham, son of
Uzziah, king of Judah, Razon the king of Aram
went up against Jerusalem with Pekah son of
Remaliah, king of Israel, to lay siege to it; but he
was unable to capture it. ● The news was brought
to the House of David. "Aram" they said, "has
reached Ephraim." Then the heart of the king
and the hearts of the people shuddered as the
trees of the forest shudder in front of the wind.
● Yahweh said to Isaiah, "Go with your son Shear-
jashub, and meet Ahaz at the end of the conduit
of the upper pool on the Fuller's Field road, ●
and say to him:
'Pay attention, keep calm, have no fear,
do not let your heart sink
because of these two smouldering stumps of firebrands,

5   or because Aram, Ephraim and the son of Remaliah
have plotted to ruin you, and have said:

6   Let us invade Judah and terrorise it
and seize it for ourselves,
and set up a king there,
the son of Tabeel.

7   The Lord Yahweh says this:
It shall not come true; it shall not be.

8a   The capital of Aram is Damascus,
the head of Damascus, Razon;

9a   the capital of Ephraim, Samaria,
the head of Samaria, the son of Remaliah.

8b   Six or five years more

and a shattered Ephraim shall no longer be a
people.
7:9b   But if you do not stand by me,
you will not stand at all.' "

10-12   Once again Yahweh spoke to Ahaz and said, ●
Ask Yahweh your God for a sign for yourself
coming either from the depths of Sheol or from
the heights above." ● "No," Ahaz answered "I will
not put Yahweh to the test."
13   Then he said:
Listen now, House of David:
are you not satisfied with trying the patience of
men
without trying the patience of my God, too?
14   The Lord himself, therefore,
will give you a sign.
It is this: the maiden is with child
and will soon give birth to a son
whom she will call Immanuel.
15   On curds and honey will he feed
until he knows how to refuse evil
and choose good.
16   For before this child knows how to refuse evil
and choose good,
the land whose two kings terrify you
will be deserted.
17   Yahweh will bring times for you
and your people and your father's House,
such as have not come
since Ephraim broke away from Judah
(the king of Assyria).

The actual Immanuel Book begins with this Scripture
selection. The prophet who speaks here is the same Isaiah
of the former chapters, the same prophet of salvation and
doom. What makes these prophecies into a separate "collection" is the fact that from now on salvation is personified
in Immanuel and doom in Assyria. Since we are reading
the Bible and not studying history, we hardly have to say

anything more about Assyria than the prophet does himself. In our own century we have experienced the phenomenon of a suddenly rising world power. We know how a whole society can be taken off guard by it. We can imagine how unsure it makes one's existence. It is enough to know that Assyria was such a world power in the ancient East.

What we are looking for is the religious interpretation which Isaiah attributes to this phenomenon. To begin with, we will attempt to place Assyria in a broader context, already somewhat expressed in the preceding chapters.

Isaiah's preaching is determined by two facts: the national sin and the national disaster.

The national sin has many sides which have been singularly and mercilessly illustrated for us by Isaiah. He has also a summary definition for it, which always amounts to the same thing: disloyalty to Yahweh. This sin is national not only because the people as a whole are guilty of it, but also because Israel as a nation came into existence through the opposite way, i.e., by faithful surrender to Yahweh. The words with which the book of Isaiah begins are literally and historically true: "I reared sons, / I brought them up."

The covenant between God and man is, and is called, the "old" Testament, precisely because it is a national covenant. In the society of that time, religion and nation were intimately bound up. Since God established a covenant with certain people, these gradually formed, more and more, an exclusive group. This exclusiveness expressed itself both socially and organizationally and had to lead to a national separation which eventually found its crowning and stabilization in the governmental form of a kingdom. Israel originated in this way.

By deserting Yahweh, Israel cut herself off from the national source of life. She exposed herself to the danger of losing her exclusiveness and being assimilated into the mass.

It had been more or less a silent defection, which had executed itself during the course of two centuries. It was a gradual hollowing out. Israel, unnoticed, slipped back to the level of ancient Eastern paganism, which she had shaken off so painfully in her growing period.

Where a national process of decay festers, the time will come when one has to say: The national society is rotten. When Isaiah came on the scene, it had reached this stage. As a gifted prophet, he could make a precise diagnosis. His task was to open the eyes of his congeners to the reality.

The national sin determined in this way the nature of his preaching.

The national disaster, the second fact which dominated Isaiah's public life, was the doom which threatened Israel and began to realize itself after some years in an ever-greater magnitude. Because of her sin, Israel was not able to survive a political fall and this doom became a national disaster in the full sense of the word, so that her national existence was at stake and was ultimately lost. This doom was personified by Assyria.

Assyria, or Ashur, had no predecessors, unless one goes back far before Israel's time. Thanks to this fact, the people believing in Yahweh could bring themselves to an independent political existence which enjoyed its high point during the undivided kingdom under David and Solomon, and later still could maintain itself in the kingdoms of Israel and Judah. The Promised Land is part of a strategic and commercial and, consequently, vital area, so that an independent political bond is excluded there as soon as a mighty power begins to grow in the Near East.

Well then, Assyria was the first real power after many centuries. Isaiah's first appearance coincided with the time when this power began to develop itself, through a series of blitzkriegs, into a world power. Assyria absorbed everything and created in this way a world power of theretofore unknown dimensions. This world power would change hands at intervals, but it would last for a thousand years. Politically, the Old Testament people of God were literally and forever wiped off the map. Assyria was indeed the beginning of the end.

Isaiah was more right than he could ever suspect. We come to the highly important discovery that Assyria made the Old Testament no longer possible: the emergence of a world power, consecutively taken over by Babylonians, Persians, Greeks, and Romans, and continuing until after Christ, naturally meant the end of the Old Testament.

The great revolution of Old to New, of which the prophet is the herald, can be viewed from the inside or the outside. From the inside: the end of the national dispensation of salvation is the logical consequence of Israel's sin, which affects the national principle of life. From the outside: the rise of the Assyrian world power means the end of a dispensation of salvation which uses a national society as a framework and organ.

However, only the inner and outer factors together can effect Israel's destruction. The factor which destroys from the outside can wipe out a political set-up, but cannot destroy an authentic religious community. Faith would have saved the nation anyway, and to a certain extent it actually did. From the sinking Israel, Judaism arises. Further, the factor undermining from the inside affects the religious community, but the exterior set-up is maintained until a power from the outside, as a "rod in Yahweh's hand," destroys it.

It does not make sense to ask what would have happened if Israel's attitude and / or the circumstances had been different. We have only summarized here what we have to say afterward when we examine the actual course of events. In light of this, if we read Isaiah's call, his prophetic commission, and his oracles, we can understand something of the miracle of prophecy. Likewise we will be able to evaluate more thoroughly the bearing of Isaiah's judgment concerning Assyria; we will have a better understanding of the essential contents of the salvation which is contained in the Immanuel message. Now we will concern ourselves with the data of this Scripture reading.

The first verse is immense because of the accumulation of proper names. If we replace all these names of kings and kingdoms with the capitals concerned, the situation is immediately clear. The first verse says then, that the combined forces of Damascus and Samaria are on their way to Jerusalem to besiege the city. This expedition is linked up with the suddenly risen Assyrian storm.

In 745 B.C. Tiglath-pileser III ascended the throne. He was the first of a series of conquerors who would build an unbelievable world power within the next half century. After having extended and established his power over the whole of Mesopotamia, Tiglath-pileser turned his attention to Syro-Palestine, the traditionally contested bridge—on the one side of which was the sea and on the other, desert sand—between Egypt, Asia Minor, and Mesopotamia. Without possession of this bridge, there could be no world power in the Near East.

Already in 740 B.C. the first kingdoms on Syrian soil were liquiated and made into Assyrian provinces. In 738 the strong northern neighbor, Hamath, was divided into a series of Assyrian provinces. Damascus and Samaria hastened to pay tribute. That cost the Northern Kingdom 1,000 talents of silver, 50 shekels per taxable man (2 Kings 15:19).

In the middle thirties, as soon as Assyria turned her back, the Syro-Palestine states formed an anti-Assyrian coalition under the leadership of Damascus. However, because of political reasons which can be presupposed, but which are not important here, Ahaz of Judah did not join the coalition. Therefore, Damascus and Samaria headed for Jerusalem to conquer the city and to replace Ahaz with the son of Tabeel (judging from the name, someone from Damascus). But, as the text says, they could not take the city.

The situation of the text here and in parallel places (Kings and Chronicles) leads one to suspect that later Judean chauvinism has tampered with this sentence, which probably said the opposite, namely, that Ahaz was not able to begin a fight against these two kings to stop their march on Jerusalem and to prevent a siege of the city. This connects nicely with the next verse, which describes the panic that had arisen as a result of the news that the two armies were advancing. Then it became clear that Ahaz had to find a solution. The second book of Kings relates what he decided to do: "Then Ahaz sent messengers to Tiglath-pileser king of Assyria to say: I am your servant and your son. Come and rescue me from the king of Aram and the king of Israel who are making war against me. And Ahaz took the silver and gold that was found in the Temple of Yahweh and in the treasury of the royal palace, and sent this as a present to the king of Assyria." The text, written after the events, continues then in a matter-of-fact and unconcerned way: "The king granted his request and, going up against Damascus, captured it; he deported its population to Kir, and put Rezin to death" (2 Kings 16:7-9).

From the Assyrian annals we know that Damascus fell in the year 732. Ahaz's measure had been effective. As far as the siege of Jerusalem is concerned, the attackers withdrew helter-skelter. Tiglath-pileser first settled with Samaria, which surrendered itself immediately and had to pay a heavy tribute. In this way the city and surrounding countryside were rescued, but all the rest of the Northern Kingdom (the coastal strip, Galilee, and the Trans-Jordan) was divided into three provinces. Damascus, however, was taken in the siege and lost its national existence. The king was killed, the elite of the population were sent into exile and replaced by Assyrian officials who ruled what was from that day forward "the province of Damascus." Everything was done according to the well-known Assyrian formula, which would be applied to Samaria in 721.

Just before these surprising events, which destroyed what had taken many centuries to achieve and dictated the situation for many more centuries, the truly historical meeting between Isaiah and Ahaz took place. Perhaps it is more appropriate to term this meeting "a collision." It is a collision between faith and politics. The religious community and the community of people who grew from

it and became the personification of it do not include each
other; they are estranged from each other. They take
shape in the dialogue-partners who, as strangers, as men
from completely different worlds, confront each other.

The prophet does not speak from political insight, but
from religious insight. Perhaps he was even politically
right, but faith can also ask things which in the given
situation seem to be political folly and even may be. The
prophet is ordered to maintain the people of God as such.
His task is not to serve a secular state, which long since
had threatened to take away from Judah its character as
people of God and with this every reason for its existence.
In this way, faith is right in the long run, even in the
political sense. This is verified by the facts, at the time of
both Isaiah and Jeremiah. These are the exact, sheer,
human speculations of Judah's kings, which entice them
to choose sides in the international complications, thereby
bringing disaster to their homeland.

Isaiah therefore advises Ahaz to keep calm. By this
calmness the prophet does not mean that the king should
not keep his wits about him, but he expresses his religious
conviction that the nation cannot be saved by military or
political settlement, especially not if, by this, she denies
her own principle of life. There is a beautiful text which
explicitly explains the biblical notion of "silence."

> For thus says the Lord Yahweh, the Holy One in
>   Israel:
> Your salvation lay in conversion and tranquility,
> your strength in complete trust;
> and you would have none.
>
> "No" you said "we will flee on horses."
> So be it, flee then!
> And you add, "In swift chariots."
> So be it, your pursuers will be swift too.

> A thousand will flee at the threat of one
> and when five threaten you will flee,
> until what is left of you will be
> like a flagstaff on a mountain top
> like a signal on a hill.
>
> Isaiah 30:15-17

In this text the tranquillity of faith, the "silent" trust, stands in opposition to horses (and chariots), with which we are already familiar as the stereotyped image of military and sheer human power in general, with all the frantic unrest of it (see pp. 94, 144). The faithful Israel of better times was saved and won in the holy war without horses and chariots, which in contrast are characteristic of Israel's pagan enemies (Exod. 15:1, 4; Josh. 11:4; Judg. 4:3; 1 Sam. 13:5). A nation which does not owe its existence to horses and chariots will also not be able to maintain itself by them. To put all trust in them speaks of a pagan mentality: "Some boast of chariots, some of horses, but we boast about the name of Yahweh our God" (Ps. 20:7). Consequently there is mention of the royal legislation in Deuteronomy that does not allow the keeping of many horses (17:16). Hence the woe of Isaiah: "Woe to those who go down to Egypt / to seek help there, / who build their hopes on cavalry, / who rely on the number of chariots / and on the strength of mounted men, / but never look to the Holy One of Israel / nor consult Yahweh" (31:1).

These texts make it clear how fundamental a decision of faith confronted Ahaz. The prophet is so sure of his business because the head of Aram is only Damascus, and the head of Damascus is only King Razon. The same holds true for Samaria: the head of Samaria is the son of Remaliah, contemptuously so called by the prophet because he was not a man of royal blood, but an invader and a regicide. Only Damascus and Samaria with all their con-

spiracies can think of ending overnight the age-old Davidic
dynasty. But the capital of Judah is Jerusalem, and the
head of Jerusalem is the Davidic king, Yahweh's anointed
One. He can count on Yahweh's promise that the throne
of David will never be shaken in eternity.

These two kings, together with the "son of Tebeel"
in the rearguard, aim precisely at the dynasty. But their
attack fizzles out: "It shall not come true; it shall not be."
Whatever these hostile kings undertake, whatever Ahaz
does, the continuation of the dynasty is assured. That was
unconditionally promised to David, and this promise remains in force.

However, there is a question as to how this dynasty
will continue. If David's successors misbehave, the dynasty
can be saved only by humiliation and judgment. The home
will become a "hut"; the cedar of the dynasty will lose its
proud top. It will realize again that it possesses royalty
only and literally "by the grace of God." This realization
will supply it with renewed vitality. This warning is echoed
in the great promise: "I will be a father to him [David's
successor] and he a son to me; if he does evil, I will
punish him. . . . Yet I will not withdraw my favor from
him, as I withdrew it from your predecessor. Your House
and your sovereignty will always stand secure" (2 Sam.
7:14). Thus, this unconditional, salvific promise to David
coincides with a conditional threat of doom. This unconditional, salvific promise is repeated again by the definite
statement of Isaiah: "It shall not come true; it shall not be."
In an equally definite statement: "But if you do not stand
by me, you will not stand at all," he affirms the conditional
threat of disaster. This Hebrew proverb contains a nice
play on words. The word for "to believe" means "to rely
on somebody," "to place one's trust or confidence in some-

one." Yahweh's statement reads literally: If you do not trust me as your stronghold, you will not have any stronghold. Or, according to a creditable translation: "If you will not believe, surely you shall not be established" (RSV).

Ahaz has already made his choice. While the prophet and the king were talking, messengers were on their way to Tiglath-pileser. With this Assyrian solution, Ahaz feels more at ease than with Isaiah's solution of faith. This situation makes clear, therefore, what faith actually is: to abandon the familiar, conveniently arranged assurances and to leap into the darkness of God—which will appear to be light itself in the leap.

Ahaz does not want to give up what he sees as the solution. The prophet has come at an inopportune moment. The king turns him away with a pious formula which belongs to the mouth of a great believer, ready to believe even without a sign. In Ahaz's mouth the formula is abused to camouflage an unbelief which is so obstinate that he attempts to prevent being disturbed in his unbelief by a sign. But in spite of this, the sign is given and it is one of salvation which unconditionally guarantees the continuation of the dynasty. But at the same time it is a sign of disaster, which Ahaz will bring upon the house of David by his attitude. Immanuel is that sign.

In three great prophecies, which compete with each other in importance (7:14; 9:5; 11:1), Isaiah calls forth his Immanuel figure. We have read the first of these. It will remain an initial approach. Chapters 7-12 form a coherent cycle. This coherence is amplified by the common historical background, namely, the Assyrian invasion. But the actual unifying principle is the Immanuel figure. This cycle is, therefore, called the Immanuel Book.

It is clear that we must first read the book in order to be able safely to say what salvific message the prophet wants to express by picturing his Immanuel figure. We are unfortunate insofar as we have to begin with the most difficult and most disputed Immanuel text. Not only the exegete but also the layman must approach such a text in a controlled manner. He should not want to know everything at once, nor to decide everything precisely. He should consider this text as his first meeting with a holy mystery which he has to leave for the time being in vagueness, a vagueness which it held for the prophet himself, or with which he consciously left it here.

This prophecy is famous and suffers, consequently, from a "splendid isolation," with the danger that it is used as a "prediction," so that one goes blind staring at what is conceived as material evidence in this prophecy. It is safer to assume that the prophet wants to say essentially the same thing here as in the following great texts. As a result we will see this prophecy in its own perspective, and the fullness of the fulfillment will surprise us again in all its newness. Meanwhile, trained by Isaiah, we will be able to give a purer answer of faith to the message related to this matter in the Gospel.

This chapter speaks in clear language only when it threatens with disaster. The Immanuel is, however, essentially a sign of salvation, but one which is placed before the eyes of those who do not want to see and before ears which do not want to hear words spoken in the name of God. The prophet leaves it, therefore, as a mysterious puzzle. Immanuel, God-with-us, is naturally a salvific sign, but only for those who can really believe in God. For those who want to do without God, God-with-us must be a sign of doom, since it includes the condemnation of belief in human means of salvation. If God-with-us is the only salvation, then all those who have thought of a road to salvation without God are beyond redemption. Immanuel is thus "destined for the fall and for the rising of many in Israel, destined to be a sign that is rejected [and a sword will pierce your own soul too] so that the secret thoughts of many may be laid bare" (Luke 2:34-35).

The Immanuel is a salvific sign which will be a greater condemnation for the unwilling and unrepentant people. This seventh chapter directly joins the former chapter in which Isaiah's prophetic commission was related. Isaiah, the great prophet of salvation—his name means "Yahweh is salvation"—is for the masses the great prophet of doom. His salvific message itself (that only Yahweh is salvation) is loaded with damnation for those who seek their salvation apart from God. His appearance becomes a condemnation of the masses. But from these masses, the prophetic word of God creates a remnant which, like the root of a felled giant of the forest, becomes the point of departure of a new people of God, for whom the salvific dealings of God turn from damnation to salvation.

The obduracy of Israel's masses now receives shape in the obduracy of David's house. The salvific sign, which was offered to this unwilling Davidic house which refused it, is given anyway. It is and remains a sign of divine salvation. But now it is at the same time the condemnation of the actual attitude of this Davidic house, which obstinately clings to human certainty of salvation. In this way Immanuel is a sign of doom for this Davidic house. This Davidic house will also have to be judged and thus will be reduced, in its own way, to a remnant. "In its own way," since Scripture does not use the word "remnant" in this case; it speaks of the "hut of David" and especially of "shoot" or "root of Jesse," as will be clear further on.

In this remnant Yahweh will realize his salvific intentions for David. Immanuel is the expressive sign of
guarantee of this remnant, which is born of belief and
maintained by a miracle of God. The new future, reserved for the remnants of dynasty and people, is both typified and assured in him; assured, since he is the real
beginning of it; typified, since the prophet pictures the
origin and the behavior of Immanuel in such a way that
they are an image of the origin and the situation of the
faithful remnant. Such a thing is called a "sign" in
prophetic language. Immanuel still appears to be what he
originally is, a sign of salvation. Immanuel is the Davidic
son of the future, exponent of the new people of God and
in all respects the opposite and, hence, the condemnation,
of the degenerated Davidic son, Ahaz, and his generation.

The ambiguity of the Immanuel sign is confirmed by
the living prophecy whom Isaiah had to carry along,
namely, his little son Shear-jashub, "A remnant-will-return."
"Remnant" assumes a preceding judgment by which only
a portion of the numerous descendants of Abraham survives, while the verb "to return" points to a new possibility
of salvation, but only after the judgment concerning the
masses has been executed.

In this seventh chapter, doom is in the foreground.
The salvific figure, Immanuel, is also the sign of this
doom on account of the obduracy of those who were
given this sign. This ominous side of Immanuel is developed in the eighth chapter, in which a figure parallel
to Immanuel appears, namely, a second son of Isaiah who
is also a living prophecy and likewise bears an ambiguous
name: "Maher-shalal-hash-baz, "Speedy-spoil-quick-booty."
It is only a question of who is the direct object of this
spoil and who will disappear with it. The function of the

sign of Immanuel in the situation of that time will receive a considerable clarification.

But the sign of Immanuel is ultimately and especially meant for the faithful. It is not given to them as a puzzle, so that they, though seeing, will not see and will not convert themselves, but as a stronghold for their faith and a source of consolation. We can therefore expect much light from the other two great Immanuel oracles, since these are not directed against the unfaithful masses but to a small circle of followers who already are the Remnant and to whom it is given to know the mysteries of the Kingdom of Heaven.

Isaiah now speaks out uninhibitedly. The second oracle pictures Immanuel as a child with the four miraculous names (9:5); the third, as the shoot from the root of Jesse, the royal descendant upon whom Yahweh's spirit rests sevenfold (11:1).

After having read these, we will be able to imagine more completely and express more accurately what a world of faith is called forth in this Scripture reading by this Old Testament Madonna, by this child and its nameless mother.

13

THE WATERS OF

SHILOAH (7:18-8:8)

7:18   That day Yahweh will whistle up mosquitoes
from the Delta of the Egyptian Niles,
and bees from the land of Assyria,

19   to come and settle
on the steep ravine, on the rocky cleft,
on the thorn bush and on every pasture.

20   On that day the Lord will shave
with a blade hired from beyond the River
(the king of Assyria),
the head and hairs of the body,
and take off the beard, too.

21   That day each man will raise
one heifer and two sheep,

22   and because of the abundance of milk they give,
all who are left in the country
will feed on curds and honey.

23   That day, where a thousand vines used to be,
worth one thousand pieces of silver,
all will be briar and thorn.

24   Men will enter it with arrows and bow,
since the whole country will revert to briar and
thorn.

25   On any hillside hoed with the hoe
no one will come
for fear of briars and thorns;
it will be pasture for cattle and grazing for sheep.

8:1-2   Yahweh said to me, "Take a large seal and
scratch on it in ordinary writing MAHER-SHALAL-
HASH-BAZ. ● Then find me reliable witnesses,
Uriah the priest and Zechariah son of Jeberechiah."

8:3-4   I went to the prophetess, she conceived and gave birth to a son. Yahweh said to me, "Call him Maher-shalal-hash-baz, ● for before the child knows how to say father or mother, the wealth of Damascus and the booty of Samaria will be carried off before the king of Assyria."

5   Yahweh spoke to me again and said:

6   Because this people has refused the waters of Shiloah
which flow in tranquillity,
and trembles before Razon
and the son of Remaliah,

7   the Lord will bring up against you
the mighty and deep waters of the River
(the king of Assyria and all his glory),
and it will overflow out of its bed
bursting all its banks;

8   it will inundate Judah, flow over, pour out,
flooding it up to the neck,
and its wings will be spread
over the whole breadth of your country, O Immanuel.

Jerusalem has been hard pressed by its mighty northern neighbors, Damascus and Samaria. But Ahaz, the king on the Davidic throne, has found a foolproof plan to shake off his enemies: he has called in the help of the Assyrian king. Ahaz, along with the city, feels safe with this plan. In a private conversation, Isaiah attempts to have the king reconsider his decision.

If this intervention of the prophet creates the impression, for contemporary readers, of political meddlesomeness, then it is because we can scarcely imagine how essentially politics and religion are interwoven in the Old Testament. The peculiarity of the Old Testament consists precisely in this, that the Kingdom of God has a national form. Here a separate people originated by becoming a people of God; this people developed itself into a state by becoming a theocratic state.

Although belief in Yahweh is naturally the principle of life of a religious community, religious apartheid actually causes social, and eventually national, apartheid. This is a law of life in the society of that time, in which every form of human apartheid and of human relations in a group finds its reflection and true copy in the world of the divine realm.

When the authentic divine atmosphere entered the human world in a new and special way by revelation, it found a given channel for the stream of revelation. The God of the world and of mankind reveals himself by becoming the God of a very particular people. One privileged believer grew into a family; the family became a people. Likewise, the God of revelation grew from a personal god of protection to the god of the family and finally became the national God of a people.

In the book of Isaiah we are exactly at the point where this God of a people began to be recognized by his believers as the only universal God. This necessary and irresistible development—the true divine realm always breaks through the limited human framework in which it reveals itself and in which it is thought and represented— this development in religious awareness, by which the believer arrives at the concept of national God of his people as universal God, actually comes about by the fact that the old ties between people and God were broken. We saw it in the vision of Isaiah's call. The salvific message that Yahweh is the God of the universe and of mankind has a reverse side which is a message of doom for Israel. Yahweh rejects the national community which up until then had been called after him ("Yahweh's people"), but for whom he is no longer a reality. Through his prophet, Yahweh is creating for himself a new faithful community which can hold out independently of the degenerated national framework.

Isaiah provides no political advice. He does not leave Ahaz two political possibilities. He gives him a choice which calls for a decision of faith. Ahaz has to choose between God-with-us and Assyria. It is a choice between the evident, human power of Assyria and the power of Yahweh, which exists only in faith and on which the believer has to rely, even against the seeming powerlessness of God. The reason is that the ancient East experiences national impotence as impotence of the national God. The weakness of God is an eternal annoyance, and only in faith is it experienced as power. Ahaz preferred a strong man above a weak god and was not willing to reconsider his choice.

Isaiah's Immanuel is indeed the personification of God's weakness, purposely so described by Isaiah: a maiden and a newborn child; a young mother who gives a name; an image of tender weakness and of complete helplessness. What a contrast with the horses and the chariots of Assyria! The eating of "curds and honey" belongs to this image, as will soon be apparent. Likewise the whole picture is a concrete expression of the tranquillity which Isaiah recommends to Ahaz and which will be characteristic for the "remnant." By the choice of a name above all names, faith confesses that "power is at its best in weakness" (2 Cor. 12:9).

After this conversation the breach between the prophet and the king is complete, since by his choice the king

breaks forever with Yahweh. By shackling himself hand
and foot to Assyria's king, Ahaz bound himself to Assyria's
god. The Bible gives a strong example of this. As soon
as Damascus was conquered, an Assyrian altar was erected
there. Of course, Ashur's god has again extended his
kingdom! When Ahaz, who came to pay tribute to
Tiglath-pileser at Damascus, saw that altar there, he sent
its design and exact model to the high priest, Uriah. Such
an Assyrian altar, destined for holocausts, had to be constructed in Jerusalem on the site of the ancient altar of
Yahweh. As soon as Ahaz returned to Jerusalem, he
ascended the new altar on which all official sacrifices had
to be sacrificed from that time on. Other changes still had
to be introduced, all, so the biblical story concludes, for
the sake of the king of Assyria (2 Kings 16:10-18).

This ending reminds us that political vassalage, as well
as political friendship and marriages, is naturally expressed
in the religious realm in the Near East, primarily in the
official state religion. In this way, quite a few "foreign"
gods also conquered a place in Jerusalem (cf. 1 Kings
11:7-8; 16:32).

Now we have a better understanding of how Ahaz's
appeal to Assyria means rejection of Yahweh. Instead of
being a believer of Yahweh he is now a superstitious
adorer of Assyria's god, which must have been a powerful
one (by Ahaz's reasoning) in view of the Assyrian successes
(cf. 2 Chron. 28:22-25).

At the same time we see clearly that Isaiah does not
make a political appearance, but champions belief in
Yahweh, through whom a theocratic state can survive in
the long run. The prophet does not speak from a political,
but from a religious, conviction. In his Immanuel figure

he confesses his faith that the Kingdom of God will continue on earth no matter what mankind may undertake. But he expresses at the same time his religious assurance that this Kingdom of God will be dissociated from Ahaz and from the whole degenerate national policy of which he is the exponent. The prophet is therefore assured by his faith that the old kingdom is doomed.

Until then the cleavage between North and South had been the greatest disaster in the history of the nation and of the Davidic dynasty, but "Yahweh will bring times for you and your people and your father's House, such as have not come since Ephraim broke away from Judah" (7:17). "The king of Assyria" was added later. It is obvious that posterity linked this text more completely to Assyria, perhaps hardly suspecting that Assyria was only a preliminary to complete destruction, a circumstance foreseen here by the prophet.

The conversation between the prophet and the king is now finished. But in the book some later oracles have been added, which one by one bear witness to what kind of an impression the Assyrian nightmare left.

Already at the end of the collection of oracles of doom an Assyrian oracle presents an apotheosis of doom: "He [Yahweh] hoists a signal for a distant nation, / he whistles it up from the ends of the earth . . ." (5:26ff.). This intentionally blurred text is now clarified: "That day Yahweh will whistle up mosquitoes / from the Delta of the Egyptian Niles, / and bees from the land of Assyria, / to come and settle / on the steep ravine, on the rocky cleft, / on the thorn bush and on every pasture" (7:18-19).

This text concerning the Assyrian invasion is amplified by an oracle which alludes to the disgraceful deportation

into Assyrian exile: "On that day Yahweh will shave /
with a blade hired from beyond the River / (the king of
Assyria), / the heads and hairs of the body, / and take off
the beard, too" (7:20).

This picture of disaster is completed by a third oracle,
which seemingly has grown into a unity by means of the
catchwords "briars and thorns," typical indication of a
depopulated country stricken by a divine curse (Gen.
3:17ff.). In this way these three oracles form an arresting
climax: invasion, exile, general desolation of the country.
The prophecy of doom finds its rest, as it were, in the
last-mentioned element, since it pictures the constant and
hopeless situation of doom (cf. Isa. 13:19-22). Hence it
concludes, saying: "That day, where a thousand vines
used to be, / worth one thousand pieces of silver, / all will
be briar and thorn. / Men will enter it with arrows and
bow, / since the whole country will revert to briar and
thorn. / On any hillside hoed with the hoe / no one will
come for fear of briars and thorns; / it will be pasture for
cattle and grazing for sheep" (7:23-25). These additions
and enlargements of the seventh chapter point to the far-
reaching consequences of this conversation between prophet
and king. Ahaz does not want to believe in the sign of
Immanuel, the sign of the pre-eminently faithful king of
the future. By his choice in favor of Assyria, Ahaz excludes
himself from the Kingdom of God, from the realm of faith,
from the messianic line of succession. The Messiah will
come, but he will come via a break with the present house
of David, that is, via a judgment over this house of David.
Not for nothing was Isaiah accompanied by his little son
"A-remnant-will-return." This living prophecy could be
applied to the house of David. Therefore Immanuel is in
the first instance, a sign of doom. To the chain of disasters

which began with the break between North and South, Ahaz himself added a new link, Assyria, the world power which will create the conditions leading to a definite catastrophe.

It does not appear that the prophet ever delivered his message concerning Immanuel to the masses of people. When he returns to the subject, it is for those who are already initiated. The people of Judah have apparently put all their hope in the Assyrian policy of Ahaz. The prophet limits himself to a condemnation of this irreligious attitude.

He does this in the presence of the king by means of the sign of Immanuel, which essentially has a far deeper and more encompassing consequence, but which in the present text is directly connected with these troubled times: "For before this child knows how to refuse evil / and choose good, / the land whose two kings terrify you / will be deserted" (7:16). Ahaz is worrying too much. Damascus and Samaria are "stumps of firebrands" which will soon be consumed and reduced to ashes (7:4). The prophet touches lightly on the actual situation at this point, but it becomes, as it were, subservient to a vision of the future which encompasses at a glance the entirety of God's action: in Immanuel the future Kingdom of God lies concentrated.

With the people, however, the prophet limits himself to the actual situation; he uses a new sign which is completely adapted to this situation. Before going into this, we draw a conclusion with regard to Immanuel from the limited character of this new sign.

Immanuel is a sign which is far-reaching, even more so than Jerusalem's trying situation of the year 735.

Consequently, the import of this sign, for example, cannot be measured by what Ahaz, in the given circumstances, was able to make out of Isaiah's words. Sometimes it is reasoned that since the sign was ostensibly given to Ahaz, it must have had a special significance for him. If exegesis recovers this significance, it has done its job.

There are substantial grounds for disagreeing with this reasoning. The significance of a passage, as it occurs in our Bibles (often after many adventures), should not be limited to the significance which the words have when they were spoken for the first time in a certain past situation. Though they are two coherent questions, still they are distinct: What was said, meant, and understood in the year 735. And: What does this statement made at that time signify, as it is transmitted, noted down and finally placed in the entirety of the Book of Immanuel?

There is, however, a special textual datum denoting the inaccuracy of this reasoning. The sign of Immanuel is closely followed by a second sign which repeats the message of Immanuel to a certain extent, but also contrasts it: the limited format of Maher-shalal underscores the exceptionality of the Immanuel figure. One compares both figures. The relationship between both signs is obvious, but still every reader feels that it would be completely wrong to put them on the same level.

Indeed, Immanuel is a salvific sign for believers and only became an ominous sign for Ahaz personally by his reaction: the immediate consequences of the sign for the year 735 do not, therefore, exhaust the sign.

The second sign is completely different. It is only a repetition of the sign of Immanuel precisely insofar as something for the special circumstances of that time follows from it. The sign of Maher-shalal declares invalid the fear of those who have little faith with regard to the two aggressors, and it elaborates on the doom aspect of the sign of Immanuel.

Now there is no longer a private conversation. The prophet has to take a seal and has to write on it in everyday (nonhieratic) writing, which can be read by everyone, a kind of dedication: to Maher-shalal-hash-baz, to Speedy-spoil-quick-booty. The prophet calls upon unexpected witnesses closely connected with the king: Uriah, known to us in relation to the new altar, and a certain Zechariah (perhaps the same one mentioned in 2 Chron. 29:1), Ahaz's father-in-law! This lends stress and reputation to the name which Isaiah gives to his son, while he brings in the suspense. Yet he leaves it unexplained for the time being. The witnesses refute beforehand the insinuation that the name had been given afterward as a quasi-prediction of facts which had already taken place when the name was chosen. Isaiah appointed these witnesses, hoping that something would be brought to the attention of the king.

Only after the boy's birth is the name explained: the boy will have to bear this name because, before he can say "father" and "mother," the treasures of Damascus and the spoil of Samaria will be brought before the Assyrian king. One can think here of a kind of victory feast: soldiers march in front of the royal table showing the spoil, as can be seen on some monuments (cf. Dan. 5:1-4). The Judean children say "my father" and "my mother," which sounds very nice in their language: **abi, immi.**

"Before the child knows how to say father or mother" is surprisingly parallel to "Before this child knows how to refuse evil and choose good" (7:16), which must signify a computation of time; before he has come to the age of reason. This is a very peculiar and even suspicious shift in significance with regard to a far richer and original sentence which we find in 7:15 (cf. 7:22). In any case, as the text now runs, the parallel is outstanding and this chapter consequently clarifies the former one.

But the difference is obvious, too. The sign is completely clear to the people, since the boy, Speedy-spoil-quick-booty, is the sign of exactly what is soon going to happen to Damascus and Samaria. The sign of Immanuel, however, is difficult and unclear, at least in relation to the direct facts of that time. This betrays its broader purport, because of which it is rather difficult to apply it to the actual situation. It is even possible that it is a later application, so that 7:16 would be an awkward imitation of 8:4. Soon after Isaiah's death, historical applications of his prophecies were common, and so the passage bristles here with glosses.

Isaiah says, concerning Immanuel, that he will eat curds and honey till he knows how to refuse evil and to choose good. This is something more than knowing how to say "father" and "mother." With these disputed words Isaiah apparently wanted to sketch Immanuel precisely as the messianic figure (not as a contemporary, but as much present as the Kingdom of God and the Day of Yahweh). The prophet probably seeks to make the connection by using an image familiar to his audience: curds and honey as food for gods and perhaps food of paradise, surely as the food of the ideal Promised Land; perhaps also as food which is a simple product of nature, food for shepherds, which, as it were, comes directly from God's hand and which suggests something of the fact that one is completely dependent on God by the absence of farming, that is, of sedentary culture and of human affluence. In a certain sense, therefore, it is an emergency food, which forms a contrast with the affluence of decadent Jerusalem, but which will set man again on the right track; food by which he learns how to refuse evil and choose good, as divine food of grace, from which the new, faithful man grows.

In connection with the food of the nomads, one should compare the prophetic idealization of the nomadic period as the time of the first love and of ardent faith, in reaction to the degeneration to which urban affluence leads (cf. Jer. 35:6-14, the Rechabites; and Gen. 4:17, where Cain is pictured as the first builder of a town). With this in mind, that peculiar "feed on curds and honey" of Immanuel can be understood as a typification of the definite new salvation of the future. This new salvation is completely different from the human salvation which Ahaz seeks. It is also understood as an ominous sign for him. It is the plain, yet abundant, food of the faithful Remnant which will share in the new salvation after all the old richness has been wiped out by a catastrophe: "That day each man will raise / one heifer and two sheep, / and because of the abundance of milk they give, / all who are left in the country / will feed on curds and honey" (7:21-22).

The food of Immanuel is in contrast with the decadent affluence of the capital. Likewise, Immanuel is, in this respect, a sign of doom. But his food, which recalls the nomadic period, sketches at the same time the situation of the faithful Remnant, and this touch likewise completes the salvific sign. The ambiguity of the sign of Immanuel becomes, in this way, visible even in its details.

The conversation of Isaiah with the king took place in two phases, between which some time may easily have lapsed. Judah has nothing to fear from Damascus and Samaria, since both will soon fall (first phase, 7:1-9). But great disasters will come upon king and people by their unbelief (second phase, 7:10-17). These two phases can also be found in Isaiah's message to the people. In a first oracle the prophet predicts, by means of the name which he gives to his son, that Damascus and Samaria soon will fall (8:1-4); in a second oracle the prophet makes clear, with the help of an arresting image, what disaster the people are in for, due to their unbelief: "Yahweh spoke to me again and said: / Because this people has refused the waters of Shiloah / which flow in tranquillity, / and trembles before Razon / and the son of Remaliah, / the Lord will bring up against you / the mighty and deep waters of the River / (the king of Assyria and all his glory), / and it will overflow out of its bed / bursting all its banks; / it will inundate Judah, flow over, pour out, / flooding it up to the neck, / and its wings will be spread / over the whole breadth of your country, O Immanuel" (8:5-8).

The image speaks for itself. The city of Jerusalem lives on **one** spring, which is at the foot of the mountain of the city. For ages the water from this spring would be transported through a canal or gutter close to the city walls, where it was collected in a pool. This pool, situated at the south side and at the lowest part of the city, is called Siloam or Shiloah.

The waters of Shiloah flow quietly, for the spring is modest and the fall of the canal is slight. It is no impressive waterway which humanly could compete with the great world rivers. But it rises at the foot of Yahweh's

sanctuary, where Yahweh himself is the source of life for
his city. Shiloah is another example of the "tranquillity"
of God. But this mundane weakness is heavenly power, as
Ezekiel's faith confesses in his vision of the life-giving and
healing stream which he saw rise from under the right
side of the Temple and swell to a paradisiacal river (Ezek.
47; Rev. 22).

Israel's power does not lie on the human level, but
in her God and her religious belief. And at this moment
the people are about to cut off their most important
source of life: "They have abandoned me, the fountain of
living water, only to dig cisterns for themselves, leaky
cisterns that hold no water. What is the good of going to
Egypt now to drink the water of the Nile? What is the
good of going to Assyria to drink the water of the river?"
(Jer. 2:13, 18).

When the man of God, Elisha, advised the leper
Naaman of Damascus to bathe himself in the Jordan, he
answered indignantly: "Surely Abana and Pharpar, the
rivers of Damascus, are better than any water in Israel?"
(2 Kings 5:12). Surely, but yet only these despised waters
heal human leprosy.

With these tranquil flowing waters of Shiloah, Isaiah
recalls the past divine loyalties and he inspires the pious
prayer of the new believers:

> Yahweh is my shepherd,
> I lack nothing
> In meadows of green grass he lets me lie.
> To the waters of repose he leads me;
> there he revives my soul.
>   Psalm 23:1-3

These waters were traditionally the joy of the City
of God (Ps. 46:5). It is a joy which the world cannot give.

It is reserved for those who dare to stake their lives on the sign of Immanuel.

The same powerful thought recurs over and over; with Immanuel despised by Ahaz, the prophet formulates in one or another way the same principal thought as with the despised waters of Shiloah. These difficult chapters can, therefore, be for every reader of the Bible a source in which he can again purify his faith.

14

THE MASTER AND
HIS DISCIPLES (8:11-9:6)

8:11   Yes, Yahweh spoke to me like this
when his hand seized hold of me
to turn me from walking in the path
that this people follows.

12   Do not call conspiracy
all that this people calls conspiracy;
do not fear what they fear,
do not be afraid of them.

13   It is Yahweh Sabaoth,
whom you must hold in veneration,
him you must fear,
him you must dread.

14   He is the sanctuary and the stumbling-stone
and the rock that brings down
the two Houses of Israel;
a trap and a snare
for the inhabitants of Jerusalem.

15   By it many will be brought down,
many fall and be broken,
be trapped and made captive.

16   I bind up this testimony,
I seal this revelation,
in the heart of my disciples.

17   I wait for Yahweh
who hides his face from the House of Jacob;
in him I hope.

18   I and the children whom Yahweh has given me
are signs and portents in Israel
from Yahweh Sabaoth
who dwells on Mount Zion.

8:19   And should men say to you, "Consult ghosts
        and wizards that whisper and mutter"—
        by all means a people must consult its gods
        and, on behalf of the living, consult the dead.

20   To obtain a revelation and a testimony,
        without doubt this is how they will talk,
        since there is no dawn for them.

21   Distressed and starving he will wander through
                the country
        and, starving, he will become frenzied,
        blaspheming his king and his God;
22   turning his gaze upward,
        then down to the earth,
        he will find only distress and darkness,
        the blackness of anguish,
        and will see nothing but night.
23   Is not all blackness where anguish is?

            In days past he humbled the land of Zebulun
        and the land of Naphtali, but in days to come he
        will confer glory on the Way of the Sea on the far
        side of Jordan, province of the nations.

9:1   The people that walked in darkness
        has seen a great light;
        on those who live in a land of deep shadow
        a light has shone.
2   You have made their gladness greater,
        you have made their joy increase;
        they rejoice in your presence
        as men rejoice at harvest time,
        as men are happy when they are dividing the
                spoils.

3   For the yoke that was weighing on him,
        the bar across his shoulders,
        the rod of his oppressor,
        these you break as on the day of Midian.

4   For all the footgear of battle,

every cloak rolled in blood,
is burnt,
and consumed by fire.

5   For there is a child born for us,
a son given to us
and dominion is laid on his shoulders;
and this is the name they give him:
Wonder-Counsellor, Mighty-God,
Eternal-Father, Prince-of-Peace.
6   Wide is his dominion
in a peace that has no end,
for the throne of David
and for his royal power,
which he establishes and makes secure
in justice and integrity.
From this time onwards and for ever,
the jealous love of Yahweh Sabaoth will do this.

This Scripture reading occupies a special place in the book of Isaiah. It explicitly says that the prophet had disciples. In addition, it gives us some idea as to how he formed them. This is valuable information, of which we have already made use. The distinction between the voices of the master and of his disciples has already clarified several passages in the above chapters. We also saw some oracles which fall into place, once we know that Isaiah delivered them in the closed circle of his disciples.

It should not be imagined that we possess in the Scripture passage a literal text of a certain speech which Isaiah addressed to his disciples. We have more than that speech. This text has originated through the conglomeration of all kinds of fragments, sometimes very badly preserved. But in this way we get, in a nutshell, a clear idea of the numerous conversations Isaiah had with his disciples. From what has been preserved for us here, we can gain an insight into what themes and in what direction, and even how personally and movingly, the prophet must have spoken with his disciples. The more we familiarize ourselves with this text, which is difficult to understand on first sight, the more we are reminded of Christ in the intimate circle of his disciples, especially as he speaks to them at the Last Supper. We get the impression of a departure, of a last exhortation, of a testament.

The evangelists, as a matter of fact, stress this parallel between Isaiah and Jesus. Christ withdrew from official Judaism and the masses of the people because they no longer seemed to be receptive to his message. During the last months of his activities, he concentrates on the twelve disciples, to fashion them into a faithful remnant amidst unfaithful Judaism, to fashion them into a "church," and to make them, consequently, the foundation of his Church. The last meeting is the climax of this: the whole Church is formed here and is present here as a separated Remnant. The evangelists mark this turning point in Jesus' activity by referring to Isaiah. It is a valuable reference, which can teach us the art of reading the Scriptures.

The parallel in indeed remarkable and not accidental (cf. p. 166). Since the royal house and the masses of the people have apparently hardened their hearts, Isaiah devotes all his attention to his disciples. He actually is the man of Providence, called to arouse life in the dead body of what once was Yahweh's people, to arouse life by the creative power of his prophetic word. We now hear that Isaiah is busy with the careful cultivation of this faithful remnant. As his words are written down, they are intended to foster the "church" in the Bible reader.

We are not yet finished with the sign of Immanuel. But the data of this Scripture reading move us in the right direction. In the midst of his disciples, the prophet speaks about Immanuel in clearer terms. This is obvious, for Immanuel apparently belongs to them; he is their sign. He is the sign from which they, as believers, will have to live. And that is already an important discovery: the alliance of Immanuel with the faithful Remnant. This was already clear from two previous readings: Immanuel typifies the Remnant; he is himself the Remnant.

Since Immanuel is the sign of surety that the throne of David will not totter, we could already surmise that he is a prophetic indication of the ideal son of David. The great benefit of this Scripture reading is that it states this explicitly. It is, therefore, clear at the same time that Immanuel is identical with the Remnant and to what extent. The Davidic king, as Anointed One of Yahweh, is the exponent of Israel as people of Yahweh. The unfaithful Ahaz is the exponent of the unfaithful Israel of his time. Likewise, Immanuel, as the new David, is the exponent of his new people of God. The situation of the Davidic monarchy is relived in him, but on a completely new scale (namely, without connection to the national and material situation). At the same time he forms a sharp contrast with the situation in Ahaz's time. This is why Immanuel is the salvific sign for the Remnant and an ominous sign for the majority, above all for Ahaz. As the true son of David, Immanuel is an ominous sign for the present dynasty in a special way.

From now on, we will write the word "remnant" with a capital letter, since the faithful remnant, in the middle of which and from which the new salvation, in the concrete shape of Immanuel, will come forth, is a holy Remnant. A small letter or capital letter is used when "remnant" means an indication of doom or salvation, respectively.

Doom: "And, though a tenth of the people remain, it will be stripped." Salvation: "The stock is a holy seed" (as we have seen in 6:13). We will add two more quotes to illustrate both aspects. Doom: "And death will seem preferable to life **to all the survivors** of this wicked race, whereever I have driven them. . . . It is Yahweh who speaks" (Jer. 8:3). Salvation: "Out of the lame I will make a remnant and out of the weary a mighty nation" (Mic. 4:7; "remnant" stands contrary to the indication of doom, "lame," which equals "weary" and is parallel to "mighty nation").

The intimate bond between Immanuel and the Remnant is expressed in the name itself, by the pronoun "us." This name signifies, indeed, that God-is-with-us. "Us" is emphasized. Yahweh is the God of the true believers. He does not want to be Yahweh and God for the unbelievers. Compare Hosea: "You are not my people and I am not your God" (1:9-10; in Hebrew it is the literal denial of Exod. 3:14). But he will be with us, says Isaiah to his disciples. The forthcoming catastrophe will be a salvific judgment for the believers, so that they will form the faithful remnant which Yahweh Sabaoth saves for himself (1:9).

Immanuel is the sign that the believer can trust in God. His name guarantees—without any danger of confusion it can be stated in this way—that the remnant will become Remnant. This Scripture reading closes, therefore, with a triumphant cry of faith: "For there is a child born to us, a son given to us." This "us," explicitly placed here and repeated, refers to the select group of faithful, in the first instance to the faithful remnant, eventually to God's community, to the Church. Now a fine detail can be appreciated. The prophet had said to Ahaz: "Ask Yahweh your God for a sign" (7:11). It is his last chance. There is not yet a break between Ahaz and Yahweh; Yahweh is still Ahaz's God. But after Ahaz's denial, the prophet immediately reacts, saying: "Are you not satisfied with trying the patience of men without trying the patience of my God, too?" (7:13). Not **your** or **our** God, but **my** God. Yahweh has ceased to be Ahaz's God. The same holds true for the people who preferred the waters of Assyria above those of Shiloah. They are no longer Yahweh's people, but "this" people (8:6; cf. 6.9).

At one time, Yahweh had selected Israel from among the peoples for himself, as "remnant" of mankind estranged from God, with the ultimate goal of building a new mankind from this remnant. Israel typifies itself in Abraham, who, as "remnant," was redeemed from a world of peoples "confused" by Babylonian paganism. Creator and King of the whole world, Yahweh chose Israel and selected it for himself to be his Kingdom (Exod. 19:5). It has now come so far with "the chosen people" that Yahweh has to select his faithful from this people to form a Remnant from this deplorable remainder, which will be a new people of God. The pronoun "us" in the name Immanuel, as well as the whole figure of Immanuel, is at once an encouragement for the believers and an ominous sign for the unbelievers.

Yahweh began by selecting Isaiah. Referring to his call, the prophet tells this to his disciples: His Hand seized hold of me, Yahweh warned me (it is actually stronger: corrected me; the verb even means "to castigate"; 8:11). Vocation is separation; it produces loneliness. Isaiah had to become different from others. Compare Jeremiah: "I never took pleasure in sitting in scoffers' company; with your hand on me I held myself aloof" (15:17). This hand overpowered Isaiah (cf. Ezek. 3:14): "The spirit lifted me up and took me . . . . and the hand of Yahweh lay heavy on me").

Isaiah had his trials of faith. He had to follow this new road. Now he has to teach his disciples this road. They will have to maintain themselves as believers amidst an unfaithful people. They have to be cautious of the opinions, practices, and reasonings of what John the evangelist will later call "the world."

They should not call conspiracy all that this people call conspiracy (8:12). This surely refers to Isaiah's condemnation of Ahaz's Assyrian politics. This must have been viewed as treacherous in the public opinion, for the same reason for which Jeremiah, 150 years later, was considered to be dangerous to the state. Isaiah therefore arms his disciples against a crisis of conscience which they could be talked into, as if a true believer of Yahweh could not be a good Judean citizen.

An unfaithful people soon panics, as was clear from the attack of Damascus and Samaria on Jerusalem. Whoever has lost the fear of Yahweh is afraid of anything. Compare Leviticus: "I will strike fear into the hearts of those of you that are left; in the land of their enemies the sound of a falling leaf shall send them fleeing as men flee from the sword, and they shall fall though no one is pursuing them" (Lev. 26:36-37).

But whoever fears Yahweh, does not have to be afraid of men. "Do not fear what they fear. . . . / It is Yahweh Sabaoth / whom you must hold in veneration, / him you must fear, / him you must dread" (8:12-13). We are again reminded of the Gospel: "To you my friends I say: Do not be afraid of those who kill the body and after that can do no more. I will tell you whom to fear:

fear him who, after he has killed, has the power to cast into hell. Yes, I tell you, fear him" (Luke 12:4-5).

"He is the sanctuary" (8:14). Yahweh is the Holy One of Israel, the divine Reality who is near and is in the midst of Israel as a consuming fire (Deut. 4:24; Heb. 12:29). It depends on the human decision of faith whether this sanctuary will be for salvation or for doom. The glowing love ("zeal") of Yahweh will be either purifying or destroying and, eventually, either heaven or hell. In Isaiah's language it runs like this: The Holy One is "the stumbling-stone / and the rock that brings down / the two Houses of Israel; / a trap and a snare / for the inhabitants of Jerusalem. / By it many will be brought down, / many fall and be broken [cf. stumbling-stone / rock], / be trapped and made captive [cf. trap / snare]" (8:14-15).

It is not accidental that in this Scripture reading we repeatedly have to think of the so-called eschatological speeches of Jesus. These are a summarizing reflection of conversations between Jesus and his disciples concerning the fall of Jerusalem and the end of the world. Jesus teaches his disciples how they will have to behave as believers in the coming divine judgment.

Isaiah does essentially the same. He is really the prophet of the nearness of God. His message amounts to the proclamation of God's coming: the times of the people come to an end; God's time, God's Day, has come. Isaiah preaches salvation and doom, because the Day of Yahweh is a salvific or ominous day. It will be a day of grace and redemption for the true belivers, but a day of punishment and judgment for the unfaithful.

The name "Immanuel" is the summarizing sign of what the prophet of the nearness of God has to say. It cannot be clearer: God-with-us is the sign of God's nearness. Immanuel is therefore a sign of contradiction, a sign in which the distinction of minds has been completed. Immanuel is actually an ominous sign to the house of David and to the masses. Both will fall in the judgment, which will be destructive of the whole people—those are the many who will stumble on Yahweh the Rock. But the judgment will be purifying and redeeming for the "remnant" which repents: A-remnant-will-return.

Jesus warns his disciples, and through them all believers, not to be misled by false signs, false prophets, and false Christs. He promises them that whoever perseveres to the end will be saved. While there will be desperate anguish among the peoples on earth because of the roaring of the sea and the breakers, while men are dying from fear and anguish of things which come over the world, the faithful will have to stand erect and hold their heads high, since their redemption is near (cf. Luke 21:25-28).

Isaiah speaks in the same vein. He wants to deposit his preaching as a valuable testimony in the hearts of his disciples. Faith must be their stronghold. They should preserve the message of Immanuel faithfully. Their faith should determine their way of life: "I bind up this testimony, / I seal this revelation, / in the heart of my disciples" (8:16). As a testament and a document, as a roll of parchment which is bound up and sealed, Isaiah deposits his message of faith with his disciples.

Isaiah refers to it with the words "testimony" and "law." "Law" (**torah**) is teaching in the name of God in answer to the question of man as to what he must do in a certain case, how he must behave. One went to the sanctuary "to consult God," that is, one had to ask the priest in office for an answer, for the law belongs to the priest from of old (Judg. 20:18; cf. Deut. 17:8-13). In this instance, the "law" can therefore be described as a line of conduct, as revealed by God. Hence the translation "revelation" or "rule of faith," namely, faith as the standard of human thinking and action. This is the reverse of "confer with flesh and blood" (Gal. 1:16, RSV), against which the prophet will directly warn.

The prophet has fulfilled his task. When he has spoken for the last time, his word will continue to live on in his disciples. There is nothing else to do but wait with confidence for God's time: "I wait for Yahweh / who hides his face from the House of Jacob; / in him I hope" (8:17). Yahweh hides himself and is silent. Some will sneer: Where is your God? When will he finally come? (cf. 1 Pet. 3:3-4). Isaiah will convey his tranquil religious assurance to his disciples. The silence of God is a trial of faith and a constant temptation to seek one's salvation elsewhere.

The believer will have to live as a lonely man among a people who search for human assurances and deceitful signs. The believer has to hold fast to the authentic signs which God himself has given: "I and the children whom Yahweh has given me are signs and portents in Israel from Yahweh Sabaoth who dwells on Mount Zion" (8:18). The names of Isaiah and his two children make them into a living and tangible prophecy. The prophets usually deposit the kernel of their message in some telling, suggestive terms, in proper names which they seemingly decide upon for this purpose. In prophetic language the person who bears such a "telling" name is called a "sign." Isaiah and his children are therefore a living picture of what Isaiah preaches, thus a "sign" of his message. Not empty signs,

but signs given by Yahweh, who has the power to con-
cretize these signs and to realize the doom and salvation
which are symbolically contained in these names.

The disciples should adhere to these signs without
being misled by the false signs to which a faithless and
all too superstitious people attach value: "And should men
say to you, 'Consult ghosts and wizards that whisper and
mutter' . . . to obtain a revelation and a testimony, without
doubt this is how they will talk, since there is no dawn
for them" (8:19-20). From this somewhat difficult and
uncertain text the antithesis between the tranquil certitude
of faith and the despondent despair of unbelief is still
explicit. For the believer there is always prospect; in the
night, from which even he is not saved, he always recognizes signs of the coming dawn. But the unbeliever "will
wander . . . and turning his gaze upward, then down
to the earth, he will find only distress and darkness"
(8:21-22a). No matter how corrupted these last verses may
be, they render an impressive picture of the man who
will not rest in God and consequently finds no rest anywhere, of the man who sins against the light and consequently is at the mercy of his own darkness.

The verse which follows is very uncertain. It looks
like an awkward attempt of later revisers to make a
transition to the next oracle. The verse says: "And they
will be thrust into darkness. But there will be no gloom
for her that was in anguish" (8:22b-23a, RSV). If this
translation is correct, the old readers of Isaiah's prophecies
have in any case had an eye for the contrast between
light and darkness, between anguish and joy, at which
the composers of the book undoubtedly aimed and which
probably date back as far as the time of Isaiah. Now we

touch on a small oracle in which the prophet pays attention to the contrast.

In days past Yahweh humbled the land of Zebulun and
Naphtali, but in the days to come he will confer glory on
the Way of the Sea on the far side of Jordan, province of
the nations (8:23-9:1).

This oracle indicates that Judah sobered up fast after
the inebriation of victory, brought about with the help
of Assyria. Within a few years an age-old situation had
radically changed. The whole northern part of the country,
which was still the land of the fathers, became an
Assyrian province, including Zebulun, Naphtali, and the
far side of Jordan. This province is called the province
(**gelil**) of the nations—Galilee. This entire district is
crossed from the northeast to the southwest by the Way
of the Sea, the famous tradeway which connects Mesopotamia with Egypt. All this has been humbled. This oracle
finds its starting point, therefore, in a very specific, local,
and historical situation. But, as often happens, the prophetic vision widens itself, without losing its starting point,
to a vision which encompasses the coming of the Kingdom
of God in one glance. In a limited event the prophet
recognizes the facts which are at work always and everywhere: Assyria is the accidental personification of world
power and the northern country calls into existence "the
country of Immanuel" (8:8), which has no geographical
borders any more.

"Days past" is the historical time in which Isaiah lives.
The North experiences the indignity of Assyrian domination. It is caught in Assyrian darkness. But the prophet
looks now at the "days to come," which is the time of
Yahweh. The country of Immanuel, the land of the future,

will be the contrast of the present situation. Yahweh will confer glory instead of indignity. In the middle of the darkness, the light breaks through: "The people that walked in darkness / has seen a great light; / on those who live in a land of deep shadow / a light has shone" (9:1).

The reference of Matthew (4:12-16) to this text confronts us again with the miracle of the prophecy (cf. p. 144). From this "light-oracle," which is the opening of the greatest prophecy concerning the child with miraculous names, nobody would dare to venture that the new son of David would stand in relation to the "northern country" in a special way. Everybody feels that Christ is the complete fulfillment of this prophecy, because he, as he says himself, is "the light of the world." It is beneficial to open our eyes to this real fulfillment which the evangelist points to as a seemingly accidental detail, a detail which can hardly belong to the prophetic message itself but, rather, belongs to the wording of it. The prophets usually speak about the future from their contemporary data (for example, the fact that Galilee now is an Assyrian province). Whoever is familiar with the prophetic way of speaking could judge in this cast that this prophecy does not point to the salvation of Galilee, but to the salvation of the world. It is not a prediction of material details, but an expression of complete religious certitude concerning the coming salvation.

We are confronted with a miraculous mystery which perhaps belongs to the mystery of the Book, rather than to the mystery of the prophet Isaiah. It is as if the Word of God, which takes shape in human words, goes beyond human limits.

Galilee is in a special way the land of him who is the true Light, for it is the land of his hidden life and especially of his "epiphany." He revealed there his glory, because it is the land of his miracles, especially his first miracles (John 2:11; 4:54). Matthew points, therefore, to the parallel of contrast between doom and salvation, which seems to be the tactics of the divine revenge. The very part of the country, where the doom of the carrying off into exile (and so the downfall of the old people of God) began, has become the starting point of the new salvation and consequently of the upbuilding of the new people of God. Isaiah has recognized that it is God's way of acting to take revenge in a similar way and, as it were, to apply his salvific action to the situation brought about by sin. This is what the prophet expresses by his contrast between the days "past" and "to come."

Isaiah 9:1-6 deserves to be read separately, and re-read. Although directed to the disciples and the climax of Isaiah's conversation with them, this oracle goes far over their heads. In this respect it can be compared to the priestly prayer at the close of Jesus' farewell (John 17). It is a strong and perfect poem which irresistibly draws us to the climax of verses 5 and 6, since in these verses the prophet actually says where the light originates and why there is such joy in the nation.

Salvation is there. The prophet sees it. He approaches it like someone who comes from afar: a great light in the land (9:1), everywhere gladness and joy. Illustrated in a reverse order (chiasm): joy as at harvest time, gladness as at the dividing of the spoils (9:2). Why? What has happened? This is expressed in a strong crescendo in three phases (three times "for") in such a way that only the third reveals the proper reason.

The foreign occupation has come to an end. The enemy has been defeated. Yahweh has repeated, on a greater scale, the miracle from the time of our religious heroes: the Day of Yahweh will be like the day of Midian when Gideon fought the battle that has the same value to Israel as the "Battle of the Spurs" has to Holland (Jdt. 7):* "For the yoke that was weighing on him, / the bar across his shoulders, / the rod of his oppressor, / these you break as on the day of Midian" (9:3).

The victory over the enemy remains a characteristic feature of the "end of the times" (eschatology) throughout the rest of the Bible. It is a prophetic indication of the ultimate victory over "the world" and its reign." This text shows where the military terminology originates, which is used by the Scriptures to point to this essentially spiritual event. Isaiah speaks about Assyria in the first instance, as Jeremiah (cf. also Isa. 13) will do concerning Babylon. That their vision reaches far beyond this is clearly shown here and will be clarified by the next scriptural passage. The prophets read the actual issue of the conflict between Israel and the big powers of the earth completely in line with the old poets who had already surmised a deeper background in the conflict between Israel and its small neighbors (Gen. 49:8ff.; Num. 24:17-19; Judg. 5:13; Exod. 15:14-18).

The second reason for joy is that finally there is peace. Here, too, Assyria clearly is the starting point of the prophecy (marching armies!). All the equipment of war can be completely cleared away, since it does not serve any purpose now that the messianic kingdom with its

*Trans. Note: Battle near Kortrijk (Belgium), July 11, 1302, where the French army was defeated by the Flemings.

paradisiacal peace has come: "For all the footgear of battle, / every cloak rolled in blood, / is burnt, / and consumed by fire" (9:4; cf. 2:4).

Only now does the prophet mention the source of all that light and all that joy, the bearer of this liberation and this peace. It appears to be Immanuel. His names reveal that he is indeed Immanuel, that in him God has indeed approached his people. They express that he is the elected instrument and the personification of the salvation which Yahweh has reserved for his people: "For a child is born for us, / a son is given to us / and dominion is laid on his shoulders; / and this is the name they give him: / Wonder-Counsellor, Mighty-God, / Eternal-Father, Prince-of-Peace" (9:5).

While doom is at hand, the prophet opens for the Remnant the vision of the future Kingdom of God, which will be established on the ruins of the old kingdom. From death springs life, from the remnant, which is a poor remainder, a new people of God has been born, and from the house of David, which has been doomed, Immanuel arises. The mysterious, divine order of this resurrection and the power of Yahweh Sabaoth, who will accomplish this, receive shape in Immanuel, whom, therefore, he calls Wonder-Counsellor and Mighty-God. He means that there has come forever an end to the tyranny and exploitation of native and foreign rulers (cf. 9:3); therefore, he is called Eternal-Father. His Kingdom does not rest on military power and waging war. He is commander, not of the war but of the peace (**dux belli, dux pacis**). His dominion not only brings an end to the war and devastation, but also is the source of a sound, happy, and flourishing society. He is therefore caller Prince-(Commander)-of-Peace (cf. 9:4). So in Yahweh's Kingdom, the great positions which, otherwise held by figures next to the king (counsellor, commander-in-chief, "father"; cf. Gen. 45:8; Isa. 22:21ff.), submerge in Immanuel, since he is the visible manifestation of the invisible, divine majesty ("Powerful God").

He is all this, since he, the Anointed One of Yahweh, is the king in the Kingdom of God. He is the fulfillment of the promise given to David. He is the fervently expected ideal son of David. Hence he bears those names deservedly, since he makes them true in the splendor and the blessings of his government. Thanks to him, his dominion is wide "in a peace that has no end, / for the throne of David / and for his royal power, / which he establishes and makes secure / in justice and integrity. / From this time onwards and for ever" (9:6).

"Justice and integrity" have been sought in vain by Yahweh in the old city (5:7). He will bring them there himself.

They will receive human and royal shape in the Just One par excellence:

> See, the days are coming—it is Yahweh who
>   speaks—
> when I will raise a virtuous Branch for David
> who will reign as true king and be wise,
> practising honesty and integrity in the land.
> In his days Judah will be saved
> and Israel dwell in confidence.
> And this is the theme he will be called:
> Yahweh-our-integrity"
>   Jeremiah 23:5-6

The coming of Yahweh's justice and integrity means judgment for the old city (1:27ff.). The prophet had to stress this up until now. But here he opens for the believer the unhindered vision of the new city of David, which will emerge from the judgment.

This vision points to the religious road which man has to travel in his troubled existence. It is a road which everyone will smooth for himself according to his personal circumstances of life. It is a road which has to be sought and conquered, since this new salvation is not brought to him from the outside, but will have to grow from within. True religion is not a system which automatically provides salvation. A complete affirmation or a complete denial, as a fully human answer to the perilous, glowing, loving zeal of Yahweh of Hosts, who will achieve all this, is here at stake (9:6b).

15

YAHWEH'S OUTSTRETCHED HAND (9:7-10:4)

9:7 The Lord hurls a word against Jacob,
     it falls on Israel.

8   All the people of Ephraim and all the inhabitants of
          Samaria know it.
     In their pride they have said,
     speaking in the arrogance of their heart,

9   "The bricks have fallen down, then we will build
          with dressed stone;
     the sycamores have been cut down, we will put
          cedars in their place."

10   But Yahweh is marshalling his people's enemies
          against them,
     he is stirring up their foes:

11   to the east, Aram, to the west, the Philistines
     devour Israel with gaping jaw.
     Yet his anger is not spent,
     still his hand is raised to strike.

12   But the people have not come back to him who
          struck them,
     they have not come looking for Yahweh Sabaoth;

13   hence Yahweh has cut head and tail from Israel,
     palm branch and reed in a single day.

14   (The "head" is the elder and the man of rank;
     the "tail," the prophet with lying vision.)

15   This people's leaders have taken the wrong turning,
     and those who are led are lost.

16   And so the Lord will not spare their young men,
     will have no pity for their orphans and widows.
     Since the whole people is godless and evil,

its speech is madness.
Yet his anger is not spent,
still his hand is raised to strike.

9:17   Yes, wickedness burns like a fire:
       it consumes briar and thorn,
       it sets the forest thickets alight
       and columns of smoke go rolling upwards.
18   The land is set aflame by the wrath of Yahweh
           Sabaoth
       and the people are food for the fire.
       Not one spares his brother,
19b   each devours the flesh of his neighbour.
       On the right side they carve and still are hungry,
       on the left they devour and are not satisfied.
19a   Manasseh devours Ephraim, Ephraim Manasseh,
       and both hurl themselves on Judah.
       Yet his anger is not spent,
       still his hand is raised to strike.

10:1   Woe to the legislators of infamous laws,
       to those who issue tyrannical decrees,
2   who refuse justice to the unfortunate
       and cheat the poor among my people of their
           rights,
       who make widows their prey
       and rob the orphan.
3   What will you do on the day of punishment,
       when, from far off, destruction comes?
       To whom will you run for help?
       where will you leave your riches?
4   Nothing for it but to crouch with the captives
       and to fall with the slain.
       Yet his anger is not spent,
       still his hand is raised to strike.

16

THE ROD IN

GOD'S HAND (10:5-27)

10:5   Woe to Assyria, the rod of my anger,
the club brandished by me in my fury!

6   I sent him against a godless nation;
I gave him commission against a people that
    provokes me,
to pillage and to plunder freely
and to stamp down like the mud in the streets.

7   But he did not intend this,
his heart did not plan it so.
No, in his heart was to destroy,
to go on cutting nations to pieces without limit.

8   He said, "Are not my officers all kings?

9   Is not Calmo like Carchemish,
Hamath like Arpad,
Samaria like Damascus?

10   As my hand has reached out to the kingdoms of
    the idols,
richer in sculptured images than Jerusalem and
    Samaria,

11   as I have dealt with Samaria and her idols,
shall I not treat Jerusalem and her images the
    same?"

12   When the Lord has completed all his work
on Mount Zion and in Jerusalem, he will punish
what comes from the king of Assyria's boastful
heart, and his arrogant insolence.

13   For he has said:

"By the strength of my own arm I have done this
and by my own intelligence, for understanding is
    mine;

I have pushed back the frontiers of peoples
and plundered their treasures.
I have brought their inhabitants down to the dust.

10:14 As if they were a bird's nest, my hand has seized
the riches of the peoples.
As people pick up deserted eggs
I have picked up the whole earth,
with not a wing fluttering,
not a beak opening, not a chirp."

15 Does the axe claim more credit than the man who
wields it,
or the saw more strength than the man who
handles it?
It would be like the cudgel controlling the man
who raises it,
or the club moving what is not made of wood!

16 And so Yahweh Sabaoth is going to send
a wasting sickness on his stout warriors;
beneath his plenty, a burning will burn
like a consuming fire.

17 The light of Israel will become a fire
and its Holy One a flame
burning and devouring thorns
and briars in a single day.

18 He will destroy the luxuriance of his forest
and his orchard, soul and body too;
that will be like a sick man passing away;

19 the remnant of his forest trees will be so easy to
count
that a child could make the list.

20 That day,
the remnant of Israel and the survivors of the
House of Jacob
will stop relying on the man who strikes them
and will truly rely on Yahweh,
the Holy One of Israel.

21 A remnant will return, the remnant of Jacob,
to the mighty God.

10:22-23   Israel, your people may be like the sand on the
             seashore, but only a remnant will return. A de-
             struction has been decreed that will bring inex-
             haustible integrity. ● Yes, throughout the country
             the Lord Yahweh Sabaoth will carry out the
             destruction he has decreed.

24   And so Yahweh Sabaoth says this:
             My people who live in Zion,
             do not be afraid of Assyria who strikes you with
                  the club
             and lifts up the rod against you.

25   A little longer, a very little,
             and fury will come to an end,
             my anger will destroy them.
26   Yahweh Sabaoth will whirl the whip against him,
             like the time he struck Midian at the Rock of Oreb,
             like the time he stretched out his rod against the
                  sea
             and raised it over the road from Egypt.
27   That day,
             his burden will fall from your shoulder,
             his yoke will cease to weigh on your neck.

The book of Isaiah goes from one extreme to the other.
The previous Scripture reading closed with the cheering
salvific oracle concerning the Child with the miraculous
names, who will establish the ideal and imperishable
Davidic kingdom. This oracle is immediately followed by
a powerful poem of doom, which pronounces in four
stanzas a great woe over the same people for whom the
prophet opened such a splendid future in the previous
oracle (9:7-10:4). But after this ominous oracle, the passage
which we now read follows.

In this one, too, a great woe is pronounced, not over
Israel, but over Assyria. This can only be to the advantage
of Israel. Although Yahweh is angry with his people, he

defends them against Assyria and therefore opens a new possibility of salvation for Israel. Yahweh is angry with the prosperous people which fell away from him. Because of this he allows foreign people to execute the punishment deserved by his people. However, his beaten and almost destroyed people does not evoke his wrath, but his mercy. Hence he stands up for the poor remnant of his people.

This turn in the prophetic train of thought has a variant, which strongly resounds in the Scripture passage. Since the defeat of a people is at the same time the defeat of its god, Yahweh's name is "desecrated" among the peoples by the humiliating situation in which his people finds itself. This is at the same time a victory for the gods of the conquerers, so that the name of "foreign" gods will be "exalted." This evokes Yahweh's "jealousy." He does not yield his glory to another (Isa. 42:8). Yahweh will, therefore, "sanctify" and "glorify" his name among the peoples by saving his people. Compare the prayer of Moses: What would the Egyptians think if we should perish here in the desert? (Deut. 9:28; 32:27; Num. 14:16; Ps. 79:10). Hence it says that Yahweh's "jealousy" (in 9:7 it is translated as "jealous love") will accomplish the miracle of regrouping Israel's remnant into a new people (Isa. 37:32). Ezekiel 36 approaches Israel's restoration completely from this angle; one finds there a very anthropomorphic and elaborate description of Yahweh's "jealous love."

This oracle against Assyria is a classic example of how the prophecy of doom against the masses turns into an ominous prophecy against the peoples at the very moment the climax of doom is reached, and turns at the same time into a salvific prophecy for those of Israel who are left, thus for the remnant.

The book of Isaiah suddenly plunges from a summit of salvation into a depth of doom, in order to climb up gradually from this to a new salvific oracle. The Bible reader should completely assimilate this stern contrast and should not weaken it by the knowledge, though correct, that these oracles are not pronouncements one after another. Each is given at a different time and also to a different audience. The tensions in the book of Isaiah are the tensions in the religious existence of man himself. Faith may sometimes appear to be easily conquered and to be in safe possession, as if it had fallen into one's lap in his early youth. But as soon as life provides situations which have to be lived fully and humanly, we positively experience that we are not able to assent to the faith of our childhood in a mature way without any conflict.

During his earthly life the believer ultimately stands between life and death, although he is perhaps conscious of these only at certain critical turning points. Man lives under a holy God; his situation is literally critical, since he stands under crisis, since a divine judgment is about to be enacted on him, because God is coming.

Faith in a heavenly hereafter is of the most suspicious character if it does not confront us more completely with the earthly realities to which it should give the right meaning. The first readers of Isaiah had their eyes opened drastically with regard to the national dream, concerning a new kingdom of David, by a merciless poem of doom, which is divided into four stanzas by a refrain from which it borrows its irresistible force: "Yet his anger is not spent, / still his hand is raised to strike" (9:11, 16:20; 10:4). This refrain sharply describes the critical situation of Judah and Jerusalem. But at the same time it becomes clear from this, as from a classic and pointed example, that man will have to work for his salvation "in fear and trembling" (Phil. 2:12). Man lives under God's outstretched hand; he lives toward an ultimate decision.

The decision of Judah and Jerusalem has not yet fallen, but the hand, which wants to heal and redeem, threatens to become a crushing hand. Once more this poem confronts us with the dilemma so characteristic of the first five chapters, where we met the refrain once before (5:25). There is no need to discuss this ominous poem, since we have delved sufficiently into the collection of doom oracles in this book, to which this poem belongs **historically**. Here we are concerned with the **literary** position which it has received in this book. By the very placing in the book, there arises the rhythmic movement from salvation to doom and from doom to salvation, which is a faithful reflection of the rhythm in the prophetic preaching itself: the God of salvation has to be too often the God of doom, God-with-us is simultaneously a sign of salvation and of doom.

The oracle concerning the Child with miraculous names was the summit. This salvific prophecy finds its natural continuation and crowning in chapter 11, in the oracle concerning the shoot from the old stock of Jesse. The composition of the book does even more justice to this oracle, since the reader has to descend to the depth of doom in order to work himself up through conversion and faith until he reaches this last culmination, which will be at the same time the apotheosis of the Book of Immanuel.

This book is divided into three main rhythmic movements, ascents and descents, which flow one from the other. We see three ever-higher arses in the well-known texts concerning Immanuel: the child of the "virgin," the child with its miraculous names, the shoot of Jesse.

These arses rise from three ever-deeper descents of doom. This doom is always the Assyrian doom. The higher the need rises, the more explicitly faith speaks: the three oracles concerning Immanuel follow alongside the three Assyrian oracles.

The prophets do not want to predict all kinds of details concerning the future doom. Ultimately they know only that it is awful to fall into the hands of the living God. They try to express this awfulness in words and to make it tangible with the aid of their contemporary data. Assyria therefore plays a highly important part in the ominous prophecy of the book concerning Immanuel.

The prophets are so sure of the new salvation that, for them, salvation is already present and they apparently describe it as eyewitnesses. The same is true for their description of the coming doom. Starting from the signs of their time, they see the destruction grow and grow until the moment of the destroying blow has arrived. It is conspicuous: as soon as the doom reaches such a height in a living description, the prophet suddenly ceases to be a prophet of doom. He sympathizes with what he sees, so much so that at the moment the water reaches his lips, he clings to Yahweh through a cry of distress or a profession of faith.

In this way it becomes clear that doom is never Yahweh's last word. When everything seems lost, Yahweh intervenes. We see this happen repeatedly here: over and over again, the prophecy of doom winds up in a prophecy of salvation; over and over again, doom appears to be the indispensable transition to salvation; over and over again, Assyria crashes into Immanuel. That, in general, is the reason why the three oracles concerning Immanuel are followed by the three Assyrian oracles.

We have seen two of these oracles, but not sufficiently enough from this angle. In his ominous prophecy against the people who despise the waters of Shiloah, the prophet saw the waters of the Euphrates and Tigris penetrate the country. He saw Assyria descend upon Judah like a giant, preying bird: "And its wings will be spread over the whole breadth of your country, O Immanuel." Judah is a helpless prey in the grip of Assyria! It seems that Judah has had it, for a cry of distress sounds here: "your country, O Immanuel." This name suddenly turns the prophecy of doom against Judah into a prophecy of doom against Assyria and against the power of which Assyria is the personification:

> Know this, peoples, you will be crushed;
> listen, far-off nations,
> arm yourselves, yet you will be crushed.
> Devise a plan, it is thwarted;
> put forward an argument, there is no substance
> in it,
> for God is with us.

Isaiah 8:8-10

The conversation of Isaiah with his disciples is connected to this. Doom suddenly turns into salvation.

We have not yet read this text. Attention should be paid to two points in passing: First, the Bible itself offers here a definite explanation of the name "Immanuel," since this text begins with the proper name, but ends with the literal translation of it. The power of the name explicitly speaks from this text. The biblical explanation of the name Maher-shalal was immediately given when this name was mentioned the first time (8:1-4). Later in this Scripture reading we finally find the authentic explanation of the name Shear-jashub (10:21ff.). Second, this text illustrates the peculiar form of the decree against the hardness of heart (6:9). Here, too, the verb is used in the imperative:

arm yourselves and be crushed. This sentence is even repeated for emphasis' sake. This imperative is not a command and, consequently, does not express what **has** to happen, but it is a Semitic way of saying what surely **will** happen. The sentence runs: although you make so many preparations for war, you will be defeated anyway; whatever plans you contrive, it is sure that they will be frustrated. The decree against hardness of heart can be understood in the same way: although you hear it so often, you will not listen.

We have met a second example of such an abrupt transition from doom to salvation in the previous scriptural fragment. Assyrian darkness has fallen, but in the middle of this impenetrable darkness the light of Immanuel suddenly breaks through (9:1-4).

The two examples are only indications, compared to what we now read. For in this third and last Assyrian oracle we again find this characteristic prophetic train of thought very explicitly and, as it were, in a reasoned form. The most telling example we will save, however, for the next Scripture reading, since it is intimately bound up with the oracle concerning the shoot of Jesse, which contrasts it.

These transitions from doom to salvation are, one by one, expressions of a miraculous faith. It is a faith which is born on the ruins of all human assurances, since it then discovers the only divine certitude. It is therefore a faith which can "glory in tribulations." The believer lives in a world which has to undergo judgment. In this very judgment God creates his believers. Throughout the history of the world this shift takes place. Over and over again, a remnant has to be rescued and separated from a perverted generation (Acts 2:40).

Assyria has changed Israel into a remnant. But then the blazing flame which purged Israel becomes a wall of fire which consumes Assyria and makes this great power, with its innumerable armies, in its turn, a remnant. From the whole Assyrian forest only a few trees will be left, so few that a child can count them (10:16-19).

One remnant evokes another one: the remnant of Israel will no longer trust Assyria on that day, but will truly put its trust in Yahweh, the Holy One of Israel. That is the return, the conversion of the rest. Isaiah's son Shear-jashub, A-remnant-will-return, is a sign of this as the prophet now explains literally: A remnant will return, the remnant of Jacob, to the mighty God. It is the Mighty God who reveals himself in Immanuel. This is also the reason why Immanuel will be called Strong God. The prophet once more indicates that the sign of Immanuel is the redemption of the remnant.

But both Shear-jashub and Immanuel are simultaneously an ominous sign for the unfaithful masses as the prophet once more stresses: Although your people, O Israel, is like the sand of the sea, only a remnant of this will return. A destruction which will be a flood of justice is surely imminent. Once more, the believer will have to undergo judgment together with the world in which he lives. But while this overflowing justice will destroy the old world as in a flood, it will at the same time carry the ark in which the believer will find safety (10:20-23).

The Assyrian doom is imminent. The blows will hurt sorely. The faithful will be hurt in what is most dear to them: their country, their city, their royal house, their Temple. All these things are dear to believers, since until now they have been connected with the name of Yahweh, since they considered these dearly loved familiar and national places as a guarantee of Yahweh's presence. In the coming doom Yahweh will be the great Absent One. He will hide his face from the house of Jacob.

From the consoling words which Isaiah addressed to his disciples on this situation, an inspiring tranquillity speaks. They are words which can give support to someone who has to clear a way of faith through the seemingly hopeless and meaningless existence in a confused and merciless world: Yahweh will redeem his people. Yet a short time ("a little longer, a very little"). Actually not quantitatively short (a small number of years and days), but qualitatively short (the time of transiency in the same sense in which Paul writes: "Brothers, this is what I mean: our time is growing short . . . the world as we know it is passing away" (1 Cor. 7:29-31). There is no human evidence which points to an approaching redemption; it is only near for him who dares to hope against all hope for a miracle. This second redemption will be as much a miracle as the first one when Yahweh made his people his personal possession by redeeming it from the hand of Egypt and Midian: Assyria will undergo the same fate as Egypt:

> And so Yahweh Sabaoth says this:
> My people who live in Zion
> do not be afraid of Assyria who strikes you with
>   the club
> and lifts up the rod against you.
> A little longer, a very little,
> and fury will come to an end,
> my anger will destroy them.
> Yahweh Sabaoth will whirl the whip against him,
> like the time he struck Midian at the Rock of Oreb,
>   the time he stretched out his rod against the
>   sea

and raised it over the road from Egypt.
That day,
his burden will fall from your shoulder,
his yoke will cease to weigh on your neck.
Isaiah 10:24-27

For more than half a century Judah had to deal with
the Assyrian doom. It is a long and moving history of
doom, as some dates can immediately clarify: 740 B.C., fall
of Arpad; 732 B.C., fall of Damascus; 721 B.C., fall of
Samaria; 711 B.C., fall of the Philistine city of Ashdod; 701
B.C., siege of Jerusalem (Isa. chaps. 36-37). There is no
doubt that the several Assyrian oracles of Isaiah have
individually had a very definite historical cause. It belongs
to the task of Scripture scholars to answer the question:
To which phase or to which episode of the Assyrian
invasion does this particular text belong? The answer is
often disputed. Although it may be an interesting question, it is not important. And that is good; otherwise one
would have to be a Scripture scholar in order to read the
Bible.

The question is not so important, since the prophet,
although he may speak as a result of very definite circumstances, aims at the essence. From a particular Assyrian
appearance he changes to the Assyrian phenomenon in its
entirety, as he considers this as the personification of the
God-hating world power of all times.

Isaiah's disciples and the editors of the book have
understood this very well. The Assyrian invasion and
even the whole Assyrian world empire rather soon passed
into history. Posterity little knew, and perhaps less than
we, to which part of the Assyrian invasion the prophet
refers in a particular text. All kinds of Assyrian texts were
strung together in greater passages, as, for example, in

this Scripture reading. And so they received their place in the book. They are, however, global indications of the bare fact of the Assyrian invasion, precisely as a particular and past form of the world power.

This book expresses a religious insight concerning the world power as such in its behavior and its function with regard to the community of God: the rod in the hand of Yahweh, Lord of Hosts, who strikes to heal. When Yahweh has completed this work of punishment and chastising with regard to Mount Zion, he will settle with Assyria.

The distinction between Immanuel and Assyria is the distinction between the Kingdom of God and the kingdom of this world, and that is a distinction which is eternal. But only faith is able to see this distinction. Isaiah is the great witness of that faith. By giving meaning to the events of his time from his faith, he hands over the key to all world events.

Jeremiah (chaps. 50-51) expresses the same religious vision concerning Babylon, while Ezekiel (chaps. 38-39) is so taken up by the apocalyptic end of time that the historical names and celebrities which he mentions completely serve this end and hardly seem to refer to a historical situation at the time of the prophet. The book of Daniel, in a grand synthesis, interprets the whole Old Testament history as the history of the faithful community of God, of the people of saints which, when the worst is reached, is snatched from the kingdom of the world in its consecutive historical personifications through divine intervention.

In the last book of the Bible, the book of Revelation, St. John summarizes both the literary and the theological heredity of his prophetic predecessors in connection with the Roman world power. Their literary heredity, insofar as he uses their terms and their illustrations as building material for his apocalyptic types and scenes; their theological heredity, insofar as his book is aimed at the witness of what properly is at stake in these sublunar events which touch the lives of believers.

The last book of the Bible is the scriptural guarantee that we are not wrong if we feel that we can apply to our own Christian existence what Isaiah—on first sight—seems to have said concerning Assyria.

THE ROOT OF
JESSE (11:1-16)

11:1   A shoot springs from the stock of Jesse,
a scion thrusts from his roots:

2   on him the spirit of Yahweh rests,
a spirit of wisdom and insight,
a spirit of counsel and power,
a spirit of knowledge and of the fear of Yahweh.
(The fear of Yahweh is his breath.)

3   He does not judge by appearances,
he gives no verdict on hearsay,

4   but judges the wretched with integrity,
and with equity gives a verdict for the poor of the
land.
His word is a rod that strikes the ruthless,
his sentences bring death to the wicked.

5   Integrity is the loincloth round his waist,
faithfulness the belt about his hips.

6   The wolf lives with the lamb,
the panther lies down with the kid,
calf and lion cub feed together
with a little boy to lead them.

7   The cow and the bear make friends,
their young lie down together.
The lion eats straw like the ox.

8   The infant plays over the cobra's hole;
into the viper's lair
the young child puts his hand.

9   They do no hurt, no harm,
on all my holy mountain,
for the country is filled with the knowledge of
Yahweh
as the waters swell the sea.

11:10   That day, the root of Jesse
        shall stand as a signal to the peoples.
        It will be sought out by the nations
        and its home will be glorious.

11   That day, the Lord will raise his hand once more
        to ransom the remnant of his people,
        left over from the exile of Assyria, of Egypt,
        of Pathros, of Cush, of Elam,
        of Shinar, of Hamath, of the islands of the sea.

12   He will hoist a signal for the nations
        and assemble the outcasts of Israel;
        he will bring back the scattered people of Judah
        from the four corners of the earth.

13   Then Ephraim's jealousy will come to an end
        and Judah's enemies be put down;
        Ephraim will no longer be jealous of Judah
        nor Judah any longer the enemy of Ephraim.

14   They will sweep down westwards on the Philistine
        slopes,
        together they will pillage the sons of the East,
        extend their sway over Edom and Moab,
        and make the Ammonites their subjects.

15   And Yahweh will dry up the gulf of the Sea of
        Egypt
        and stretch out his hand over the River,
        and divide it into seven streams,
        for men to cross dry-shod,

16   to make a pathway for the remnant of his people
        left over from the exile of Assyria,
        as there was for Israel
        when it came up out of Egypt.

This last scriptural passage is indeed a finale—the finale of a symphony, one could say. The comparison with a great musical composition can help us to account for the character of the twelve chapters, which we have read and have meditated on in this book. This does justice both to the deep and unmistakable untiy of the cycle of prophecies and to its colorful composition.

The most important themes of this symphony could already be recognized in the overture; after this they were elaborated in all kinds of variations. The general theme of the approach of God was twofold from the beginning. God's approach is both ominous and encouraging, the announcement of his coming is a message of both doom and salvation.

From the central sixth chapter it was clear that this ambiguity of the prophecy actually takes root in the meeting of the holy atmosphere with the human and earthly one. Only outside the context of factual history, which is salvation history—so only on an abstract and un-real level—man as creature seems to have unobscured relations with his God. Faith, however, has realized from of old that God has created man for eternity. To this corresponds completely the fact that the frailty and transi-ency of being man are experienced as inscrutably coherent with sinfulness. The relentless dominion of mortality and death refer to a fundamental alienation from the God who is the source of all life (Gen. 3). This becomes a more acute experience as soon as the earthly mortal man be-comes more explicitly confronted with the realm of the holy.

This generally human situation has taken the shape of the concrete, historical dialogue between Yahweh and Israel: the Holy One of Israel lives among a sinful people. This special national situation was lived in its turn in an intensified form by Isaiah: he experienced the deeply painful and simultaneously redeeming nearness of the Holy One of Israel in the very core of his personal existence. Then the sacred, national signs of this Nearness became transparent to the prophet and thus it became an unam-biguous spiritual meeting. He was able, therefore, in the classical story of his call, to record the essential elements of the meeting between God and man and, in the first instance, of the existential situation in which Israel found itself as a people of Yahweh.

In the first five chapters the themes of doom and salvation are couched in rather general terms; in the last six chapters, however, salvation receives shape in Immanuel and doom in Assyria. The first five chapters were characterized as the collection of doom oracles, since the motif of doom dominates and the theme of salvation resounds only a single time. But in the last six chapters, which form the Book of Immanuel, the theme of salvation is more and more elaborated, namely in three great rhythmic movements. This Scripture passage is the highest and last movement, which will broadly flow into a completely satisfying closing accord in which all tensions dissolve themselves.

These twelve chapters in their magnificent entirety can be compared with a cathedral on which many generations have built, a sanctuary with many naves and chapels and a colorful variety of monuments. But all these parts go back to the inspiration of the first architect and are the manifold expression of his original thought. One arch rises after the other, always higher and farther until they merge, as it were, and find their crowning in the triumphal arch, to which the visitor finally gazes in meditation. This Scripture passage, is, then, comparable to the triumphal arch.

The liberating effect of this salvific message is considerably heightened by the preceding oracle in which the depth of doom is reached. This oracle describes a successful march of the Assyrian army on Jerusalem. Only at the very last moment, when the city seems hopelessly lost, does Yahweh intervene.

The prophet mentions the names of fourteen places which must have been familiar to anyone in Jerusalem. They are the last fourteen villages or prominent places which one meets approaching Jerusalem from the north. In the prophetic description, the Assyrian march starts in the neighborhood of the northern border of the Southern Kingdom, something like a three-hour walk from the city. At every place name, the Assyrian comes some miles closer; the enemy advances closer and closer to the city. The last name is Nob, known in the pilgrim stories as Scopus ("view"), the most prominent point in the wide perimeter, one mile north of Jerusalem, where the traveler suddenly sees for the first time the panorama of the city lying at his feet. There is no obstacle hindering the enemy, and the city is there to be seized.

The following text contains fourteen geographical names, most of them followed by a short note, which usually contains an untranslatable play on words. The prophet continues by saying about the Assyrian:

> He advances from the district of Rimmon,
> he reaches Aiath,
> he passes through Migron
> he leaves his baggage train at Michmash.
> They file through the defile,
> they bivouac at Geba.
> Ramah quakes,
> Gilbeah of Saul takes flight.
> Bath-gallim, cry aloud!
> Laishah, hear her!
> Anathoth, answer her!
> Madmenah is running away,
> the inhabitants of Gebim are fleeing.
> He will shake his fist against the mount of the
>   daughter of Zion,

against the hill of Jerusalem.
See, the Lord Yahweh Sabaoth
hews down the boughs with a crash.
The topmost heights are cut off,
the proudest are brought down.
The forest thickets fall beneath the axe.
Lebanon and its splendours collapse.
Isaiah 10:27-34

This text is followed, in the same breath, by the oracle concerning the shoot of Jesse. The Assyrian army, dispersed on the hills around Jerusalem, resembles the cedars of Lebanon. The silent budding of the shoot of Jesse forms a nice contrast with this Assyrian forest, which collapses with a crash: a shoot springs from the stock of Jesse, a shoot buds from its roots. The thickest forest crashes; the inconspicuous shoot sprouts (cf. Isa. 53:2): in a telling image we meet here the entire contrast between the Kingdom of God and the kingdom of the world.

This contrast dominates the whole of Isaiah's preaching, but here he brings it to a culmination: we get the impression of a decisive, final fight between the two powers that seek domination over men's hearts. We are not unjustly reminded of the apocalyptic final fight as St. John describes it in the book of Revelation, for the prophet and the apostles see essentially the same scene. They recognize what actually is at stake in the unequal battle between Assyria and Jerusalem, between Rome and the Christian community.

Isaiah does not predict the route which the Assyrian army will travel—it will surely come from the South—but he uses geographical names to indicate that the fight will come to the worst. He does justice to Assyria and the kingdom of this world. Assyria is successful; the kingdom of this world seemingly triumphs; the City of God seems beyond redemption. The prophet wants to arm his disciples with this description against what we now call the scandal of the cross. Only faith in the resurrection from death can make human existence meaningful. This faith was asked of, and rendered by, Abraham who, because of this, is the father of all believers (Rom. 4). This faith is asked of Judah and Jerusalem.

Only along this way of faith can people born in Jerusalem, to whom Isaiah speaks in the first place, find a possibility of existence when the city lies in ruins. Nobody knows what fate the city can expect, but it is certain that Jerusalem can be what it essentially is only by faith: the City of God. The degeneration of Jerusalem has now progressed so far that the upbuilding of the City of God is best served by the destruction of the material city. The true believers will have their privilege of being born in Jerusalem returned a hundredfold, since faith will give them the birthright of the Holy City which will arise from the ruins of material Jerusalem. He who will be purged by the judgment over his earthly city, will acquire the birthright of the City of God (Ps. 87) which will still be the continuation and realization of what God intended by his election of the old Jerusalem.

God builds his city among the people by judging the city which man has built for himself. This judgment is portrayed once and for all in the story of the Tower of Babel, with which is very meaningfully connected the story of the call of Abraham, of whom it is written that "he looked forward to a city founded, designed, and built by God" (Heb. 11:10).

We have heard Isaiah speak in all kinds of keys concerning the judgment which will come over every form of human pride. Once more he portrays in Assyria the extremity to which human megalomania can come. As if by a final effort, the kingdom of this world attempts to prevent the definite establishment of the Kingdom of God, not realizing that it will be established thanks to this effort. The power of darkness is apportioned her hour, but it will simultaneously be the hour of the Redeemer; what looks like its victory is its definite defeat. From the side of the slain Messiah, the Church is born.

As a rod in Yahweh's hand, Assyria executes the divine judgment through which will be generated the religious energy that will make the City of God everlasting. There is the merciless borderline of the powers of the earth: the more they rage, the purer will be the Remnant, which will be spiritually intangible by faith.

The world power will also execute judgment over the house of David. Deprived of human glory, of royalty, it is reduced to its initial humble state: the nameless farmer's family of Bethlehem. The prophet will indicate this with this peculiar expression: the root of Jesse. It is the poor remainder of the dynasty. The proud cedar of the dynasty is brought down; only a remnant, the old family root, is left. But here also a-remnant-will-return applies. In and through the judgment, Yahweh of Hosts himself creates a family remnant, that from it may bud forth a new David after his heart. Reference to this was made in the sign of Immanuel, who, thanks to the judgment, returned to the plain food of the time of the nomads, who ate curds and honey but who learned in this way to choose the good and to reject the bad, rediscovering the faith of the nomadic times by living their way of life.

The remnant will become the Holy Remnant by faith.

As "remnant" turns from the idea of doom into the idea of salvation, so "the shoot of Jesse," too, though it reminds us of the judgment over the dynasty, becomes an indication of salvation. This prophecy has come that far. Parallel to "Remnant" as pure idea of salvation, the "Branch of David," rather than the "Shoot of Jesse," has become the classical term of Israel's salvific expectations with regard to the King of the future (Jer. 23:5; 33:15; Zech. 3:8; 6:12).

What Ahaz still was in name, the new royal descendant will be in reality: the Anointed One of Yahweh. The spirit of Yahweh will rest on him (11:2). The oracle expresses how complete this anointment by the spirit will be in the septenary gifts, which are so divided that together they cover the living and working atmosphere of the king. The spirit which seized hold of this son of David expresses itself in three times two pairs of spiritual gifts which are attuned to the function of ruler and make him the ideal king of the Kingdom of God. Equipped with "a spirit of wisdom and understanding—two gifts which Solomon requested (1 Kings 3:9)—"he does not judge by appearances, / he gives no verdict on hearsay" (11:3); equipped with "a spirit of counsel and power," he is indeed the Wonder-Counsellor and Mighty God by protecting the poor with equity from suppression and exploitation (11:4).

These two pairs of gifts, by which the king attains the right attitude with regard to his subjects through insight, conduct, and effectiveness, rest on the last pair, by which he attains the right attitude with regard to his God: "a spirit of knowledge and of the fear of Yahweh" (11:2). Knowledge of Yahweh and fear of Yahweh are often two concurrent notions, though the stress differs: fear expresses distance; knowledge expresses union and surrender. Both encompass the whole religious sphere and are the classical definition of the authentic ideal of piety. "Integrity is the loin cloth round his waist, / faithfulness the belt about his hips" (11:5).

From the fact that he is the champion of "the wretched" and "the poor of the land" and takes action against "the ruthless," we notice that Isaiah is, in this oracle engaged in forming a faithful remnant amidst unfaithful Israel. As always, the prophetic word is encouraging for the believers who had to acquire—often in the school of economic poverty and of a hard earthly existence—the spiritual attitude of complete surrender and total availability with regard to Yahweh, an attitude which, mainly in the prophets and in the psalms, is called "poverty." These "poor" are the reverse of the "proud," the "princes," the "rich" (Luke 1:51-53), whose unbelief consists exactly in this, that they feel safe only with their earthly possessions and human means. For them, this oracle is ominous, since they are the "ruthless" to whom the prophet refers. They are responsible for the social abuses in Israel. The designation "shoot of Jesse" points as much as the name Immanuel to the "ideal of poverty," which will be characteristic for the "spirituality" of the Remnant and likewise belongs to the fundamentals of the faithful community of God of all times, since this will only be able to endure as Remnant in "the bad world" (Matt. 5:3-12). These words completely fit, therefore, in Isaiah's time.

The miraculous aspect of this oracle is actually that it was proclaimed in a situation which was completely contrary to the one it described. The Book of Immanuel ends, therefore, with a triumph of faith. It is a faith which accumulates all possibilities of expression in order to give concrete shape to the certitude which it contains regarding the future. This future is in God's hand. That is the basis for religious certitude. But the future is known only to God. Therefore, the prophets express religious certitude by furnishing the future with the very best recollections of the past. This chapter is a classical example of this. The oracle of the shoot of Jesse is enriched by the paradise theme: in the messianic Kingdom, sin will no longer exist (11:9); man will live in harmony with God, and hence the paradisiacal harmony among the people, and even in the whole of the subhuman world, will be restored (11:6-8).

There is also (second theme) peace again between North and South (11:13): the splendor of David's monarchy returns. The neighboring nations which David subjugated are conquered once more (11:14). The residence of the new King is the world center which attracts all nations (11:10).

Finally, we have the theme of the second exodus, which is a repetition on a grand scale of the delivery from Egypt and the crossing of the Red Sea (11:15-16): from the four winds Yahweh convokes his new people (11:11-12).

Then the hymn of thanksgiving resounds. It is a new song of the future. But amidst suppression and despite his earthly exile, the believer can sing it with unwavering certitude:

> That day, you will say:
> I give thanks to you, Yahweh,
> you were angry with me
> but your anger is appeased
> and you have given me consolation.
> See now, he is the God of my salvation.
> I have trust now and no fear,
> for Yahweh is my strength, my song,
> he is my salvation.
> And you will draw water joyfully

from the springs of salvation.

That day, you will say:
Give thanks to Yahweh,
call his name aloud.
Proclaim his deeds to the people,
declare his name sublime.
Sing of Yahweh, for he has done marvellous things,
let them be made known to the whole world.
Cry out for joy and gladness,
you dwellers in Zion,
for great in the midst of you
is the Holy One of Israel.
Isaiah 12

This psalm, and therefore this whole cycle of twelve chapters, closes with an expression which is the signature of Isaiah's message: "in the midst of you is the Holy One of Israel." That is his first and last word.

His first word. It is his message of doom for ancient Zion, already present in the beginning of the first chapter: "They have . . . despised the Holy One of Israel" (1:4).

By the proclamation of this aspect of holiness, Isaiah shows himself to be an authentic prophet, in contradistinction to the ordinary representatives of the class of prophets, who, as pillars of society (3:2), share in and facilitate the degeneration of it by conforming—completely after the fashion of pagan prophetism—to the listeners who demanded from their prophets: "Take the Holy One out of our sight" (30:11). That is a total denial in its rudest form of the man who does not want to be reminded of God because he wishes to go his own way undisturbed. This Holy One became, therefore, a destruction to ancient Zion, for Yahweh put fire in Zion and his furnace in Jerusalem (31:9).

The proclamation of this Holy One is also Isaiah's last

word. It is, as in this psalm, his salvific message for the inhabitants of the new Zion. The certainty that the Holy One of Israel lives in their midst is the great anchorage and the consoling experience of the faithful pilgrims who attempt to follow their road of "silence" and "poverty" and who realize by a complete affirmation of their lives the Kingdom of God on earth. They can justly say: Immanuel, God-with-us. Isaiah is therefore, from start to finish, the Prophet of the Nearness of God.

EPILOGUE:

IMMANUEL AND HIS

MOTHER (7:14)

7:14   The Lord himself, therefore,
      will give you a sign.
      It is this: the maiden is with child
      and will soon give birth to a son
      whom she will call Immanuel.

A sign was offered. Even a sign outside the reach of
every man: "coming from the depth of Sheol or from the
heights above" (7:11). That sign was refused. The sign
was given all the same: the child Immanuel.

We think spontaneously of a sign as a "proof," as a
miracle. Besides, one apparently does not have to look
so far for the miracle. When Matthew mentions Mary's
virginal maternity, he refers to the sign of Immanuel (Matt.
1:22).

Likewise there originated a current way of approaching
the seventh chapter of Isaiah: Immanuel is a sign because
he is a miracle and the miracle consists of the fact that
he was born of a virgin. Of this—perhaps strangely
enough—no mention has been made in this book so far.
It was restricted to a cautious and global approach: we
purposely restricted ourselves to what the prophet, at
least and in any case, wanted to say.

Methodically this is always needed and absolutely re-
quired in an overfreighted question like this one. He who
wants to understand Isaiah should not start with Matthew,

although he might fruitfully wind up with him. The reverse is true, too: he who wants to understand Matthew does well by ending with Isaiah, according to the example of the evangelist himself.

This epilogue is typified by this: it goes back and forth, from the prophet to the evangelist and from the evangelist to the prophet. We hope that in this way—for that is the purpose here—a synthesis between the current approach and that followed so far, will grow.

Just because this book has kept a distance, it rests on a solid foundation about which not everything has been said, yet from which the popular ideas concerning Immanuel should be understood meaningfully or, insofar as this does not work, can be revised. Besides, there are still some data which have hardly been used in the previous chapters and which justify a further specification of the figure of Immanuel; also along this road the distance between both ways of approach will be bridged, more or less.

Sign and/or Miracle?

To penetrate to the core of the matter, we make here some observations on the current ideas which give one food for thought.

Since God is free to reveal what he wants, one does not feel it as an objection that the omniscient God would reveal very definite, in this case even biological, details of a future event to a man. One is inclined to attribute the same material contents to Isaiah's prophetic knowledge as to Matthew's historical knowledge.

However, it is not and never has been a question of what God can do, but what he actually and usually does.

Well then, the current ideas are in conflict with the character which the Old Testament revelation actually shows: it presents man with certain religious certitudes regarding the future, but least of all an anticipating historical knowledge of it. The prophecy points to the future, it points in a certain direction like an arrow, which follows a very definite course: it points to the core and essence of what is coming without knowing when and how it will be realized. The fulfillment surpasses the prophecy. Still, the later facts, with all their historical circumstances, are the fulfillment and the concrete form of what the prophet saw, so that, in this case for example, Matthew can justly call on Isaiah.

With the current approach we inevitably end up in a labyrinth in which we get completely stuck. It does not matter how one turns or swings the matter—and that has been done quite a bit in competent circles—it remains an insoluble puzzle as to how the virgin birth of Christ can be a sign for King Ahaz or for any of his contemporaries.

What is worse, the text of Immanuel is, even for the Scripture reader, hardly a sign if he considers it only as a miracle of prophetic foreknowledge. At best I can speak about a sign insofar as the text helps me with a proof, which proves me right against people of different beliefs. That is rather different from a sign which lets me understand my concrete situation of life, as a divine appeal to which I have to answer. Yet, Isaiah used this sign as a two-edged sword which penetrates so deeply that it separates the soul and the spirit, the joints and the marrow, since it sorts out the calculations and thoughts of man's heart! (Heb. 4:12). The sign "means" nothing to us. That is precarious, and shows better than any reasoning that a too massive idea of sign blinds us for the actual sign value of it. We are now trying to account for this. We discover, indeed, some weak sides to the current notion. Upon further consideration it particularly appears that the starting points are not good, namely "sign" and "miracle" are naturally accepted as equal.

This book has taken a cautious and safe stand concerning the sign character of Immanuel, which can be completely maintained, although it needs some addition. We understood the sign of Immanuel as the concrete formulation of the religious attitude and the religious claim and simultaneously as the concrete condemnation of the unfaithful attitude of human calculation. In other words, Immanuel is first of all a sign, since he "signifies" the main contents of Isaiah's preaching.

At this point we will have to clarify better that Immanuel is more than a "literary" personification of Isaiah's message. He is this, but he is more. Such "literary" personifications frequently occur in the prophets and it is certain that such a personification is, in their opinion, a "sign." Isaiah himself and his two sons, by the names they bear, are therefore "signs and portents in Israel from Yahweh Sabaoth": their names are a signifying personification of Isaiah's salvific and ominous message (8:18).

As the prophets often illustrate and underscore their message with actions—sometimes real, sometimes fictitious actions—so they can do the same by portraying to their audience a visionary picture. All these signs do not "prove," but are the illustrated and graphic repetition of one or another oracle.

A single example. In order to warn Judah, already long groaning under Assyria, not to seek its salvation in Egypt, Isaiah predicts (chap. 20) that Assyria will soon defeat Egypt and that the Egyptians will be carried off into exile naked and barefoot. The prophet now receives the order to walk about without cloak and barefoot, as "a sign and portent for Egypt." Isaiah's behavior is a sign, since it is the symbolic translation of his warning oracle.

In Jeremiah 1:14 the ominous oracle says: "The North is where disaster is boiling over." The sign of this is "a cooking pot on the boil with its content tilting from the North." Isaiah really walked around without cloak, but a cooking pot has in reality never turned up from the north. Yet, the enemies who would overrun city and country showed up from that direction. Jeremiah saw the sign of this in a vision, thus a visionary sign.

The difference between Immanuel and Isaiah's two children consists in this, that the latter are contemporaries and thus signs which everyone can see. Immanuel, however, is principally a figure of the future. He is a sign in a vision of the future; he is a visionary sign.*

Immanuel, however, is not merely a sign; he is not a figure constructed by the prophet as illustration of his preaching. He is someone well known, a familiar figure of the future. It is already clear from our Scripture reading that the seventh chapter of Isaiah is very much related to the promise to David as formulated in 2 Samuel 7. This promise dominates the biblical history of kings: it is prophetic historiography in which we fully recognize Isaiah's vision concerning the dynasty. Immanuel is more than merely a sign, since Isaiah, confronted with the degenerated

*This aspect of the sign of Immanuel is very well clarified in the enlightening article by Stefan Porubcan in the *Catholic Biblical Quarterly* 22 (1960) pp. 144-149.

dynasty, proclaims his religious certitude concerning the future, ideal "son of David." He does not merely refer to this familiar figure, but he depicts him in such a way that he is at the same time the concrete personification and illustration of the salvation and doom which the prophet preaches; in other words, he makes him a "sign."

In Immanuel we recognize all kinds of "signlike" traces. We already took Immanuel's eating of "curds and honey" in this way: a certain behavior which depicts a situation in which the faithful remnant will find itself; we could call it a symbolic action. Also, the conspicuous way in which Immanuel came to the fore with his mother, must be understood as a sign of miraculous, divine interference. First and foremost the prophet stamps him as a sign by having attributed to him—always on the visionary level—a significant name.

From this constructive criticism, in which we anticipated somewhat our subject, it is sufficiently clear that the current approach is at least one-sided. The complete sign is not justifiably dealt with while it is still not clear how the one side, which is overexposed, harmoniously fits into the entirety of Isaiah's train of thought.

The Prophet and the Evangelist

After this preparatory work we will once more approach in another way what is at stake here. This book stressed that the name "Immanuel" is the expression of the religious certitude that the Holy One of Israel is near to his people in a certain way and will come near. In this general sense we called this name, in the last Scripture reading, Isaiah's first and last word.

The prophet, however, does not limit himself to this definite but general conviction. He also grasps something of the way in which God will come near. He is convinced that the concrete way in which Yahweh came near to his people in times past, will find its continuation, fulfillment, and crowning in his ultimate coming.

He is a prophet, since the past becomes transparent to him; the past becomes for him a revealing sign which introduces him into the mystery of God's ways. Well then, by choosing David as his Anointed One and Jerusalem as the place where he will live eternally, Yahweh approaches his people in the closest possible way and forever. The covenant with David, which inseparably binds the house of David and the house of Yahweh with each other, seals and, at the same time, crowns Yahweh's alliance with his people.

The religious conviction of this pre-eminently Jerusalem prophet professes, therefore, the more definite conviction that God will be with his people in the future through a purified shoot of the dynasty, who will realize the original intentions of God, thwarted by the historical kings of the house of David: to be the instrument of divine salvation for the people. This more definite conviction is not so much expressed in the name "Immanuel" as in the mysterious figure who is the bearer of it, as has been indicated previously.

It is obvious that the New Testament, where it describes the fulfillment of the prophetic expectation, does not stop at the vague indication which is contained in the name "Immanuel." This name is, as is known, also the first and the last word of Matthew's Gospel. In this instance, however, the name is filled with the entire tangibility of the historical reality which the evangelist wants to witness. Seeking clarity concerning the relation between prophet and evangelist, we particularly question how far the details of the fulfillment are the extension of certain details in the expectation. After relating the conception, the birth, and the naming of Mary's son, Matthew says that "all this" is the fulfillment of Yahweh's word as it is written in Isaiah 7:14 (Matt. 1:20-23). Much could be learned from the correct answer to the difficult question of how this prophecy refers to this particular detail of the Christian fact with regard to understanding both the Old and the New Testaments.

The close of Matthew's Gospel, too, is characterized by the sign of Immanuel. We see the Risen Lord amidst "the eleven disciples." They are the faithful remnant which he has formed for himself and from which he wants to build the Universal Church. He commands them to do so and for that purpose he impresses them with his message concerning Immanuel: "And know that I am with you always; yes, to the end of time" (Matt. 28:20). It is the short summary of all he has told them, and he had to tell them in the forty days between resurrection and ascension. The message of Immanuel in its most general meaning, namely, as the assurance that God will be with his people, has here become strictly christological: Christ will be with his faithful. Within the framework of the general fact that the New Testament ascribes to Christ what is characteristic for Yahweh in the Old Testament, the Old Testament promise that Yahweh will be with his people receives here its pure New Testament translation. The deep harmony between both Testaments belongs to the very contents of the Christian conviction. The many detailed similarities, to which the New Testament refers by quotations from the Old Testament and by all kinds of allusions, must first be seen in the function of this conviction.

Both Testaments live the same faith and give the same faithful interpretation to human existence. In the prophet the accent is on the future: the Old Testament witnesses to faith in the Christ who is to come. Precisely since it does not possess any historical knowledge of details, it can only go by the essential structure of the coming salvation. The New Testament witnesses, in the first instance, to the Christ who **has** come; in order to discover the essential bearing of this Christian fact, which now is known with an abundance of historical details, the New Testament seeks knowledge from the Old Testament.

The Master himself opened the eyes of his disciples by referring them to the Old Testament (Luke 24:25-27, 44-47). The New Testament bears all traces that the young Church gradually realized the importance of the facts which the eye- and ear-witnesses had experienced, only by meditation on the message of the Old Testament. Its religious insight into the Christian fact shares the apostolic preaching by formulating the Christian proclamation of salvation in terms of the prophetic proclamation of salvation. The Old Testament still has the function of making the Christian mystery accessible. It enriches our religious knowledge of it. It is the source of revelation through which Christian faith originates and is maintained. In this framework the nativity story of Matthew is nothing else than a telling example.

Although it is true in a certain sense that we can have a better understanding of the full sense of the words recorded by Isaiah in Matthew, the reverse truth deserves at least as much attention: we need Isaiah to understand Matthew well. That is also clear.

Already from 7:14, but especially from the entire Book

of Immanuel, it is clear that the name Immanuel is the most important element of the prophecy: the child is a sign especially by his name. It is an element which can easily be overlooked in the evangelist. Isaiah helps us, therefore, to read Matthew well. The name Jesus is indeed for him an important point of fulfillment, and therefore an important reason why he quotes Isaiah. Joseph has to give the son of Mary the name Jesus "because he is the one who is to save his people from their sins" (Matt. 1:21). The reason is in the significance of the name Jesus, which is: Yahweh saves or Yahweh is salvation. Israel experiences Yahweh's nearness since it is saved by Yahweh; Yahweh therefore makes true his promise: "I will be with you." The name Jesus has essentially the same content as the name Immanuel. The prophecy concerning the child who will be called Immanuel was, therefore, fulfilled by the child who is called Jesus.

If Matthew wants to connect the name Immanuel with Jesus' miraculous conception—as Luke does by the expression "son of God" (Luke 1:35)—he follows Isaiah's train of thought, although Isaiah is less explicit concerning the nature of the miracle. This is the very value of his prophecy for our religious insight. Reading the evangelist in our modern way, we are easily occupied by the biological fact of virginal conception. The prophet widens our scope, precisely because he wants to underscore God's action in the future fact indicated by him and only touches on the essential structure of salvation. He does not speak of a birth from a virginal, or even a barren mother: the biological aspect does not play any role with him, and he wanted least of all "to predict" a biological fact. The most important thing he does is to give a religious interpretation of a particular motherhood, however it may have come about. We will have to transport ourselves into Isaiah's train of thought.

Mater Admirabilis

The Remnant did not come into existence by "flesh and blood," but by faith. The new future people of God is the tangible proof of the creative power of resurrection of Yahweh, who brings the dead to life and calls into being what did not exist (Rom. 4:17). From dying Israel, Judaism and eventually the Christian Church buds forth. Immanuel is the sign of this new people of God, particularly the way in which he receives his existence: not the fruit of flesh and blood, but of faith.

The ancient people of God had already come into being by faith. The Scriptures indicates this by stressing the barrenness of Israel's ancestresses. On behalf of God it is then announced that what seems impossible to men will actually happen. In this way there originated in biblical historiography a more or less stereotyped formula, which Isaiah uses to announce the birth of Immanuel (cf. Gen. 16:11 and Judg. 13:3). This stereotyped formula points to divine action. This is what the name of the child explicitly states. This name is therefore important: the name enforces the fact that a special significance is attached to the mother, the birth, and the behavior of Immanuel. A name is often inspired by circumstances surrounding a birth, and this name marks the whole situation of Immanuel as a sign.

The great pioneer of faithful modern exegesis, Fr. Lagrange, wrote in the first volume of the famous **Revue Biblique** (pp. 481ff.) in 1892, that the rationalists of his century have to decide for themselves whether or not to accept a miraculous maternity, but that Isaiah definitely had it in mind: to the wrong of their unbelief they add the wrong of their exegesis, as if Isaiah shares their point of view concerning the impossibility of a supernatural factor in something as human as motherhood.

Although it may be clear from Isaiah's language and from the line of salvation history that the mother of the Messiah is a "miraculous" mother, the structure of the seventh chapter and the context which the book of Isaiah offers lead clearly to the same conclusion.

One should pay attention particularly to the contrast between the first part (vss. 1-9) of the seventh chapter, which is completely wrapped up in the human situation of that time, and the second part (vss. 10ff.) in which the prophet is completely taken up with the situation that will originate on the day on which the time of man passes and the time of God comes: Immanuel is the beginning of God's time!

Although Ahaz did not want a sign, the sign was given, a sign of divine ways, of which verse 11 indicates the measure and magnitude.

The relation between 7:14, on the one hand, and 9:5 (the child with its miraculous names) and 11:1 (the shoot of Jesse), on the other, is of definite importance.

From this relation it is not only clear that Immanuel is Messiah—and according to the classical picture of the Messiah, namely the Messianic King of Davidic blood— but also that he originates from a depth of human impotence and misery through a creative miracle from God. For a people which had to seek its road in darkness, the light suddenly radiates; from the dynasty which had fallen into the oblivion of Bethlehem's farming family of Jesse, a new shoot appears. We always remember the situation of the text: human power does not bring salvation; the believer cannot trust in it and is likewise doomed to human powerlessness. But against all odds he counts on a miracle from God. The text of Immanuel expresses this belief: God's power breaks through in the intermundane event; in the Messiah man's frailty becomes God's power. The prophet stresses the origin of the salvation: consequently, a picture of motherhood and birth. Salvation breaks through **because of** God: consequently, a miraculous motherhood. In short, since mother and child together are the concrete image of the budding of God's salvation amidst and from the faithful remnant, nothing can be done here with the **neutral** announcement of a birth.

The famous text of Micah (5:1-4) runs parallel in many respects. Also present here is the classical picture of the Messiah (the new David), the Remnant, doom and salvation, and even Assyria. A thing which is most striking is the humble origin of the new salvation. If we are not mistaken, the prophet points to the humble—therefore unnoticed by men—origin of the still so famous Davidic dynasty (hidden in God's eternal plans), in order to convince his audience that from the calamitous situation, which now is inescapably imminent, a new salvation will come forth, since God calls forth a new David: "But you, Ephrathah, [Bethlehem] the least of the clans of Judah, out of you will be born for me the one who is to rule over Israel; his origin goes back to the distant past to the days of old."

A most remarkable thing, however, is the continuation of the text: "Yahweh is therefore going to abandon them till the time when she who is to give birth gives birth." It continues with a description of the new salvation. Great calamity will come first. But the end of the calamity and the beginning of salvation is a mother-figure. Any anonymous mother cannot be a satisfactory explanation of this text. The text presupposes a figure that is well known; a more or less familiar picture is at issue: only "the messianic mother" makes sense.

It is unnecessary to investigate how the rural Micah and the city-dweller, Isaiah, who were contemporaries, can have influenced each other (cf. Isa. 2:2-4 and Mic. 4:1-4). However it may be, both texts clarify each other: there is no single human guarantee to salvation; the new salvation is from divine origin, and this is tangibly indicated by the prophets in the figure of the messianic mother who is pre-eminently a miraculous mother. Pre-eminently, for she is not the only one. She crowns the succession of miraculous mothers who are the living sign that God's salvific intervention has established Israel.

Fruitfulness of Faith

The New Testament refers to the motherhood of the infertile Elisabeth as a sign of the motherhood of the virgin Mary (Luke 1:36). This reference is important because it places Mary's virginal motherhood in the line of the past actions of God.

The believer was always born from God. That is a spiritual birth. But in the Old Testament—it is old on this account—this birth happens even on a physical level: a people is here, at the same time, a faithful community, and becomes a separated people only by forming itself into a religious community. Hence, an entire nation is born from faith.

Through faith in Yahweh's power to raise from the dead, Abraham became patriarch of the ancient people of God and father of all the faithful, even from the start of the Old Testament. He experienced this faith in his own burned-out body and in Sarah's barren womb, and reached the climax of this in the sacrifice of Isaac (Rom. 4; Heb. 11). Abraham is pictured as the primordial type of the believer: from his figure the "church" of both Testaments should discover its own existential situation. It is explicitly implicated in it ("In you and your descendants all generations will be blessed"), five times in the book of Genesis, so that Israel would not understand this Abraham story as past history of the patriarch, but as its own actual history.

At the beginning of the New Testament there is, as exponent of Israel's silent remnant, the figure of Mary who becomes the mother of the Messiah and, through him, the mother of all believers, through her "yes" of faithful obedience. Assuming the song of the miraculously fertile Anna as her own, Maria sings the Magnificat of her virginal motherhood, pre-eminently the song of the "poor," in the presence of Elisabeth who had become fertile ("Blessed is she who believed!"). Precisely as the type of the Remnant, she is type of the New Testament Church, which is explicitly implicated once again: "Yes, from this day forward **all generations** will call me blessed" (Luke 1:48).

The road which leads from Abraham, the father of faith, to Mary, the mother of faith, is marked by seven miraculous mothers. In this framework the sign of Immanuel belongs.

In Isaiah's time, Israel had degenerated to spiritual infertility, namely to unbelief. Hence—characteristic consequences in the national economy of salvation—Israel was infertile even physically: the people perished. Only a remnant was left of the people which was innumerable as grains of dust and sand and the stars, according to the fertility blessing given to Abraham. This remnant is, humanly speaking, infertile—"she who was said to be barren"—but they will be fertile by faith, so that of this remnant it can be said: "Shout for joy, you barren women who bore no children! / Break into cries of joy and gladness, you who were never in labour! / For the sons of the forsaken one are more in number / than the sons of the wedded wife, says Yahweh" (Isa. 54:1). Immanuel himself is pre-eminently a fruit of faith, and, as such, firstborn and sign of this holy Remnant, of that new Israel which is born from faith.

Both people and dynasty are still upright, but they are almost dislodged from the faith in which they were rooted. Stubbornly clinging to human guarantees of salvation, they are doomed in such a way that the royal house will drag them down in its calamity. The prophet sees this clearly and proclaims it. Opposed to this, he puts his religious insight into what is still the only redemption: by divine interference new salvation will shoot from the beaten and purged remnant, namely by means of a new shoot from the beaten and purged dynasty. Lady X from the humbled family of David will become the mother of a child; it will be a child of pure faith, a child from God. Hence it will be called Immanuel. In this way Mary's virginal motherhood, not as a biological fact, but in its deepest sense, is completely the extension of Isaiah's prophecy. Matthew tells us the fact; he is an evangelist for that. But Isaiah renders the meanings of it; he is a prophet for that. The fertility of faith is the primary fact with regard to Mary and blossoms forth in her bodily fertility (cf. Luke 11:27ff.; Matt. 12:50), as the Church's tradition expresses so well: **prius concepit mente quam ventre!**

Future Figure and/or Contemporary?

It should not be excluded beforehand that the prophecy concerning Immanuel points, in the first instance, to the motherhood of Ahaz's wife, even if this (seen without faith) is merely "out of human stock or urge of the flesh" (John 1:13). Fertility of faith, by definition, cannot be established physically. In the material fact of Hezekiah's birth, only the believer can see the hand of God who keeps his promise to David: "You shall never lack for a man to sit before me on the throne of Israel" (1 Kings 8:25). If this motherhood is faithfully understood as a sign of God's unwavering trust in the house of David, the fruit of this can then be called Immanuel. In his oracle concerning the descendant of David, the prophet would then summarize the actual call of the royalty and map out the road of faith which will somehow lead the house of David through the catastrophe, but with the help of the divine trust.

Immanuel is a name which the prophet chooses himself or coins—this type of name is available in the ancient Near Eastern world—as the summarizing sign of the entire coming salvation, of the entire future Kingdom, which already is beginning its hidden growth in the days of the prophet. In the bearer of this name his expectation culminates in the embodiment and the instrument of that new salvation, the "Messiah." The word "messiah" signifies "Anointed One" and renders to the future figure of salvation the character of a king, since the title "Anointed One of Yahweh" is used for the reigning king in the Old Testament. Only the New Testament uses the word "messiah" in an exclusively messianic meaning, so familiar to us. The Aramaic term (John 1:41 and 4:25) occurs twice, but we find the Greek term ("the Christ," e.g., John 7:41) very often. In Isaiah the word is not used in this sense, but the idea is completely there: his Immanuel is the royal child of the house of David. It is unmistakably present in the seventh chapter which is completely addressed to the "house of David"; it is affirmed in the eighth chapter by the expression "your country, O Immanuel" (vs. 8). Finally, it is very explicit in the passages concerning the Child with the miraculous names and concerning the shoot of Jesse.

This special attention to the dynasty can be best explained by a "happy event" in the royal house. There is nothing against, and much in favor, of the birth of a successor occasioning the prophet to express his messianic expectation, especially since nothing can be expected from the reigning king.

It has already been noticed in the past, and it is now an attainment of the discipline, that the prophet speaks about the future without leaving the present (Jerome). This is very clear in the "messianic psalms," particularly in this group of them, which equally can be called "royal psalms," as they are more and more so called. This signifies a new approach to the psalms. The current exegesis of the psalms, which has received much new inspiration from the research of their "Sitz im Leben" (Gunkel), has cast a new light on the classical "messianic" psalms by discerning the dynastic events which occasioned the psalms, if not of every one separately, then surely of this kind of psalm and of their literary form and structure. As illustration, Gunkel's suggestions follow here: enthronement (Pss. 2; 101; 110); anniversary of enthronement (Pss. 21; 72); anniversary of the establishment of the dynasty in Zion (Ps. 132); wedding (Ps. 45); departure for battlefield (Ps. 20); triumphant return (Ps. 18).

It is outside the framework of this book to delve into

the historical question. It is sufficient to ascertain that the birth of Ahaz's son and successor, Hezekiah, was the occasion for the prophet to express his profession of faith. This seems also to be the conviction of the historiographer, both in the books of Kings and those of Chronicles, since he describes Hezekiah's reign in terms which hardly correspond only by accident so completely to Isaiah's picture of the ideal son of David: "He [Hezekiah] did what is pleasing to Yahweh, just as his ancestor David had done. . . . . He **puts his trust in the God of Israel.** No king of Judah after him could be compared with him—nor any of those before him. **He was devoted to Yahweh** never turning from him, but keeping the commandments that Yahweh had laid down for Moses. And so **Yahweh was with him** [Immanuel=God-with-us] and he was successful in all that he undertook" (2 Kings 18:3-7).*

Here the historiographer does not do much justice to the bearing of Isaiah's prophecy. Further, he has the right to interpret faithfully Hezekiah's reign in the light of this prophecy. But we who can survey the further course of history would be wrong in considering what was initially the fulfillment and application of Isaiah's religious vision as the authentic and complete contents of it. We noted before, in the editors and compilers of Isaiah's prophecies, the inclination and the need to apply the prophet's words to history. From a second text the relation between Hezekiah and Immanuel can be better defined:

> This shall be the sign for you [Hezekiah]:
> this year will be eaten the self-sown grain
> next year what sprouts in the fallow,
> but in the third year sow and reap,
> plant vineyards and eat their fruit.

*My attention was drawn to this text through a statement by Fr. Clemens Epping, O.F.M.

The surviving remnant of the House of Judah shall
    bring forth
new roots below and fruits above;
for a remnant shall go out from Jerusalem,
and survivors from Mount Zion.
The jealous love of Yahweh Sabaoth shall accom-
    plish this.
                    2 Kings 19:29-31; Isaiah 37:30-32

This text is a clarification in three respects:

1.   The oracle starts from a specific situation and
answers the question of the moment (term of three years).
But then it broadens into a global vision of the future,
namely, in terms which Isaiah usually employs for this.
This oracle can therefore give us an idea of how the text
concerning Immanuel, despite its broad effect, can still
point to persons and circumstances at that time, as is clear
from the indication of a short term in 7:16 (cf. 8:4).

2.   Once more the affinity, according to contents and
atmosphere, between this oracle concerning Hezekiah and
the oracle concerning Immanuel, the parallel between Hezekiah and Immanuel, is clear.   In the light of the previous
point, this second point makes more sense.

3.   It is probably that the historiographer saw the last
real Isaian sentence fulfilled in his hero Hezekiah.   It even
seems possible that he is responsible for placing this
sentence at this exact spot.*   Although it may be a somewhat one-sided application of the text, the author has the
right to use the text in this way and by this to correct our
one-sidedness.   This reveals itself in our understanding of

*2 Chron. 29-32 may convey an impression of "priestly" his-
toriography; the lines of the "prophetic" story concerning Hezekiah
(Isa. 36-39; 2 Kings 18-20) are extended in such a way that he is
now the model of the ideal of piety as it was lived in the second
Temple.

both the biblical historiography and the biblical prophecy. A marginal note to the current notion of history may clarify how the messianic explanation of the text concerning Immanuel does not exclude, but rather includes, its application to Hezekiah.

History and Prophecy

David, Moses, Abraham, and even Adam, are often completely and exclusively understood as figures of the past. This is one-sided, since Scripture, in the way in which it prortrays these figures, gives at the same time— and sometimes in the first place—a religious outlook on certain actual events.

Adam is not first of all a man of past times, but the man of now and all times. The story concerning Adam is graphic theology concerning the phenomenon of man; in his figure Israel's religious thinking concerning man is concentrated.

We would not half understand the story concerning Abraham if the theology regarding the believer should escape our notice in this figure: Israel's situation as people of God finds its graphic theological expression in the patriarch of faith.

In the person of Moses, who is not a prophet at all— in a historical technical sense—the biblical theology concerning the prophetic phenomenon is crystallized. Moses is signified as one of the greatest prophets, since Israel's religious awareness, perhaps forced by the decay of prophecy, expresses in his person what authentic prophecy is and how prophecy should function among the real people of God (Exod. 4:15ff.; 7:1; Num. 12:6-8; Deut. 18:9-22; 34:10-12).

Finally, in the biography of David, the prophetic vision

—which marks the story of the introduction, the fortunes, and the decline of the royalty as a separate history—culminates. It is a theological synthesis concerning royalty and dynasty. In the person of David the historiographer creates the ideal, i.e., the actual divine design of a king such as this fits into the structure of a people which already belongs to Yahweh and already has been constituted completely as such. Although the Pentateuch, in the form of an elaborate history of Israel's origin, offers a theology of the covenant people without including royalty, the historical story which follows this brings a new synthesis about: royalty, through which the covenant people were completely constituted nationally and historically, is theologically located, so that it can be harmoniously fitted into the Pentateuch theology. The covenant with David is the crowning and confirmation of the Sinaitic covenant (2 Sam. 7:26; 1 Kings 9:4-9). The ancient Eastern "ideology of the king" is here completely transformed to the Yahwistic theology concerning the king.

It is only a small step from the religious insight into what royalty is supposed to be according to God's intentions to the religious expectation of what it will be on the ground of these same intentions of God. The Davidic theology dissolves itself in the expectation of Messiah-King just as (though less explicit) the Mosaic theology dissolves in the expectation of the Messiah-Prophet.

It is not accidental that this marginal note to a too one-sided idea of biblical historiography is naturally attached to the prophet. History and prophecy are intimately related in Scripture. That was already clear in another connection in the beginning of the tenth Scripture reading. They can even flow into one another. Perhaps since they are both related to the present time: the historiography does not limit itself to the past; the prophecy does not limit itself to the future. An exegesis which understands Immanuel exclusively as a figure of the future runs a great risk of being one-sided. As the figures of the past are portrayed as a religious orientation for the present, so prophecy portrays its figures of the future in such a way that they are at the same time a religious interpretation and norm of belief of actual phenomena.

Immanuel is likewise a norm of faith and a touchstone of the dynasty. The text gives a religious orientation for the entire further history of the house of David, whatever course this may take.

This is still expressed too weakly. As all prophecy, this is also creating and defining the future; in a real sense it makes the future, because it is the Word of God: "Yes, as the rain and the snow come down from the heavens and do not return without watering the earth, making it yield and giving growth to provide seed for the sower and bread for the eating, so the word that goes from my mouth does not return to me empty, without carrying out my will and succeeding in what it was sent to do" (Isa. 55:10-11).

The prophecy concerning Immanuel is therefore a divine word which allowed new salvation to originate in and by means of the Davidic family. The prophecy renders a divine salvific will which, as a never-ceasing energy, sets up and maintains a growing process of salvation through all the fortunes of the house of David, until the salvation which God has designed will be completed.

From the moment that this prophecy was proclaimed, it began to work; it began to realize itself in Isaiah's time, although it was only completely realized in Christ. Only

this fulfillment corresponds to the breadth and depth of
Isaiah's religious awareness, because it still surpasses this.
Isaiah expressed this divine answer to the human question
—in the shape of Israel's national expectation—in this
prophecy, since his faith, via the Davidic king Hezekiah
or someone else, wanted tangibly to encompass him who
is pre-eminently the Son of David.

Hezekiah or whoever! That sounds suddenly very indifferent. Still we did not search in vain. One needs to
know that Isaiah's prophecies take root in very definite
historical circustances. In this way one is prevented from
using them as so many "predictions" from which, with the
New Testament in hand, he could make demands while,
staring himself blind at material details, he has no eye
for the grandeur of a religious vision which can even help
to gain a better understanding of the bearing of the New
Testament fulfillment. Hence the argument with regard
to Hezekiah. On the other hand, however, the reader of
the Bible should not pass over these particular historical
circumstances simply because they are not of any specific
importance in the Bible as we know it today. We can
accept for certain that the great texts (7:14; 9:5; 11:1),
as they were proclaimed by Isaiah, had a very definite
"Sitz im Leben." It is the task of scholars to find out
which "birth" occasioned these prophetic remarks. It has
become an inextricable question which takes us far, very
far, from the Scriptures. It is happily a peripheral question.
The main question involved is: What is the "Sitz in der
Bibel" of these texts? And that is a completely different
question.

It is possible that the compilers of the Book of Immanuel were already unfamiliar with the exact historical
occasions of the separate oracles. Besides, it is certain

that Isaiah looked far beyond his contemporary situation; he is a prophet precisely because he sees the essential issues in the events which occur in his time and which everyone observes. He interprets what seem to be only history as salvation and damnation history, as a moment in the dialogue between Yahweh and Israel, between God and man. It is precisely this vision of faith which stands out and, as it were, is liberated by the fact that the exact circumstances of the events vanish into the past. In Scripture, the three great texts together have become in this way the expression of Isaiah's expectation of salvation. It even appears that the beginning of chapter 11 was not yet proclaimed in reference to a historical descendant of David. We would like to consider this text as a further meditation on, and an elaboration of, the message which was mentioned in the two other texts in connection with a particular descendant.

The Scripture reader should therefore be able to use the three great messianic texts in the same way that he handles the great Assyrian texts which contrast them. As we have noted before, the particular episode of the Assyrian period which occasioned Isaiah's pronouncement of a certain Assyrian oracle, was only of secondary importance. First of all, Assyria was for Isaiah the embodiment of the "kingdom of this world" to which, as witness of the faith, he actually refers. Second, as we see in Isaiah, the separate Assyrian oracles, however historically they may have been situated, became the global indication of the Assyrian nightmare for posterity—beginning with the generation which linked these oracles together. This nightmare is in its turn understood as a classical symbol of the power which is opposed to Immanuel's Kingdom.

Likewise, the Book of Immanuel can become completely

accessible to any Scripture reader. He does not need to reconstruct the historical circumstances. It is sufficient to know that they were as complex as those of our own day. It is sufficient to know that they were human situations, i.e., situations in which man has to take his stand as a free person. Of principal importance is the understanding of the interpretation which Scripture gives to these situations, for the religious insight, as formulated by the prophet, touches the human situation as such.

The biblical words make me realize that, together with God, I will have to write the history of my life; that I have to understand my human situation as a word from God, to which I actually answer with an affirmation or denial, so that even **my** life inescapably becomes salvation history or damnation history.

This is for everyone a Yes or No with regard to Christ, probably very implicit, but nevertheless real. This was also true for the Old Testament man. The prophecy concerning Immanuel is a culmination of Old Testament belief in Christ. However explicit this text appears now, in our opinion it must still be called an expression of implicit faith in Christ, though a very remarkable expression. It is so remarkable that it confronts us once again with the mystery to which we referred in the tenth Scripture reading.

The Mystery of the Book

Christ is more literally God-with-us and more literally child of a "maiden" than Isaiah can have intended according to Old Testament usage. Though his religious **awareness** has encompassed the entire mystery, Isaiah could not **imagine** explicitly or formulate what we know from the Gospel and consequently what we can read into the Isaiah text.

Matthew, and the apostolic community of which he is the voice, knows himself to be of one faith with Isaiah; he adores Isaiah as one of the greatest among the fathers of the faith. It seems as if those living at the time of the fulfillment wanted to underscore this continuation of faith by literally realizing the tangible expressions of Isaiah's faith. It was not enough for them to preserve the spirit and intention—which is the most important fulfillment— but they even used his words and images in their own formulation.

This epilogue has sought to free the reader from a delicate problem; it will have reached its goal if we can replace the problem with mystery. This mystery has three sides, if we consider it well: the prophecy, the fulfillment, and the link which connects these two: the Book.

The Scriptures of the New Testament have been built on those of the Old Testament. These Scriptures needed a thousand years to become what they are since the beginning of our era. The Scriptures consist, therefore, of many layers. Consequently, Scripture has repeatedly read and re-read its own ancient text, i.e., written and rewritten and understood anew and more fully. Consequently, there are two different questions: What did Isaiah want to say? And: What does the Isaiah text mean?

The Septuagint, the Greek edition and enlargement of the Hebrew Old Testament, is an indispensable link between the documents of both Testaments. It offers innumerable examples of progressive religious insight into the texts that it translates and often rewrites. It is a strange and extremely irrational situation that the current theology does not include it within the mystery of the Book: its witness, precisely insofar as it is strictly its own, does not count as Scripture!

The conviction of the ancient Church that the Septuagint (in itself and also where it does more than translate) was authentic Scripture, will inevitably and soon be a recovered conviction and attainment of the present theology. Faith, with which "inspiration" is so ultimately bound, did not die with Hebrew. It lived and grew, further expressing itself in Greek as it also did, for that matter, in Aramaic. Greek-speaking Judaism was the most important organ of the authentic community of God and the actual manifestation of the faithful Remnant for at least three centuries. In this Remnant the Scripture "lived" and grew as it had lived and grown in the preceding centuries. Only now, this growth was accomplished in Greek. By "translating" it, a new spiritual richness began to share in the Hebrew inheritance and a Greek emotional value was added, particularly to the biblical terminology. Precisely in this form, the Old Testament became the soil of the New Testament.

In the framework of this development, the Greek translation of 7:14 forms the missing link between Isaiah and Matthew. Although it does not say more than Isaiah, it introduces the definite term which will be taken in the strict and literal sense in the New Testament.

Isaiah does not use the word "virgin," although the Hebrew has a word for this; he uses a word which refers to youthful power—he actually says less than "virgin," but also more: there are, after all, young and aging virgins —a word which also appears in Proverbs 30:19 and Genesis 24:43 (cf. vs. 14) and which refers to a marriageable girl who has not yet been touched by a man.

The Septuagint employs the word "virgin" (**parthenos**). Since this is also done in Genesis 24:43, the word has a flexible meaning, comparable to the usage in English (maidservant=servant girl) and even in the New Testament (the wise and foolish "virgins" are bridesmaids). Anyway, the word itself is now in the text. It is an important gain. But when it comes to furnishing proofs, the Septuagint is not of much use.

The explanation of the texts on their conclusive evidence is, happily enough, the last thing a reader has to do, for that means the end of Scripture reading. It remains to be seen what Scripture proves, usually other and more important things than we look for. But if I want to prove a particular position with the Scriptures, I will approach it from a limited point of view, since its point of view will surely differ from mine. Do I find, however, my position in it? Then it is a question of whether I understood it well. If I do not rediscover the point to be proved, the disappointment will be the greater, since this one point blinds me to what Scripture actually says. This seems to be the case in our question.

It is remarkable that the entire New Testament does not return to Christ's virgin conception in the rest of the book. Apparently it is a datum about which the apostolic proclamation observed a certain restraint. Under the impression of this fact we can get a greater view of the reverent restraint with which the childhood story surrounded this fact. It is there clearly and unmistakably, but in a completely functional context. Matthew and Luke both speak about it in order to express the mystery of Jesus' descent from the Father: his birth, however much it may be from a woman, is the work of the Spirit. Notice the emphasis (Matt. 1:18, 20; Luke 1:35). Mariology is possible only within the framework of Christology! The "overshadowing" by the Holy Spirit refers to a miracle

of creation and is reminiscent of the first creation, when
the Spirit of God hovered over the water to fertilize it.
Matthew also recalls the story of creation. The beginning
of his Gospel—"A genealogy of Jesus Christ"—leans on
the Greek text of Genesis 2:4: "Such were the **origins** of
heaven and earth."

Both evangelists and Isaiah are surprisingly close to
one another, as soon as we delve into the texts and taste
their particular atmosphere. Each of them stresses in his
own way the creative intervention of God.

If we now, at the close of this epilogue, look back to
the beginning of it, we see perhaps that something is
lacking in the current approach. Perhaps we also see its
chief mistake: a certain biological datum, in this case, is
taken out of its biblical context and turns up in all kinds
of theology defined by the spirit of the times over the
centuries—next to high-level and profound theology there
existed a theology inclined to curiosity and sensation, not
to mention piety—and is finally possessed by the contemporary believer as a hard, loose datum. This could be
the disadvantage of a brief catechism, if the teaching of
this is not accompanied by an increasing familiarity with
Scripture from one's youth or, what amounts to the same
thing, if the truth of the catechism is not carefully integrated with the scriptural data by the catechist.

This book argues in its entirety that the Scriptures
have something irreplaceable for the ordinary believer.
Whether they have opened themselves for him, is another
question. We hope that it eventually does, namely, via
those who have read all of this patiently.